SÉRIE
PESSOAS E CONTEXTOS

PSICOLOGIA
CIÊNCIAS DA EDUCAÇÃO
SERVIÇO SOCIAL

IMPRENSA DA UNIVERSIDADE DE COIMBRA
COIMBRA UNIVERSITY PRESS

COORDENAÇÃO EDITORIAL

Imprensa da Universidade de Coimbra

Email: imprensa@uc.pt

URL: http://www.uc.pt/imprensa_uc

Vendas online: http://livrariadaimprensa.uc.pt

DESIGN

Carlos Costa

EXECUÇÃO GRÁFICA

KDP - Kindle Direct Publishing

ISBN

978-989-26-1619-3

ISBN DIGITAL

978-989-26-1620-9

DOI

https://doi.org/10.14195/978-989-26-1620-9

© MARÇO 2019, Imprensa da Universidade de Coimbra.

Cristina Pinto Albuquerque
Ana Maria Seixas
Albertina Lima Oliveira
António Gomes Ferreira
Maria Paula Paixão
Rui Paquete Paixão
COORDS

HIGHER EDUCATION AFTER BOLOGNA

Challenges and Perspectives

IMPRENSA DA UNIVERSIDADE DE COIMBRA
COIMBRA UNIVERSITY PRESS

MAIN EDITOR
Ana Paula Rodrigues da Fonseca Relvas

ADJUNCT EDITORS
Maria Isabel Ferraz Festas
Helena da Silva Neves dos Santos Almeida

EDITORIAL COORDINATOR
Maria João Padez de Castro

EDITORIAL BOARD
NACIONAL BOARD
Ana Maria Magalhães Teixeira Seixas
Carlos Manuel Folgado Barreira
Clara Maria Rodrigues Cruz Silva Santos
Joaquim Armando Gomes Alves Ferreira
Maria Paula Barbas de Albuquerque Paixão

INTERNACIONAL BOARD
Fathali Moghaddam | Georgetown University
José Luis Linares | Universidade Autónoma de Barcelona
José Maria Peiró | Universidade de Valência
Marco Depolo | Universidade de Bolonha
Roberto Pereira | Universidade de Deusto
Sandra Jovchelovitch | London School of Economics and Political Science
Terezinha Nunes | Universidade de Oxford

CONTENTS

INTRODUCTION 7

CHAPTER 1. 15
Bologna Process and the rethinking of the role
of higher education: Teaching strategies
focused on students' skills achievement
Ana Souto e Melo

CHAPTER 2. 51
Quality as politics and as policies and the
importance of instruments
Amélia Veiga & António Magalhães

CHAPTER 3. 77
The concept of quality within the European Higher Education
Area (EHEA): Dimensions and discourses
Sandra Milena Díaz López, Maria do Rosário Pinheiro & Carlos Folgado Barreira

CHAPTER 4. 103
The human factor as a differential in the teaching learning
relationship: Sense built on the Bologna Process in higher education
Eliana Nubia Moreira

CHAPTER 5. 139

The influence of Bologna Process and Lisbon Strategy
on the rhetoric change in Government' Programs in Portugal

Jorge Lameiras

CHAPTER 6. 179

The training of educators and teachers in Portugal in the framework
of the European Space for education and training (2007-2018)

António Gomes Ferreira & Luís Mota

CHAPTER 7. 199

The antinomies of post Bologna's higher education.
Critical appraisals on the "social dimension" of the reform

Cristina Pinto Albuquerque & Ana Cristina Brito Arcoverde

CHAPTER 8. 237

Profiles of Mobility Students

Liliana Moreira & Rui Gomes

CHAPTER 9. 265

Making Bologna Really Work!

Elmer Sterken

INTRODUCTION

After the nine hundredth anniversary of the University of Bologna, which gives name to the reform implemented in the last two decades, several changes occurred in the European space of higher education, either in what concerns the philosophy underlying its scientific, social and educational aims and responsibilities, or in what refers to the ways in which these aims can be operationalized, in terms of: the structure and duration of training, the pedagogical strategies, the link between study cycles, the relationship between research and teaching, among many other aspects.

In fact, the so-called Bologna Process was embodied in a set of agreements and prerogatives that culminated, in 2010, with the creation of the European Higher Education Area, having as one of its central objectives being the guarantee of a relatively homogeneous structure of academic degrees, facilitating the comparability of training and accreditation systems and thereby encouraging the mobility of students and graduates. The result was, in fact, a profound, yet not uncritical, reform in European higher education. Today, almost two decades after the signing of the Bologna Declaration (June 19, 1999), the reform merits a more critical, conscious and informed reflection not only on the metamorphoses unleashed and their impact, but also on the new challenges facing higher education in Europe and around the world.

The signing of the *Magna Charta Universitatum* by the Rectors of some of the most prestigious European Universities, in 1988, marks a first step towards a voluntary membership in view of a transformation of higher education aiming at: first, a closer rapprochement between the University and the social and economic contexts; second, a better articulation between European higher education institutions and the research they are developing. Within this scope was implicit a questioning and an attempt to overcome a higher education system anchored in rigidified and often anachronistic knowledge, searching for a higher, quality of the teaching-learning processes – the pedagogical dimension – and its adequacy to the specificities of the European space.

Despite the several benefits that arose in higher education following the Reform, namely the increasing in international mobility and knowledge exchange, there is also an acute awareness that several changes deserve today a much more profound reflection and revision. The quality assurance and the consistency of apprenticeship preserving the identity of university knowledge in contemporary societies is one of the main challenges, discussed in several contributions in this book.

Currently, the higher education reform has been appropriated by political systems, becoming not only a central point of the political-educational agenda and rhetoric since the 1990's, but also an essential strategy for stressing the assumptions of European competitiveness and "effectiveness" inherent to the Lisbon Strategy. With the signing of the Bologna Declaration by Ministerial initiative this "passage" from strictly academic concerns to political and technical matters was achieved. Several examples may be highlighted concerning this subject: the association of financing systems to higher education institutions with criteria of effectiveness and efficiency in their management; the determination of knowledge parameters and learning contents by priority criteria of utility and functionality for the labor market; the comparability between institutions (translated into international rankings, often with debatable and allegedly universal criteria), based on quantified and quantifiable results; the competitiveness between institutions and teachers henceforth evaluated, not only by criteria of pedagogical and scientific quality, but also by systems of recognition (not always translators of quality), are just a few paradigmatic examples of the politicization of the Bologna process and the possible loss of focus on what is essential: a University oriented by universal and humanistic values, as teleological and axiological references of its existence and of the respective activities and axes of its development. To this end, it is necessary to preserve the assumptions embodied in the *Magna Charta* of the Universities: their scientific independence, in the fields of education and research, in the face of political and economic power; the close link between research and education so that it can respond more adequately to social demands and scientific advancement; freedom as the fundamental pillar of teaching and research and the nuclear principle of the University; the universality anchored in the tradition of European humanism and translated in the search for a universal, non-autistic knowledge, but a promoter of mutual apprenticeship and cultural pluralism.

Therefore, to think about Bologna's Process today is mainly to recover and rebalance its initial purposes and to assume, in a way of critical reflection about its constitutive ambiguities: the sense attributed to the student's autonomy; the comparability of grades and accreditation systems very differentiated; the meaning of quality, and the paradoxes and perverse effects of its operationalization – for example, the rhetoric of functional skills for employability; the "productivist autism", that is to say, a scientific production enclosed in an impact publication logic, thus destined almost exclusively to the academic community, evaluated by itself and for itself; and the 'comparative dissonance', based on the weighting, under supposedly equivalent criteria, of non-equivalent elements (in particular, comparison and evaluation of higher education institutions and research units without regard to its contextual specificities and constraints).

The present book aims to highlight the importance and gains of the Bologna reforms, but also to reflect on the unfulfilled promises and the technical and substantive ambiguities that they may bear. A necessary debate in a moment of profound reflection on the pertinence, place, consistency and usefulness of the knowledge produced in higher institutions and on how it is disseminated and replicated. In the background a renewed discussion on the cultural and normative patterns of contemporary societies: what kind of knowledge is being produced today? How the relationship between teachers and students has changed? How the issues of plurality and respect for difference are placed in contexts of greater mobility and internationalization? How the equity in access and attendance of higher education is ensured within greater pressures for effectiveness and comparability? These and other issues are addressed in the various chapters of the book.

In the first chapter, Ana Souto e Melo discusses the transformations in the role of Higher Education and the teaching strategies focused on students' skills achievement. As the author underlines with Bologna Process a new paradigm emerged based in labour market skills training. The chapter presents the main results of a comparative case study on the impact of this process on a course taught in two Portuguese higher education institutions through the opinion of participants and analysis of institutional documents, highlighting, in particular, the valued skills in the current course.

In the second chapter, entitled *Quality as politics and as policies and the importance of instruments*, Amélia Veiga and António Magalhães intend to discuss the development of European higher education quality assurance politics and policies. The argument presented by the authors is that the principles construing the politics of quality assurance at the European level are being diluted in the enactment of quality assurance policies, practices and their instruments. This is a case of goal displacement with regard to the major political objective of a more integrated higher education in Europe. Discursive institutionalism allowed identifying the role of normative and cognitive ideas in the shift from the centrality of ultimate political values to instrumental ideas reflecting proceduralism. This shift illustrates the process of goal displacement of quality assurance policies coordinated at the European level.

The subject of quality in the EHEA is also discussed in chapter three, authored by Sandra Milena Díaz López, Maria do Rosário Pinheiro and Carlos Folgado Barreira. From the conceptualization of what quality implies and taking into account the important role of discourse in the implementation of ways to view reality, and consequently, in social transformation processes, this chapter offers an analysis of different dimensions of quality underlying EHEA discourses. The presented analysis identify two main tendencies of quality: discourses promoting an excision between quality and equity, calling for an understanding of education not as a product but as a right

Chapter four, authored by Eliana Nubia Moreira, debates the search for a new meaning in the act of teaching, learning and research, in an attitude that transforms, learning from living experience, reflecting on the paths that the phenomenological method points to didactic-pedagogic in higher education and contributing to the understanding of subjectivity, from which emerge aspects of the human being singularity and its essence as a possibility of reading the reality, the phenomenon and the lived experience, without forgetting the objectivity that permeates it.

In the chapter five, Jorge Lameiras presents a historical evolution of the transformations in the Portuguese higher education system after 1974, showing that during all the period economic issues have been present in discourse and practices about higher education, either as the essential issue of funding to assure the sustainability of institutions, or as a contributor agent through knowledge transfer to increase productivity and economy. The author defends however that, in Portugal, Bologna Process triggered a reform of the higher education system, from legal framework to pedagogical methodologies in the classroom, and so it is an opportunity to improve quality and deepen the identity of higher education institutions.

In the sixth chapter, António Gomes Ferreira and Luís Mota present the evolution of the educational policy on the initial training of educators and teachers, namely with respect to recruitment, training structure and the professional profile in Portugal, taking also into account the contemporary processes of "Europeanisation" and its impact on the nation-state and its educational policies.

The seventh chapter, authored by Cristina Pinto Albuquerque and Ana Cristina Brito Arcoverde, presents some critical appraisals on the 'social dimension' of the Bologna's Reform. The main purpose of the chapter is to discuss the presupposition of equality in the access and attendance of higher education in the European higher education area and Brazil, as well as the issues associated with the so-called social dimension of the Bologna Process, both in a historical and substantive perspective.

In the eighth chapter, Liliana Moreira and Rui Gomes present some data concerning the mobility student profiles of a university located at a central country (University of Groningen, in the Netherlands) and a semi-peripheral country (University of Coimbra, in Portugal). Data show that the mobility and regular students differ in terms of country of origin and family education capital. The profiles allow a clearer explanation of the differentiating characteristics of the student population and are important landmarks for new research on academic mobility.

In the last chapter, Elmer Sterken presents an optimistic view on the Bologna process, underlining its potentialities in the framework of internationalization and defending that academic development benefits from cooperation and collaboration. The author states also that the European universities should work on inclusion – making all students feel welcome in their system – and activation – getting students in an active mode in the educational process.

DOI | https://doi.org/10.14195/978-989-26-1620-9_1

CHAPTER 1

BOLOGNA PROCESS AND THE RETHINKING OF THE ROLE OF HIGHER EDUCATION:
teaching strategies focused on students' skills achievement

Ana Souto e Melo

CI&DETS, Instituto Politécnico de Viseu (Portugal)

Email: anamelo@esev.ipv.pt

Emerging labour market training needs have foreseen a new educational paradigm, under the Bologna Process, based on skills development. This article aims to present the main results of a comparative case study on the impact of this process on a course taught in two Portuguese higher education institutions through the opinion of participants and analysis of institutional documents, highlighting, in particular, the valued skills in the current course.

Introduction

The reformulation of the aims of Higher Education in the countries of the European Union (EU) has emerged as one of the main intentions of the Bologna Process in the face of the challenges and opportunities that emerge in a context of increasing global economic integration. One of its objectives was therefore to make the European area attractive, compatible and competitive (Bologna Declaration, 1999) and it is therefore essential to ensure training in the face of the difficulties inherent in a globalized society.

It is considered that the Magna Carta, signed by the Rectors of the European Universities in 1988 in Bologna, was in the genesis of the Bologna Process. This document refers to the university as being the focus that generates cultural, scientific and technological knowledge of society, thus giving it an important responsibility with regard to the economic and social development of the countries. The Bologna Process can be understood as arising from the European conjuncture, above all by the interest of the Member States in defining a common strategy, both politically and socially, with the ultimate aim of achieving higher levels of competence, productivity and competitiveness Relative to other countries in the world, namely the United States of America and Japan.

The approximation of Higher Education to the world of work requires the formation of properly qualified human resources, endowed with skills that are considered necessary for the technological, economic and cultural development of the current society. The role of universities in the production of intellectual knowledge in academic freedom, particularly those defended by the Humboldtian model (Neave, 1998), was replaced by the professional functions with the implementation of the

Bologna Process (González & Wagenaar, 2008; European, EACEA, & Eurydice, 2015).In order for higher education institutions to adjust their training offer to market laws, the emergence of useful knowledge as a convergent support of the whole structuring and organization of knowledge and, consequently, of the respective training courses that, in this sense, are aligned with the compatibility of the educational dimensions with the demands of the labor market, giving shape to a new educational paradigm based on the development/acquisition of competences, as evidenced in one of the studies developed in the scope Tuning Project[1] (González & Wagenaar, 2008).

The production of knowledge is no longer solely directed at the academic world, reconciling knowledge with its effective professional application, boosting productivity and competitiveness, highlighting the balance between the acquisition of specific and generic/transversal competences in the professional success of citizens. The higher order skills are considered, according to Lebrun (2008), essential in a quality training, since they will promote the acquisition of knowledge and key points in the Bologna Process, in learning to learn and in lifelong learning.

It is in this context that this research article is inserted, whose main objective is to reflect and disseminate the results obtained in a study on the impact of the Bologna Process on a master's degree course in teaching, taught at two Portuguese Higher Education institutions, patenting, in the first moment, the legal and historical framework of the challenges and opportunities brought about by the Bologna Process and the reflection on the

---

[1] It is an initiative working group of the European Commission within the framework of the Socrates and Tempus programs, which is of great relevance in assessing the impact of the Bologna Process on higher education institutions in the Member States.

concept of competence within the same Process; in a second moment, we intend to highlight what the meaning attributed to the competence by the participants and what competences valued in the course under study.

1. Main focus of the chapter

The Bologna Process has had an extraordinary impact (European Commission, 2010), an aspect which we can foresee is still far from over. This is related to the persistent updating and adaptation of a system that has as main objective a greater articulation between the member states to reach their strategic objectives to face the increase of the levels of social, cultural and economic competitiveness in the European space. In fact, the objectives underlying the whole process have been adjusted over a period of approximately twenty years, since the practical realization of the innovation of the educational paradigm that has persisted for decades in our educational systems and which forms an integral part of a mentality rooted by all (both trainees and trainers) is a step that "may well take the time of a generation" (Feyo Azevedo, 2004, p. 1).

During this period, an effort has been made in reflection and discussion, as well as in the production of documents, which set out some of the fundamental principles in pursuing this path and political decision making in order to converge towards a common European dimension. Although results from more recent studies point to a clear cooperation and convergence of European Higher Education systems, there are still many difficulties underlying its actual implementation, which makes us consider the Bologna Process as a set of opportunities and challenges that only the persistent efforts of students, teachers and employers can guarantee their effective implementation in a continuous process of search, shared reflection, discovery and effective renewal of Higher Education systems. In other words, Bologna is a biggest challenge will be to fulfill the assumptions already outlined in the various meetings of the member states, namely the effective development of generic competences to specific ones, bringing with them the true scope of one of the most ambitious the objectives of the Bologna Process are the approximation of the knowledge developed in the scope of Higher Education to the current labor market needs, thus giving it the effective responsibility with regard to the economic and social development of the countries, which we intend to trigger with the present investigation.

1.1. The Bologna Process: Opportunities and Challenges

The Bologna Process has had a great impact and expansion which has not been limited only to the countries belonging to the EU. This aspect confirms a consolidated view of its success assumptions and, to that extent, also insists in its consequence several opportunities that highlight the renewal of Higher Education systems. In addition to the emerging opportunities, there are numerous challenges brought by the goal of a consolidation and convergence of enormous scope that has been considered as a process yet to be completed, but throughout its implementation has been shown to follow an evolutionary line and of conclusive realization. We come to reflect on the achievements and challenges of the various meetings of member states within the framework of the Bologna Process, taking into account more recent results on their implementation.

Cooperation and adequacy for competitiveness

The main impact of the Bologna Process is that starting from a strategy of common interest and organization for the social, economic and cultural development of European countries, it acts as an incentive for Higher Education reforms, a unique opportunity for confronting and solving problems that affect the organization of Higher Education and that Bologna calls into question. In this sense, the Bologna Process has been affirmed as a generalized harmonization of the educational structures of Higher Education in Europe, translating itself into practice in the identical structural and organizational organization of the Higher Education systems, offering similar and comparable training courses, both in terms of contents and in terms of duration and conferring diplomas of equivalent value at both academic and professional levels (General Direction of Higher Education, 2008). In this way, we have adapted the various Higher Education systems through the cooperation and convergence of common strategic objectives linked to the transformations demanded by the new market economy (Sobrinho, 2005). This idea has its origin in the Magna Carta of the European Universities (1988) in which the protagonism of the universities was acknowledged as the main source of knowledge of the society and responsible for its cultural, scientific and technical development, with a well various meetings of the member states of the European Higher Education Area within the framework of the Bologna Process, which establish lines of action to be achieved by the year 2020 (Yerevan Declaration, 2015).

We are therefore faced with a functionalist conception of university (Dréze & Debelle, 1983) in which Higher Education turns to social and economic needs in order to serve the Nation and in which it is considered as a fundamental instrument in vocational training of citizens emphasizing the utilitarian value of knowledge, reconciling educational dimensions with professional requirements. The fundamental objective of Higher Education is to provide students with knowledge based on market laws, defending the notion of useful knowledge as the unifying axis of all the structuring and organization of the courses, with the intention of curricula being Market needs measured through interinstitutional cooperation with employers.

Taking into account this necessary link between higher education systems with employers, the European Qualifications Framework for Lifelong Learning (EQF) and its National Qualifications Frameworks (NQF) are set up by Parliament and the European Council (2008, May 6), which reaffirmed the interest in a European Higher Education system based on the diversity of academic profiles for each cycle of studies, stating the corresponding competences and professional exits. The main objectives of these frameworks were to help member states, Higher Education institutions, employers and citizens compare the qualifications awarded by the different European education and training systems, as well as to understand the relevance of the qualifications to meet the needs of the labor market of each country. Its purpose is not only to determine the level of student learning but also to identify the country's needs in the labor market (European Commission, 2010).

According to the results of the most recent Implementation Report of the Bologna Process in the European Higher Education Area (European Commission, EACEA & Eurydice, 2015) and with regard to the national qualifications system, it can be seen that in most of the participating countries there has been a growing correspondence between training cycles and levels of qualification stemming from the EQF. While some 15 countries in the European Higher Education Area have stated that they have not yet joined the EQF, some 32 countries (plus 10 countries over the year

2012) have adapted the descriptions of the common framework to their specific characteristics and needs. The aforementioned report also states that only half of the NQF implemented include levels corresponding to all levels of education (from Elementary to Higher Education) and that the other half of the countries relate the NQF only to Higher Education, an aspect that in our view impedes the relationship between higher education and other levels of education, and on the other, prevents the accreditation of informal learning, which is often responsible for the acquisition and development of generic skills.

Compatibility as a common qualification support for mobility

Also in the scope of cross-border cooperation, one of the most outstanding aspects of the Bologna Process is the proposal to increase mobility in Higher Education and for this purpose it is advocated the generalization of a credit system with the implementation of the European Credit Transfer and Accumulation System (ECTS) in order to ensure greater transparency and ease of understanding and recognition of the academic equivalence of learning outcomes among several higher education institutions. This academic recognition promotes a more open European area, which in turn stimulates student mobility, both between institutions of the countries themselves, regions and cities, and between institutions in different countries, a matter evidently defended in several meetings held in the Bologna Declaration (1999), Prague Declaration (2001), Salamanca Declaration (2001), and Helsinki Seminar (2001).

Recent results show that the majority of the countries of the European Higher Education Area, around 80%, followed the said pattern of ECTS award, with around seven countries allocating ECTS based on a combination of student work (hours of autonomous work) with the teacher's work (contact hours) (European Commission, EACEA & Eurydice, 2015). Portugal is one of those cases, where the number of hours allocated for self-employment and for contact respectively is sometimes made casually and taking into account the nature of the course. In addition, about 19% of the member states do not guarantee that the allocation between the number of ECTS, the learning outcomes and the defined evaluation criteria has been achieved. According to the same report, this combination of credits based on the student's learning outcomes and workload is not reconcilable with the ECTS system, since it undermines the desired objectivity in the compatibility of training and qualifications between the various systems and demonstrates the persistent difficulty in implementing mobility. In addition to this obstacle to mobility, more than half of the higher education institutions do not yet have a well-established mobility strategy and their funding remains the main obstacle to their implementation, with only a minority of about 5% of students from the European Higher Education Area, benefits from this experience (European Commission, EACEA & Eurydice, 2015), data demonstrating that mobility is still a purpose to be achieved in the future.

European strategy for the development of the knowledge-based society

Another challenge brought by Bologna Process was the idea that research is an irreplaceable factor for social and human growth in order to face increasing competitiveness (Barcelona Declaration, 2002; Magna Carta of the European Universities, 1988). The dynamization of the knowledge society was one of the dimensions evidenced as being strictly necessary for the pursuit of the objectives outlined for the implementation of the Bologna

Process which resulted in the implementation of the European Research Area. In this regard, we can see that, over the last fifty years, we have been witnessing an increase in the production of knowledge incomparably superior to any other period in the history of mankind, more oriented towards the practical application of it (Sobrinho, 2005). In the Leuven (2009) and Bucharest (2012) Declarations the idea was expressed that research should be closely linked to teaching and learning, addressing the problems of today's society through the production of practical solutions to solve them and reaffirming its strengthening as a necessary precondition for the consolidation of the European Higher Education Area. Later, the Yerevan Declaration (2015) establishes research as a priority for action to be achieved by the year 2020.

Despite this desire to strengthen research in higher education systems, there is a lack of investment in most EU countries, particularly in Portugal. Only countries such as Finland, Sweden or Denmark have an investment in research of more than 3% of GDP (Ferreira, Silva, & Firmino, 2014). On the one hand, Bologna argues that one should invest in research; on the other hand, the funding of higher education institutions is reduced so that they can make such an investment. In fact, in Portugal, from year to year, the number of research fellowships decreases and the hours of research or research accompaniment are no longer counted as teaching time, difficulties that must be reconsidered along with the financial autonomy of the institutions Higher Education, since they clearly hamper the achievement of the aforementioned objective.

Quality and certification assurance

Quality assurance for the professional qualification of citizens is also one of the most ambitious challenges laid down by the Bologna Process. In most European university systems, a relevant tradition of autonomy persisted, which in some cases resulted in the absence of external monitoring and certification mechanisms for the courses taught and, in other cases, the lack of implementation of forms of academic quality control government inspection. However, this is a situation that is being changed with great agility, by the growing consolidation of the European Community process and the consequent demand for the economic and cultural integration of Europe, through which the adoption of forms of academic quality assurance and systems external evaluation and accreditation. The purpose of this action was, on the one hand, quality assurance and recognition based on comparable data; on the other hand, the establishment of adequate indicators to describe the different profiles of Higher Education, institutions and study programs (Berlin Declaration, 2003; Leuven Declaration, 2009; Prague Declaration, 2001; Salamanca Declaration, 2001).

The European Association for Quality Assurance in Higher Education (ENQA) has played an important role in promoting European cooperation for quality assurance in higher education, bringing together the main government and private accreditation bodies of all EU countries, thus providing forms of dialogue and interaction between the various agencies involved. The purpose of this action was to create a set of measures, procedures and guidelines related to quality certification, to establish a common frame of reference, to test systems suitable for quality certification (agencies or institutions) and to disseminate good evaluation practices.

As the Report on the impact of the Bologna Process on the European Higher Education Area demonstrates, quality assurance in Higher Education is in full expansion and dynamism, recognizing that the Bologna Process and the consequent development of the

European Area of Education have contributed significantly to this expansion. However, the question is whether quality assurance is achieving the desired results and, in this field, there is a growing awareness that there is still a lot of progress to be made, student-centered learning. In the above mentioned Report, regarding student participation, no positive evidence was found, that is, as systems are reorganized, there is a prospect of a decrease in student participation, which is not desirable since In Bologna the student is an intervening part of the whole formative process (European Commission, EACEA & Eurydice, 2015). The effective participation of the student in the evaluation systems is still a challenge to be concretized. Further progress is being made towards the possibility for Higher Education institutions to be evaluated by international agencies and, in this area, reforms at national level are slow, since until the Bucharest Declaration (2012) only twelve countries of the European Higher Education Area have been integrated into ENQA. Portugal obtained full status as a member of ENQA in 2014.

Lifelong Learning as a basis for the democratization of training

In a world that develops at a faster rate, there is a recognition that it is absolutely necessary to develop skills continuously and permanently throughout life. Knowledge is seen as a transmutable, continuous and forever unfinished basis, placing education and training in the face of great challenges, which go through the preparation of the new generations to orient themselves creatively in the face of this constant change. In this sense, the new concepts of education, training and learning go beyond a purely individual duty, to a broad global responsibility to all citizens. This question of interdependence develops new educational meanings, paving the way for issues such as solidarity, humanism and civility, being fundamental aspects for the survival of the individual in society. In this way, a concept of citizenship is born that holds the individual responsible for active participation and collective life, and the idea that usefulness will not only be what is appropriate to the individual as an individual, but above all what makes him / With the world around them, strengthening a truly participatory democracy.

Lifelong learning has become a fundamental need for the continuity of learning and training, ultimately contributing to the democratization of education. In this sense, it will be indispensable to assume a renewed spirit that leaves stereotypes of knowledge as exclusive patrimony of training institutions and that allows the dynamization of multiple hypotheses for its construction, proving fundamental for the achievement of ambitious strategic objectives driven by Bologna (Berlin Declaration, 2003; Bologna Declaration, 1999; Budapest-Vienna Declaration, 2010; Bucharest Declaration, 2012; Leuven Declaration, 2009; Magna Charter of European Universities, 1988; Prague Declaration, 2001).

Education and Training Monitor (European Commission, 2015) considers that one of the current challenges for member states will be to convince Higher Education institutions that acquired skills and qualifications are not relevant forever in a changing world, promoting lifelong learning, especially in the adult population. According to the same study, only about 10.7% of Europeans (between 25 and 64 years old) participate in training actions, down to 4.4% for those with lower levels of education. In addition to these results, the report on the impact of the Bologna Process states that while member states recognize the importance of lifelong learning in overcoming Europe's economic and financial crisis, it is not properly legislated in operational terms and insists on several obstacles, notably in terms of their funding (European Commission, EACEA &

Eurydice, 2015). Given the results presented, we can see that lifelong training, which provides adequate training for the public with a new, more diversified profile, has not yet materialized as desired. Today, Higher Education maintains a student reality of growing heterogeneity, which also has implications for the social dimension.

Social dimension and the implementation of the democratization of higher education

With the Bologna Process, there was an awareness among member states of the need to increase competitiveness by balancing it with the aim of improving the social characteristics of the European Higher Education Area. The aim is to strengthen cohesion and reduce social inequalities, both at national and European level. A joint effort has been made to democratize education and, consequently, the society manifested through the various meetings in the framework of the Bologna, and one of the most recent meetings in Yerevan (Yerevan Declaration, 2015) establishes as priorities the strengthening of critical and tolerant thinking, gender equality in access and attendance in higher education, the development of values democratic and civic values of European and world citizenship, the development of more inclusive societies, also referring to the fact that the economic conditions of the students can't condition the possibility of attending Higher Education.

On the consolidation of the social dimension within the framework of the Bologna Process, although some progress has been made, the latest studies show that the goal of providing equal opportunities in access to higher education is far from being achieved. In all countries, the children of uneducated people are less likely to attend Higher Education, despite the commitment made in the Leuven Declaration (2009), to set measurable targets to increase the frequency of the most disadvantaged groups by 2010 only seven countries in the European Higher Education Area do not charge students fees and there is a large difference in the value of scholarships awarded between the various participating countries (European Commission, EACEA & Eurydice, 2015).

From the analysis previously outlined to the challenges and opportunities brought about by the Bologna Process, we can highlight two aspects: firstly, it is clear that despite the fact that a recognized advance in the pursuit of Bologna's assumptions and consensus the need for its consolidation, its complete implementation is still a challenge to be achieved; a second aspect, refers to the fact that in all of the assumptions we have previously analyzed and which we consider to be the most relevant in Bologna, they are all found in the fundamental reflection of our work, which focuses on the importance attributed to the meaning of competence and its acquisition, in particular from generic to specific, thematic that we will develop next, namely analyzing its impact on the Portuguese Higher Education system.

1.2. Teaching centered on the acquisition of competences within the framework of the Bologna Process

The central issue in the Bologna Process is the "paradigm shift from a passive model, based on the acquisition of knowledge, to a model based on the development of competences" (DL n°74/2006, Preamble). In order to achieve the aforementioned objective, combined with the idea of an investment of Higher Education in the formation of human capital, it will be necessary to integrate the knowledge acquired by the training with the knowledge required by society in general and by employers in particular. The competences set forth in the educational programs must therefore take into account the graduates exit profile after completing a course of study.

In spite of the above-mentioned need, according to a study carried out under the Tuning Project, we can verify that, in the context of European Higher Education, curricula and their development process demonstrate that the skills required are (González & Wagenaar, 2008), which hindered the continuation of the strategic measures adopted and demonstrated the persistent resistance to the profound reform that is intended implement in Higher Education.

In the context of globalization, and faced with the challenges arising from the underlying competitiveness, competencies have gained prominence in relation to the teaching objectives. The objectives were, so far, set as goals to be achieved by the student through his training. Competence reinforced "the meritocratic character of our societies and accelerate the appeal to individual mechanisms of social mobility" (Fernandes, 1998, as quoted in Azevedo, 2007, p. 23), thus developing a culture that revolves around the most competent are those who obtain the best jobs and, in the limit, that the competent ones are those who obtain employment (Azevedo, 2007).

The conceptual debate in Portugal around the terms objective, competence and knowledge has been taking shape in the last years, evidenced, first, by a discourse marked by the valorization of the organization of the teaching and learning process around the acquisition of competences, namely in the Basic Education with the publication of the National Curriculum of Essential Skills (Ministry of Education, 2001), and in Higher Education with the Bologna Process. However, this idea is later refuted by Office no. 17169/2011, which repeals the aforementioned document for Basic Education, and by Law-Decree no. 115/2013, which questions the notion of competence given by the previous decree for Higher

Education. That is to say, in Portugal we are witnessing, at the present moment, a certain contradiction of the legislation in force with respect to what has constituted the central motto of the current higher education with the Bologna Process. In our opinion, these advances and legal recalls have made it impossible to understand the importance of the acquisition of competences by the various actors and the consequent implementation in the portuguese Higher Education system of an agreement of supranational commitment, and to reflect on their concepts.

The attainment of a particular educational goal presupposes that a student learns a content or knowledge in a given teaching and learning situation. The acquisition of a certain competence is verified, in turn, when the student, before a given situation, is able to adequately mobilize different prior knowledge, selecting them and integrating them in a certain practical situation (Roldão, 2003).

The verbs associated with these two concepts (achieving goals and acquiring competences), although they have the same meaning in the written expression, refer us to different meanings. While achieving something evidence to be achieved in the future, something to be achieved, the acquisition, in turn, sends us to something achieved, as a condition required to complete a certain training. In other words, while the term objective refers to the type of knowledge that the student must achieve, personalizing a certain staticism in relation to the knowledge to be achieved in the theoretical scope, competence, on the other hand, presupposes a transposition of the knowledge reached for the practice of demonstrating a certain performative dynamism. It should be noted that competence does not neglect the value of knowledge, but adds to this static knowledge a dynamic that enables the student to adequately mobilize different prior knowledge, selecting them, integrating them and adjusting them to a particular activity. That is, competence implies mastery of content knowledge as a fundamental prerequisite, but with the added value of properly contextualizing it to practical situations, an idea that is closer to real professional needs.

Within the current context of formation, the simple static, disintegrated and decontextualized reach of knowledge is no longer sufficient, if one does not know how to integrate this knowledge in a given dynamic context of professional action. What is at stake here is therefore the abolition of a mode of learning based on the student's passive acquisition of certain knowledge. We want to implement a practical application of knowledge in the various contexts of working life, thus making the connection of this knowledge with previous life experiences, building an effective integration between knowledge, scientific innovation and actual professional practice.

In the context of higher education, the concept of competence is often associated with a broader and generic notion, such as ability or strategy, although these terms have different meanings from the previous one (Simão, 2002). Effectively, the term capacity refers to a given set of generic provisions which, once developed through contact with a particular cultural context, will give rise to the acquisition of several individual competences. In this sense, while "competence is seen as an inner potentiality [...] capable of generating a multitude of behaviors" (Simão, 2002, p. 21), assuming itself as the attested capacity to employ knowledge, skills and Social and / or methodological skills in occupational situations or in study contexts and for the purpose of professional and / or personal development (European Commission, 2006, December 18); capacity, in turn, is part of the process of acquiring competencies, in order to become more or less competent, depending on the possibilities and opportunities we will have to develop them at the practical level (Simão, 2002).

As regards the distinction between competence and strategy, while the term competence is revealed through the manifestation of behaviors, that is to say through the application of certain procedures in a conscious way, in the case of knowledge acquired in a more profound and consolidated form, the strategy requires A conscious and rational response to reach an end (Simão, 2002). The strategy will be linked to a form of application of skills already acquired. In short, both the capacity and the strategy integrate the development of a given competency, the first being directly related to its acquisition and the second with the form to be achieved.

Along with the idea of competence, the idea of learning outcomes has begun to emerge in Higher Education, with the same meaning, referring to the "statement of what a learner knows, understands and is able to do when the learning process is completed learning" (European Commission, 2006, December 18, p. 3). That is, the learning outcomes refer to the minimum knowledge, skills and competences for obtaining credits.

Within the scope of the Tuning Project, a project on the benchmarking of the kind of competencies evidenced as fundamental by the participating European institutions was developed, a kind of preliminary project was carried out at the European level, in consultation with employers, graduates and teachers, in order to identify the generic competences that should be taken into account in the implementation of any study plan. Two major groups of competences emerge: specific competences, which relate to the type of particular knowledge related to a certain area of knowledge, and the generic or transferable competences, more directed to know how to be and know how to become (Lebrun, 2008), in order to prepare students for their future role in society, both in terms of employability and citizenship (González & Wagenaar, 2008).

These generic or transversal competences were, in turn, subdivided into three types: instrumental skills, which relate to cognitive, methodological, technological and linguistic skills; Interpersonal skills, which are related to individual capacities for personal, social and cooperation interaction; And systemic competencies, which refer to a holistic approach to knowledge, requiring their interrelationship with a more global perception of the processes of managing the same knowledge (González & Wagenaar, 2008). In Portugal, through the publication of Law decree no.74/2006, of March 24, the five groups of competences are shown as reference points for the reorganization of portuguese Higher Education and for the achievement of the objectives established by the Bologna Process, the importance of acquiring transversal competences alongside the specific ones was highlighted, with the publication of Law Decree no. 107/2008.

The results of the study carried out by the Tuning Project (González & Wagenaar, 2008) demonstrated that although generic or transferable competences are considered by the thematic groups consulted, they are of great relevance for the qualification of future graduates, which corroborates results from a another study carried out by Marcel Lebrun (2008) in the same context, the results show that European Higher Education institutions also privilege specific competences to the detriment of generic or transferable competences. That is, knowledge (referring to memorized knowledge) still occupies a prominent place in the academic world relative to other types of knowledge; making the correspondence with the taxonomy of Bloom (1956), perpetuates a level of lower complexity of skills.

The continuous process of search and refinement of knowledge allows to develop competences in the scope of learning to learn, being this one of the most innovative aspects in the scope of

Higher Education pedagogy and that promises to give letters regarding the desired change of educational paradigm. We understand, therefore, that learning to learn, when properly developed, will respond to essential aspects of professional preparation: it develops a sense of autonomy, arouses interest in lifelong learning, triggers critical, reflexive and creative sense, strengthens problem solving and familiarizes the student with the possibility of error, which is often the starting point for the consolidation and / or renewal of learning.

Learning to learn, rather than providing the reach of knowledge, is objectified in the process of this search, in the strategies and attitudes that the student finds to achieve it. Thus, the current educational and training objectives of Higher Education go through learning to think, through learning to learn, that is, through learning to be. This is not a new idea, since the 1990 attitude skills have been seen as priority areas in educational development (Sprinthall & Sprinthall, 1993).

If we refer to the taxonomy of Benjamin Bloom (1956) educational goals for cognitive domain, and to convey it to the current formative goals of higher education, we can see some correlation. For Bloom (1956), the definition of what the student is expected to acquire as knowledge will be essential to ensure an adequate selection of the specific procedures or means of teaching to be implemented in the classroom. In this sense, Bloom (1956) presents six stages of educational objectives that equate to levels of increasing complexity: Basic Knowledge (level one) adjusts to the type of competencies of lower complexity level in which the students assimilate the information of form passive and little reflected, tending to dominate facts, concepts, terms, specific methods without questioning or pondering, appealing to the memorization and automation of knowledge; Understanding (level two) adds to the previous stage the need for students to understand what they have acquired as knowledge; The Application (level three) refers to the use of knowledge in real situations, with a view to integrating theoretical knowledge into practical knowledge; Analysis (level four) refers to a more advanced level two level (Understanding) and requires students to organize information into the various components and understand the relationships between them and the organizing principle; Objective Synthesis (level five) corresponds to learning to select the material and the most important ideas of the same, building a new theory beyond what is known, thus impelling new ways of understanding; Objective Assessment (level six) implies all previous levels and therefore corresponds to the highest degree of complexity, presupposing the creation of patterns of appreciation and their use in a reflected way.

Lebrun (2008) adds another one, in the scope of the knowledge extracted from the taxonomy of Bloom (1956), where high-level skills are classified by increasing degree of complexity: the know how to become. This knowledge, according to the author, corresponds to the stages Synthesizing and Evaluating and adds to the knowledge to be "a dynamic and temporal perspective" (p. 32), demonstrating how the individual projects to find his future, that is, the effort that prints to achieve your goals.

Being the knowingness and the knowledge to be interdependent of the other two knowledges, they are located in a higher level of competences, by the degree of personal and social complexity. Knowledge is intervened in the way the individual analyzes a given situation, according to his or her points of view and values, and the ones that he or she will withdraw according to their experience. Knowing becoming, in turn, intervenes in the way the individual evaluates his situation and evaluates himself with regard to the objectives or the project to which he has surrendered (Lebrun, 2008). It will be fundamental for higher education institutions to rethink and renew their practices in order to develop higher level skills in the teaching and learning process.

In view of the above, it is clear that knowledge is only valid if it is integrated into a dynamic context of action. That is, the students receive the knowledge with an attitude of true involvement in the achievements they achieve, thus looking for the integration of this knowledge in their lives and needs, awakening their critical sense, creativity in problem solving, the sense of responsibility and the readiness to learn, enabling them to learn throughout their lives. We refer, therefore, to the higher order skills, which we have explored previously in this study, which by the increasing degree of complexity have to do with knowing, knowing how to do and knowing how to be. According to the most recent results of the 2009 International Program for Students Assessment (PISA), Portuguese students have revealed their weaknesses in particular at the level of high level skills (understanding, interpreting, evaluating, reflecting). At the most elementary level, related to the type of questions that only require memorization and automation of knowledge, the Portuguese students revealed to be fit (Office of Educational Evaluation, 2010).

In the context of the new educational paradigm driven by the Bologna Process, the specific learning goals for Higher Education go through the development of several generic and transversal competences in students, an objective extended to all courses or areas of knowledge and provided for in Law-Decree no. 107/2008. These competences require the development of reflexive and critical thinking, implying the exercise of reasoning, the formulation of judgments, openness to new ways of thinking, autonomous action in diverse contexts, respect for the people around us, subordinate to the performance as a person under ethical principles and citizenship. They will also imply that the student is an active element in the learning process, developing the ability to know how to direct their own learning according to their professional interests and expectations (Garrison & Archer, 2000).

2. Methodology

In the scope of our study, we intend to answer the following research question: What competences are valued in the course under study? In order to answer this question, it is intended to achieve the following objectives: to confront the legislation decreed at national level, the regulation decreed at institutional level with the actual practice of the courses under study and with the assumptions of Bologna; Know the meaning attributed to competence by the various actors and what kind of competence is most important for them; To identify the incidence of the type of competences in the programs of the curricular units under study.

Taking into account the objectives set forth for the present study, we chose to carry out a naturalistic and phenomenological study taking into account the context of the courses under study that was understood through the analysis of documents and through the experiences and personal opinions of the various stakeholders being closely linked to the experiential dimension of the study situation, as it is perceived and manifested through the language that comes from it (Fortin 2003; Lincoln & Guba 1990; Patton 1990).

We carried out a comparative case study of a course taught in two Portuguese university and polytechnic higher education institutions, denominated by institution A and institution B, respectively. We analyzed two particular cases of formation and proceeded to their subsequent description, understanding and comparison (Yin, 2003; VanWynsberghe & Khan, 2007).

In the present research, we opted for the qualitative approach, since we studied two training contexts through the application of qualitative data collection techniques and data analysis techniques, namely semi-structured interviews with teachers and course coordinators (Ghiglione & Matalon, 2001; Tuckman, 2002), focus groups to the students (Krueger & Casey, 2009; Zuckerman-Parker & Shank, 2008;), to a total of twenty-four subjects, and to the documentary analysis of institutional documents. The emerging data analysis technique used was the analysis of conventional and directed qualitative content (Hsieh & Shannon, 2005; Mayring, 2000;).

2.1. Presentation and Discussion of Results

In the Regulations of the two institutions, the acquisition of competences is one of the presuppositions for the organization of teaching and learning of the courses, highlighting them as fundamental for a "high level" training. However, in the analyzed programs of institution A they are objective statements, denominating them "Specific Objectives of the Discipline", and a curricular unit does not clarify about the objectives or competences to be developed in the students, stating instead the contents to explore in the same. Aspects that, on the one hand, collide with what is institutionally regulated and with Bologna's presuppositions, and on the other hand, it is assumed that the student who knows what is expected of him at the learning level can develop an effort more accurate and adequate to achieve the expected results.

As regards the definition of the concept of competence, it is not defined in any document of the institutions under study. From the results obtained from the teachers interviewed in institution A, they associated the concept of competence with a continuous process of development of know-how. However, this knowledge for teachers refers only to the ability of the student to transmit a certain concept, one of the teachers adding that competence and knowledge may not coexist, contrary to what we have explored in the theoretical framework. In institution B, there is no consensus on the definition of competence among teachers. If some are close to the concept associated with Bologna's assumptions, others distance themselves from it, relating it to economic issues, even demonstrating a reactive attitude towards their development. A teacher in the area of education said that the skills cannot be measured, as we questioned, since we do not understand, then, what is evaluated by the teacher. That is, although the acquisition of competences is one of the mottos of the Bologna Process, it is not understood in this way by the majority of the teachers participating in the study.

Although the acquisition of competences is one of the mottos of the Bologna Process, it is not understood by some teachers in this way. In our view, this aspect compromises the achievement of one of the most important objectives of Bologna. The students of institution A stated that the concept of competence is reductive because it does not cover all the aspects that relate to training. One of the students of institution B, in turn, considers that competence has to do with the ability to apply knowledge in the execution of scientific work. In view of the above, we risk saying that in both institutions students are unaware of the true scope of the concept.

In the programs of institution A, the tendency is for the formulation of objectives rather than competences, namely of specific competencies. Of the emerging generic competences, the most relevant are the instrumental ones, referring to the capacity of analysis, reflection and research. The following are interpersonal skills, such as critical ability, and systemic skills such as the ability to investigate. In institution B, in curricular unit programs, the objectives are stated in a timely manner, but the specific competences to be acquired by the students prevail. However, the generic ones appear more frequently than in the other institution. As in A, the instrumental skills are the most referenced, such as the capacity for analysis, research and organization of information and mastery of basic knowledge for the exercise of the profession. In the instrumental ones, the critical capacity and mastery of the basic knowledge of the profession prevails. In systemic terms, the ability to apply in practice the acquired knowledge and the ability to open and adapt knowledge to different contexts prevails. There seems to be in this institution a better understanding of the concept of competence bound up by the Bologna Process.

Although in the programs of the two institutions the specific competences were highlighted, the type of competences mentioned by the professors interviewed as being the most valued were, curiously, the generic ones. The teachers of institution A mentioned that, given their complexity and the high number of students per class, they found many difficulties in the evaluation of these competences, so they assume not to use a formal evaluation instrument. The majority of the teachers of institution B stated that it evaluates the generic competences through the personalized support of the student in the execution of the work, and one teacher referred to resort to the definition of personalized criteria, meeting what is recommended by Bologna Process.

However, in the programs we have seen that the specific competencies are the most valued, since they present higher percentage weights than the generic ones. These results are in line with those obtained by the Tuning Project (González & Wagennar, 2008) and Marcel Lebrun (2008), confirming that, although generic competences are considered by teachers of great relevance for the qualification of future graduates, specific competencies Are still privileged in practice. Corroborating with what was developed in the theoretical framework, knowledge still occupies a prominent place in the academic world relative to other types of knowledge. These results also collide with one of the objectives set forth in Decree-Law no. 107/2008, which calls for the effective development of generic competences in students.

3. Final Comments

The study demonstrates a certain lack of knowledge of the various players in relation to the main assumptions brought by Bologna Process, namely on the real scope of the meaning of competence and its potential for quality training, ignorance that can be extended to many other aspects. Interpretations on the Bologna Process collide and call into question the operationalization of its main premises. This was a difficulty recognized in the most recent meetings of the member states (Bucharest Declaration, 2012, Budapest-Vienna Declaration, 2010; Yerevan Declaration, 2015), where it was found that the proposals made by Bologna in many Countries were not correctly implemented, a call was made for a better understanding and global involvement of the various actors in Bologna's presuppositions, and the countries of the European Higher Education Area were called upon to commit their political leaders to the effective implementation of the Bologna in all its aspects. In fact, although there has been a commitment by Member States to the implementation of the Bologna Process in higher education systems, the policies implemented at national level are not always the most appropriate in achieving the objectives of harmonization and consolidation advocated in the framework of this Process, since this sense of convergence does not always rule the wills of political leaders, as it is seen in the conceptualization of the meaning of competence in Portugal.

In short, although the Bologna Process has had a huge impact on the European Higher Education Area, there is still a clear demonstration that this impact has been better achieved in its structural and administrative implementation than at the level of its practical implementation, Corroborating with Sampaio da Nóvoa (Queirós, 2009, April 28), who mentioned that in the Bologna Process there is a lot of "cosmetic" and little effective change, and this is surely an important reason for reflection by all stakeholders.

For Portugal, and for the great majority of European countries, the implementation of a system of credits translated into the acquisition of a set of competences considered essential for the achievement of quality in the professional performance of the citizens, implies in itself a profound change In the educational paradigms traditionally assumed by higher education institutions. This change brings, therefore, innovations in the structuring of the training courses, at the level of the roles now assumed by the teacher, in the teaching and assessment dynamics that provides, and by the student, in the learning dynamics that develops. It is necessary, therefore, to reformulate the whole organization and instructive action of Higher Education. This restructuring involves a consequent adaptation of the teaching, learning and evaluation methodologies for the acquisition of competences that, in the last instance, make possible a greater effectiveness in the professional responses to the labor market.

The reflection that we have developed here intends to find in the critical points of the implementation of Bologna explored, ways of interpreting the needs arising from the complexity that the paradigm change imposes, constituting an important reason for reflection of the institutions of Higher Education, its leaders, teachers And students, since any transformation with this reach entails disorders of a different order, which only time can dispel with the commitment and participation of all those involved.

References

Azevedo, J. (2007). *Sistema educativo mundial. Ensaio sobre a regulação transnacional de educação.* Vila Nova de Gaia: Fundação Manuel Leão.

Barcelona Declaration (2002). Convention of European Ministers of Education meeting in Barcelona on 15th to 16th March 2002.

Berlim Declaration (2003). Convention of the European Ministers of Education meeting in Berlin on 19th September 2003.

Bloom, B. (1956). *Taxonomy of educational objectives, handbook 1: cognitive domain.* Nova Iorque: Mckay.

Bolonha Declaration (1999). Convention of the European Ministers of Education meeting in Bologna on 19th June 1999.

Bucharest Declaration (2012). Convention of the European Ministers of Education meeting in Bucharest on 26th and 27th April 2012.

Budapest-Vienna Declaration (2010). Convention of the European Ministers of Education meeting in Vienna on 10th to 12th March 2010.

Dréze, J., & Debelle, E. (1983). *Conceções da universidade.* Fortaleza: Universidade Federal do Ceará.

Education Ministry (2001). *Currículo nacional do ensino básico. Competências essenciais.* Lisboa: Ministério da Educação.

European Commission (2006, december 18). Recomendações do parlamento europeu e do conselho relativas à instituição do quadro europeu de qualificações para a aprendizagem ao longo da vida. *Jornal Oficial da União Europeia*, 962/CE. Recovered in 2011, january 7th, to http://eur-lex. europa.eu/LexUriServ/LexUriServ.do?uri=OJ:L:2006:394:0010:0018:pt:PDF

European Commission (2015). *Education and Training Monitor 2015*. Recovered in 2015, november 11th, to http://ec.europa.eu/education/library/publications/monitor15_en.pdf.

European Commission, EACEA, & Eurydice (2015). *The European Higher Education Area in 2015: Bologna Process. Implementation Report.* Recovered in 2015, october 7th to http://www.cnedu.pt/pt/noticias/internacional/1015-relatorio-eurydice-the-european-higher-education-area-in--2015-bologna-process-implementation-report.

European Parliament and Council (2008, may 6th). *Quadro europeu de qualificações para a aprendizagem ao longo da vida. Jornal Oficial C111.* Recovered in 2010, october 28th, to http://europa.eu/legislation_summaries/education_training_youth/lifelong_learning/c11104_pt.htm

Ferreira, N., Silva, S., & Firmino, T. (2014, janeiro 18). Investigadores não sabem para onde vai a ciência portuguesa. O Público. Recovered in 2015, october 16th, to http://www.publico.pt/ciencia/noticia/ciencia-em-tempos-de-crise-1620237.

Feyo de Azevedo, S. (2004, november). *Os novos paradigmas de formação no espaço do ensino superior e as actividades profissionais*. Comunicação apresentada no Seminário – Reflexos da Declaração de Bolonha. Recovered in 2009, december 3rd, to http://paginas.fe.up.pt/~sfeyo/Docs_SFA_Publica_Conferences/SFA_OP_20050601_Bolonha_Forum_CNPL.pdf

Fortin, M-F., (2003). *O processo de investigação: da conceção à realização* (3ªed.). Loures: Lusociência (Original work in French, published in 1996).

Garrison, D. R., & Archer, W. (2000). *A transactional perspective on teaching and learning: A framework for adult and higher education*. Oxford: Pergamon

General Direction to Higher Education (2008). *Estratégia de Lisboa*. Recovered in 2010, may 12nd, to http://www.dges.mctes.pt/DGES/pt/Reconhecimento/Uni%C3%A3o+Europeia/Estrat%C3%A9gia+Europa+2020/Estrategia+Lisboa.htm

Ghiglione, R., & Matalon, B. (2001). *O inquérito* (4ªed.). Lisboa: Celta Editora.

González, J., & Wagenaar, R. (Eds.) (2008). *Tuning project. Universities contribution to the bologna process. An introduction.* Recovered in 2010, march 30th, to http://www.unideusto.org/tuningeu/images/stories/Publications/ENGLISH_BROCHURE_FOR_WEBSITE.pdf

Helsinki Seminar: Seminar on the Degree of Degree of the European Ministers of Education meeting in Helsinki on 16th and 17th February 2001.

Hsieh, H-F., & Shannon, S. C. (2005). *Three approaches to qualitative content analysis.* Recovered in 2011, november 26th, to http://qhr.sagepub.com/content/15/9/1277.full.pdf.html

Krueger, R., & Casey, M. (2009). *Focus group: a practical guide for applied research* (4 ª ed.). Thousand Oaks, Califórnia: Sage Publications.

Law-Decree no.107/2008, 25th de june. Importance of the acquisition of transversal competences in higher education.

Law-Decree no.115/2013, 7th august. Stipulation of teaching staff requirements to teach in Higher Education.

Law-Decree no.74/2006, 24th de march. Regulation of the changes introduced by the LBSE regarding the new organization model of Higher Education.

Lebrun, M. (2008). *Teorias e métodos pedagógicos para ensinar e aprender.* Lisboa: Instituto Piaget (Original work in French published in 2002).

Leuven Declaration (2009). Convention of the European Ministers of Education meeting in Leuven on 28th and 29th May 2009.

Lincoln, Y. S., & Guba, E. G. (1991). *Naturalistic inquiry.* Newbury Park, Califórnia: Sage Publications.

Magna Charter of European Universities (1988). Convention of the Rectors of European Universities meeting in Bologna on 18th September 1988.

Mayring, P. (2000). Qualitative content analysis. *Forum: Qualitative Social Research, vol. 1, número 2.* Recovered in 2011, november 24th, to http://www.qualitative-research.net/index.php/fqs/article/view/1089

Neave, G. (1998). *Modelos de éxito. Los sistemas de cuatro países han influído en la educación superior del mundo entero? Qué han aportado?* Recovered in 2010, march 29th, to http://www.unesco.org/courier/1998_09/sp/dossier/txt12.htm.

Office no.17169/2011, 23rd december. Revocation of Skills in Basic Education.

Office of Educational Evaluation (2010). *PISA 2009. Competências dos alunos portugueses. Síntese de resultados*. Recovered in 2011, may 20th, to http://www.gave.min-edu.pt/np3content/?newsId=346&fileName=Sintese_Resultados_PISA2009.pdf

Patton, M. Q. (1990). *Qualitative evaluation and research methods*. Newbury Park, Califórnia: Sage Publications.

Prague Declaration (2001). Convention of the European Ministers of Education meeting in Prague on 19th May 2001.

Queirós, M. (2009, april 28th). Ensino superior devia voltar ao ministério da educação. *Diário Económico*. Recovered in 2011, march 11th, to http://economico.sapo.pt/noticias/ensino-superior-deveria-voltar-ao-ministerio-da-educacao_9097.html

Roldão, M. C. (2003). *Gestão do currículo e avaliação de competências*. Lisboa: Editorial Presença.

Salamanca Declaration (2001). Convention of the European Ministers of Education meeting in Salamanca on 29th and 30th March 2001.

Simão, A. M. V. (2002). *Aprendizagem estratégica. Uma aposta na auto-regulação*. Lisboa, Ministério da Educação: Autor.

Sobrinho, J. D. (2005). Educação superior, globalização e democratização. Qual universidade? *Revista Brasileira de Educação,* Brasil, 28. Recovered in 2010, may 23rd, to http://www.scielo.br/scielo.php?pid=S1413-24782005000100014&script=sci_arttext.

Sorbonne Declaration (1998). Convention of the European Ministers of Education meeting in Sorbonne on 25th May 1998.

Sprinthall, N. A., & Sprinthall, R. C. (1993). *Psicologia educacional*. Lisboa: McGraw-Hill (Trabalho original em inglês, publicado em 1990).

Tuckman, B. W. (2002). *Manual de investigação em educação* (4ª ed.). Lisboa: Fundação Calouste Gulbenkian (Original work in English, published in 1994).

VanWynsberghe, R., & Khan, S. (2007). Redefining case study. *International Journal of Qualitative Methods, 6(2)*. Recovered in 2010, june 2nd, to http://www.ualberta.ca/~iiqm/backissues/6_2/vanwynsberghe.htm

Yerevan Declaration (2015). Convention of European Ministers of Education meeting in Romania on 14th to 15th May 2015.

Yin, R. K. (2003). *Case study research: design and methods* (3ª ed.). Thousand Oaks, Califórnia: Sage Publications.

Zuckerman-Parker, M., & Shank, G. (2008). The town hall focus group: a new format for qualitative research methods. *The Qualitative Report,* 13, 630-635. Recovered in 2011, december 4th, to http://www.nova.edu/ssss/QR/QR13-4/zuckerman-parker.pdf

CHAPTER 2

QUALITY AS POLITICS AND AS POLICIES AND THE IMPORTANCE OF INSTRUMENTS

Amélia Veiga

Centro de Investigação e Intervenção Educativas,
Centro de Investigação de Políticas do Ensino Superior e Faculdade
de Psicologia e de Ciências da Educação da Universidade do Porto.

António Magalhães

Centro de Investigação de Políticas do Ensino Superior e Faculdade de Psicologia e de Ciências da Educação da Universidade do Porto.

This chapter aims at contributing to understand the development of European higher education quality assurance politics and policies. Drawing on discursive institutionalism, it analyses policy documents (reports, recommendations and guidelines) on quality assurance issued by institutions at the European level underlining the role of ideas in the construction of quality as a political driver. The argument is that the principles construing the politics of quality assurance at the European level are being diluted in the enactment of quality assurance policies, practices and their instruments. This is a case of

goal displacement with regard to the major political objective of a more integrated higher education in Europe. Discursive institutionalism allowed identifying the role of normative and cognitive ideas in the shift from the centrality of ultimate political values to instrumental ideas reflecting proceduralism. This shift illustrates the process of goal displacement of quality assurance policies coordinated at the European level.

Introduction

Quality assurance is an enduring topic in the construction of the European Higher Education Area (EHEA). The European dimension of quality assurance is visible in the European level dynamics developed since the 1990s. European quality assurance policy is an instrument of European governance as it relies on the interaction of policies at the institutional, national and European levels. In this sense, a common grammar has been developed privileging accreditation to ensure coherence to evaluation policies (Magalhães, Veiga, Ribeiro, Sousa, & Santiago, 2013). However, from the perspective of the European Commission (2009), the membership of higher education quality assurance agencies in ENQA (European Association for Quality Assurance in Higher Education) and their registration in the EQAR (European Quality Assurance Register for Higher Education) is not fulfilling the objectives of encouraging mobility as is one of the aims of European cooperation in the fields of education and training. In order to deal with this goal displacement (Hood, 2000), European Standards and Guidelines (ESG) for quality assurance were revised in 2015 with the explicit aim of improving readability and user-friendliness of quality assurance systems.

Goal displacement occurs when major goals initially defined are replaced in favour of new goals in the political process. Quality as a political driver of European coordination of higher education area aims at consolidating the EHEA on the basis of comparative quality and it is translated into policy goals focusing the promotion of mobility. This translation of the politics (consolidation of EHEA) into policy (mobility policies) may result into goal displacement as "an instrumental value becomes a terminal value in a way that defeats the objective" (Hood, 2000, p. 214).

This the case of quality assurance politics and policies developed within the EHEA as efforts towards convergence of procedures are lagging behind European values and principles. The argument is that the principles construing the politics of quality assurance are blurred in the enactment of quality assurance policies. Quality assurance practices and their instruments become the ultimate value hindering the major political objective of a more integrated higher education in Europe. The literature on policy instruments underline precisely that the instruments used to serve a policy impinge on the nature of the policy itself (Lascoumes & Galès, 2007).

With the purpose of understanding the European higher education politics and policies of quality assurance we will draw on discursive institutionalism to underline the role of ideas in the construction of quality as a political driver. Policy documents (reports, recommendations and guidelines) on quality assurance issued by institutions at the European level were analysed to characterize the political enactment of quality assurance policies.

In the first part of the chapter, we will identify the discourses or system of meaning that constitute the identity of the politics of quality. In the second part we will use Schmidt's distinction between normative and cognitive ideas to analyse the construction of European quality assurance politics and policy. Quality standards are the core instrument for comparative quality and are used as a reference for internal and external quality assurance systems in higher education and for the registration of quality assurance agencies that comply with the ESG (European Commission, 2009). The aim is to grasp the ends/means reversal in the ESG definition (2005) and their revision (2015) of quality standards of the EHEA.

1. Ideas Matter

Ideas are embedded in political action and discursive institutionalists (Schmidt, 2008) ascribe to them the role of constituting political action. This is not to deny that institutional frameworks play a role in the production and the dissemination of ideas (Mehta, 2011).

Ideas are located at different levels and ideas convened by public philosophies or *Zeitgeist*, ideas about problem definitions and ideas about problem solutions (Kingdom, 1984; Mehta, 2011) contain normative and cognitive ideas (Schmidt, 2008). Normative ideas are those that "attach values to political action and serve to legitimate the policies in a program through reference to their appropriateness (see March and Olsen 1989)" (Schmidt, 2008, p. 307) and cognitive ideas "provide the recipes, guidelines, and maps for political action and serve to justify policies and programs" (Schmidt, 2008. p. 306). While the former uses principles and values to legitimate social compliance to policies and programmes (e.g. quality of higher education), the latter provides taken-for-granted assumptions on political procedures that justify political action (e.g. evaluation of quality).

Public philosophies drive normative ideas that tend to dominate policies. They are meta-ideas providing "a heuristic that tells political actors what aspects of the issue to emphasize and what side to take" and function "as a kind of changing cultural touchstone to which actors can appeal in their efforts to advocate for a particular policy or symbol" (Mehta, 2011, p. 42). In turn, the role of ideas in shaping problem definition and ideas shaping problem solution promote chiefly cognitive ideas. While the latter provides the means for solving the problem and accomplishing policy objectives, the former configures policy responses "that will seem desirable, and hence much of political argument is fought at the level of problem definition" (Mehta, 2011, p. 27).

Public philosophies function as metanarratives and are embedded in political actors and "operate at a presuppositional level of social science epistemology or beyond our awareness" (Somers & Gibson, 1996, p. 63). This is the case of 'knowledge society' as an ideograph shaping politics and of 'quality' as one of its elements. Actually, quality is construed as a value on the basis of ideas configuring policy responses and providing the means for solving the problem. In spite of the fact that quality became a keyword in structuring political action, it assumes the features of an 'empty signifier'. Discourse analysts define this type of signifier as 'pure' as it possesses consensual subjective or ideal value. In this sense, quality is subjectively associated with which is good and worth to pursue within the 'knowledge society'.

From our perspective, quality as a normative idea prevails in the translation of public philosophies into policies as it is referred to a desirable and unquestionable value. Already in the 1990s, Barnett referring to the UK experience, distinguished between 'enlightenment' and 'surveillance' purposes in quality assurance questioning the consensual desirability of quality. The author underlined that the meaning of quality was contingent to the development of instruments to evaluate it. In this regard, evaluation of quality plays the role of the definition of the policy problem and its solution. On the one hand, evaluation of quality appears discursively as a means to solve the problem of comparative quality associated with the political goals (e.g. increasing mobility); on the other hand, evaluation of quality frames policy solutions relying, for instance, on accreditation. Hence, evaluation of quality as an instrument affect the meaning of quality assurance practices. These instruments developed on the basis of a technicist approach that reduce "the possibility of evaluation having hermeneutic or dialogic value within the academy and which could enable the academic members of the higher education system to become more genuinely a professional community" (Barnett, 1994, p. 165).

The instrumentality of evaluation with regard to quality challenged the prevalence of normative ideas of quality and its statute of an 'empty signifier' as its meaning is being struggled for by competing discourses, in Barnett's terms: 'enlightenment' *versus* 'surveillance'. Guy Neave (2012) attributed to quality assurance procedures a key role in the development and workings of the 'Evaluative state' underlining the 'surveillance' purposes of quality assurance policies at the European, national and institutional levels. This *proceduralist* and technical approaches to quality assurance has been assuming a problem-solving perspective that fails to recognize its influence on the reconfiguration of the idea of quality in shifting from normative to cognitive nature. This is a major ingredient for turning quality into a means rather than a goal in itself.

Arguably, ideas matter as they contribute to understand how politics and policies of quality on higher education turn into instrumental and procedural approaches. Following from discourse theorists, articulation is "any practice establishing a relation among elements such that their identity is modified as a result of the articulatory practice" (Laclau & Mouffe, 1985, p. 105) and will be useful to understand how the struggle over the meaning of quality revolves around normative and cognitive ideas.

1.1. The role of ideas in constituting action

In the establishment of the EHEA the prominence of cognitive ideas relies on the link established between quality assurance and the enhancement of mobility to further European integration. The statute of ideas as either *explanans* (the explanation) or *explanandum* (what needs to be explained) (Mehta, 2011) reveals key dimensions at work in policy action. When scrutinizing 'why European cooperation in quality should be promoted?' - 'because quality is a undeniable need' - 'quality' appears as playing simultaneously the role of the *explanandum* and of the *explanans* for cooperation. As *explanans* it assumes a normative stance legitimizing cooperation and as *explanandum* quality is diluted into a cognitive approach based on practices and instruments. These practices and instruments were created and legitimized by the value of quality and justified on the basis of their feasibility.

In the EHEA, European Standards and Guidelines (ESG) reflect this pragmatic policy approach and as a policy instrument they influence the nature of quality as a politics and as a policy. Actually, as argued by Guy Neave the focal points in the politics of quality are determined by the evaluation agencies which "are, *par excellence*, the arena where 'politics of quality' are fought out and laid down" (Neave, 1994, p. 129). The fact that evaluation of quality is put in the hands of external and bureaucratic power dilutes the normative nature of quality in the cognitive stance of its instrumentality.

For the purpose of understanding the risks of seeing quality from an instrumental and procedural perspective into detriment of its major normative assumptions, it is of utmost importance to find out where the power lies. The power relationships develop in the tension between education as a national prerogative and the interest of European institutions in promoting a more integrated political action. Under this framework, higher education institutions are deemed to be in control of quality assurance of their activities.

Driving the shift from normative to cognitive ideas is these power relationships between the European, national and institutional levels of policy action. Barnett underlines that there are quality processes and structures falling under the control of the academic community and those that "come to the control of agencies external to academe" (Barnett, 1994, p. 172). And Amaral adds that "European higher education is in a kind of schizophrenic situation, as on the one hand there is a rhetoric of promotion of cooperation, trust and the European dimension and, on the other hand, quality mechanisms are apparently based on suspicion" (Amaral, Tavares, & Cardoso, 2011, p. 2).

On the basis of these power relationships the analysis of the politics must take into account the mandate addressed to quality, the capacity to materialize this mandate and the influence of the instruments in driving politics making the case of the importance of ideas in construing political action in the field of quality assurance.

2. Mandate addressed to quality

Ideas driven by the European Commission with regard to quality captured by the centrality of cooperation between member states to reinforce mobility in higher education as a value and a principle. In the 1991 Memorandum on Higher Education in the European Community (1991) European excellence was articulated with quality of higher education on the basis of the assumption that public expenditure "makes assurance of quality a necessary part of political accountability" (European Commission of the European Communities, 1991, p. 13). At the same time, mutual recognition is articulated with comparative quality opening the way to

> Quality viewed as a larger issue than comparison within and between Member States and that the potential for exchange of experience and for the cooperation at Community level in the determination of the parameters of quality and in their assessment be exploited as fully as possible (European Commission of the European Communities, 1991, p. 14).

The subsequent initiatives at the European level articulated mutual recognition with cooperation for the reinforcement of mobility in higher education (Conclusions of the Council and the Ministers of Education meeting within the Council of 25 November 1991 (91/C 321/03) and the transparency of national quality assurance systems in higher education with cooperation in quality assurance (Council Recommendation of 24 September 1998 on European cooperation in quality assurance in higher education / 98/561/EC).

The mandate addressed to quality, as reflected in the 1998 Council Recommendation on European cooperation in quality assurance in higher education (98/561/EC), set the foundations of a European network of national quality agencies (ENQA). The articulation between quality and principles such as 'accountability', 'mutual recognition', 'comparative quality', 'cooperation', and 'transparency' drove the definition of the ESG. These articulations legitimize the function and the structure of the European dimension of quality assurance for the EHEA.

The meanings of quality were fixed by a managerial perspective underlying a technical approach on the basis of the association between 'quality' and 'accountability', 'comparative quality' and 'transparency'. In turn, the articulation between 'quality' and 'mutual recognition' and 'cooperation' promote ideas about problem-definition and political arguments in favour of 'cooperation' are fought for at this level. The problem of 'mutual recognition' is contingent to 'quality' and it is to be dealt with by means of 'cooperation'. However, these articulations also trigger ideas about problem-solutions ascribing to cognitive ideas an important role in the reconfiguration of quality. In this sense, the problem definition of mutual recognition is associated with the existence (or not) of quality being 'cooperation' a key mean to this end.

This tendency to deprive quality of normative meanings culminates with the acknowledgement that "since 2005, considerable progress has been made in quality assurance as well as in other Bologna action lines such as qualification frameworks, recognition and the promotion of the use of learning outcomes, all these contributing to a paradigm shift towards student-centred learning and teaching". (ENQA, 2015, p. 3).

These achievements are then presented as ideas about problem-solutions justifying cognitive ideas with vested interests. However, the articulations between 'quality assurance', 'quality frameworks', 'recognition' and 'learning outcomes' are cognitive ideas shaping simultaneously problem-definition and problem-solution in dealing with the paradigm shift towards student-centred learning and teaching. In this sense, the cognitive ideas about quality, as argued before, promoted 'quality' as playing simultaneously the role of the *explanandum* and of the *explanans,* in this case not for cooperation, rather endorsing student-centred learning and teaching approaches. As *explanans* it assumes a normative stance legitimizing the paradigm shift; as *explanandum* quality is diluted into a cognitive approach based on 'quality assurance', 'quality frameworks', 'recognition' and 'learning outcomes' procedures. These ideas reconfigure the mandate addressed to 'quality' underlining instruments justified on the basis of their practicability. Actually, drivers for a revised ESG version are to be found on the need "to improve their clarity, applicability and usefulness, including their scope" (ENQA, 2015, p. 3) reiterating justifications for political action.

Normative ideas attaching values to political action faded away as 'cooperation' or 'mutual trust' are not seeing as worthy to pursue by themselves, they essentially have a meaning in articulation with the development of procedures. The idea of 'cooperation' appears associated with the idea of team work "with other institutions, quality assurance agencies and the national ENIC/NARIC centre with a view to ensuring coherent recognition across the country" (ENQA, 2015, p. 10) and ESG purposes and principles limit themselves to reinforce "mutual trust, thus facilitating recognition and mobility within and across national borders" (ENQA, 2015, p. 6). In this sense, appropriate recognition practices are dependent on *proceduralism* permeating institutional processes. Ideas convened by public philosophies or *Zeitgeist* around the principle or value of student-centred learning and teaching also reflect the dominance of the cognitive approach about the design and delivery of study programmes and the assessment of learning outcomes (standard 1.2 – Design and approval of programmes) and "flexible modes of learning and teaching, are taken into account when allocating, planning and providing the learning resources and student support" (ENQA, 2015, p. 11).

2.1. Endeavouring the mandate addressed to quality

The political goal of contributing to the 'common understanding' of quality assurance is articulated with teaching and learning across borders (space) and among stakeholders (ESG, 2015). The idea that 'common understanding' makes possible *common* quality assurance practices is a normative idea legitimating the definition and use of ESG. In this sense, the ESG are deemed to provide "actors with common 'reference points' that orient and make sense out of their interactions" (Glynos & Howarth, 2007, p. 58). At the same time, the terms in which ESG are expressed bring forward their instrumentality in pursuing policies associated with increasing "transparency, thus helping to build mutual trust and better recognition of their qualifications, programmes and other provision" (ENQA, 2015, p. 4) and in "a broader context that also includes qualifications frameworks, ECTS and diploma supplement that also contribute to promoting the transparency and mutual trust in higher education in the EHEA" (ENQA, 2015, p. 4).

At the national level, governments and evaluation agencies assume that ESG are promoting transparency, mutual trust and better recognition. However, these normative ideas develop in the tension between education as a national prerogative and the interest of European institutions in promoting a more integrated political action. At the same time, cognitive ideas drive policy responses and political arguments at the level of problem definition and bring to the fore European and national interests and their conflicts.

ENQA aims at functioning as a European policy forum for developing and proposing standards, procedures and guidelines on quality assurance and finding common points of convergence between European quality assurance systems. At the national level these ideas feeding accreditation policies dilute in 'purposes' and 'improvement', 'enhancement', 'monitoring' and 'control' of quality of higher education. In this sense, quality tends to be dealt from a managerial perspective driven by these cognitive ideas.

Actually, following from the review of the Portuguese quality assurance practices the recommendations by ENQA in 2006 were to combine accreditation with institutional academic audit and to establish a strong independent national agency for quality assurance while underlining that "the legal framework should be formulated in a way that allows a certain degree of flexibility in the development and operation of the agency, e.g. determination of standards, adjustments in procedures, etc." (ENQA, 2006, p.10). The emphasis on flexibility of operationalisation is seen as a doorway to the fulfilment of ESG by national agencies making the issue of the distribution of power relationships problematic as there is a need to comply with European standards and guidelines. Actually, national quality assurance agencies that apply for inclusion in the European Quality Assurance Register (EQAR) undergo an external review for which the ESG provide the criteria. ENQA also relies on compliance with the ESG when it comes to granting quality assurance agencies full membership status (ENQA, 2015). Significantly, at the same time, the review of the Portuguese system underlined that the "consequences of accreditation and follow-up procedures in connection with academic audit should be clearly defined in the legal framework, and the agency should be responsible for providing the higher education institutions with proper information concerning the practical implications" (ENQA, 2006, p. 10). However, to be part of the European quality club the agencies should to continue actively support the fulfilment of ESG in higher education institutions.

The mandate addressed to quality is driven by the European institutions that subsume national and higher education institutions by pragmatically promoting the quest for quality. In spite of the fact that ESG are controlled by the national evaluation agencies, there is an uneven distribution of power between European and national institutions. It is rather complex to retain a sense of the "collective or public arena that takes you beyond the narrow machinations of the political elite" (Stoker & Marsh, 2010, p. 8) as the institutions involved in endeavouring the mandate addressed to quality are representatives of European quality assurance agencies (ENQA, ESU, EUA, EURASHE) of higher education institutions' leaderships (EUA), of students (ESU) and of stakeholders (Education International (EI), BUSINESSEUROPE). The issue of representation of interests comes to the fore as there is the need to find ways favouring a more inclusive and fair representation of interests. Actually, politics refers to power relationships that bring forward "the manner in which we constantly constitute the social in ways that exclude others" (Phillips & Jørgensen, 2004, p. 36) and to the interests of the academic communities, the state and the market (de)regulation, one must add the one of the European institutions.

2.2. Instruments carrying out the mandate addressed to quality

EU institutions have been promoting the idea of better governance through the enhancement of participation of the interests involved in the mandate addressed to quality. The literature on governing and governance refers to the 'governance turn' and the "official adoption of 'governance semantics' in 2001" (Kjaer, 2010, p. 1) in the European political coordination implying that closer integration is to be achieved on the basis of enhanced political coordination. In this sense, the Open Method of Coordination (OMC) has evolved around this turn in the EU and it is the main instrument carrying out the mandate addressed to quality in higher education. On the one hand, normative ideas legitimating its adoption are to be found on the assumptions of 'democratic institutions' and the 'representation of the people'. These ideas "must try to connect Europe with its citizens. This is the starting condition for more effective and relevant policies" (European Commission, 2001, p. 4). To these type of ideas, one can add principles such as 'voluntarism', 'subsidiarity', and 'flexibility'.

On the other hand, cognitive ideas justifying the OMC on the basis of the need of 'co-operation', 'best practices', 'common targets' and 'guidelines' articulate with the 'regular monitoring' of progress. This articulation supports the enhancement of the European Commission in playing "an active co-ordinating role already and is prepared to do so in the future, but the use of the method must not upset the institutional balance nor dilute the achievement of common objectives in the Treaty" (European Commission, 2001, p. 21). Since 2000, the EU consolidated as a political system underlining the existence of European governance. This system consists of the political management of rule, both formal and informal, driving values and norms affecting behaviours and attitudes of actors (Hall & Taylor, 1996; Kjaer, 2010).

Under this framework, political coordination of higher education has been promoting discourses basing, for instance, the evaluation common grammar to guarantee consistency in higher education policies (Magalhães et. al., 2013). This common grammar articulates normative ideas of quality with cognitive ideas associated with 'accreditation'. The primacy given to 'accreditation' as a privileged instrument of evaluation of quality, the dissemination across Europe of independent quality assurance and accreditation agencies are a result of European governance strategy. The EC sees the proliferation of quality assurance agencies across Europe as "a marked success as most countries have indeed set up a quality assurance system and European cooperation in the quality field has been intense" (European Commission 2004, p. 7).

Key in the development of the evaluation common grammar is ENQA, which is considered by the European Commission a "concrete outcome at European level and as a starting point (...) for future developments" (European Commission, 2004, p. 5) as much as it was determinant in drafting of the ESG. The centrality of ENQA in the governance of quality policies has assumed 'accreditation' as a cognitive idea. Furthermore, this feature and its pragmatic characteristics were enforced going beyond the role of national and higher education institutions. Actually,

> although none of the successive communiques from the meetings of the Ministers of Education (Prague, Berlin, Bergen) gives primacy to accreditation, and although the Recommendation of the European Parliament and of the Council (2006/143/EC) of 15th January 2006 refers to both quality assurance agencies and accreditation agencies, the fact [is] that accreditation has been pushed forward against the opposition of a large number of higher education institutions [...] (Sarrico, Rosa, Teixeira, & Cardoso, 2010, p. 39).

This makes visible the power imbalance within European governance actors and institutions in carrying out the mandate addressed to quality. However, and contrary to what the European level institutions, aimed at, European governance is not generating the desired levels of mutual trust. On the one hand, the opposition of higher education institutions was disregarded but, on the other hand, they were expected to actively work "to establish coherent internal quality assurance systems and align them with external assessment procedures" (European Commission, 2009, p. 4). This power imbalance is translated into the hegemony of cognitive ideas feeding pragmatism and *proceduralism* making quality policies as problem definition and problem solution issues.

So far, according to our argument, the mandate addressed to quality, the processes of endeavouring the mandate and its instruments show that there is the prevalence of cognitive ideas over normative ideas. Pragmatic and procedural approaches to quality while underlining the importance of the instruments impinge on the nature of the politics of quality itself. This entails a political goal displacement, as the instruments (accreditation structures and procedures) become a value by themselves shifting away from the initial political objective, i.e. the consolidation of the EHEA. Furthermore, quality itself is diluted in the instruments and procedures used to evaluate it.

2.3. Policies of quality: problem definition, problem solving, and the legitimacy by instruments

While the evaluation of quality is a contested terrain, the European institutions further enhanced the coordination of policies of quality underlining the priority of ideas about problem solution and problem definition, rather than ideas than normative ideas about European cooperation, citizenship, democracy, and participation.

The centrality of a pragmatic and instrumental centred approach to quality policies in Europe is visible in the 2009 report where the normative stances of the political endeavour are practically absent with regard to recognition and trust. On the contrary, recognition is articulated with 'quality assurance infrastructure', 'transparency for users and the society', 'sufficient level of comparability', 'cooperation with the NARIC-ENIC network is likely to enhance the database's potential', 'conventions of mutual recognition', 'portability of national accreditation'. In turn, trust is articulated with 'public access to the assessments made by the agencies' making them "transparent and trustworthy for European citizens and employers as well as for students and scholars from other continents" (European Commission, 2009, p. 3).

Along with these lines, the 2014 report on the progress in quality assurance in higher education the normative idea of transparency was diluted into the development of tools such as learning outcomes, qualifications frameworks, the European Credit Transfer and Accumulation System (ECTS), and the Diploma Supplement. In turn, the normative idea of an 'European area' is translated into an European area of skills and qualifications, contributing to the pragmatic approaches of policies for teaching and learning. The same goes with regard to trust as it is expected to be enhanced by 'quality assurance mechanisms' (European Commission, 2014) such as the publication of the results of quality evaluation.

Problem definition and problem solution are gathered in this instrumental approaches to quality policies. Actually, the problem of building "a higher level of trust between agencies" is dealt with the "need to convince their European peers that they offer a sufficient level of comparability". To this end, ideas about problem solution come from quality assurance infrastructures that must provide reliable data and proof of comparable practices as "a precondition for cross-recognition of degrees and the promotion of student mobility" (European Commission, 2009, p. 10). This represents an ends/means reversal where the initial political goals of social equity among European citizens is captured by the instruments developed for the purpose. With regard to trust, the problem definition matches the problem solution as "publishing QA results stimulates quality enhancement and helps build trust and transparency" (European Commission, 2014, p. 5).

This shift from normative goals to the centrality of instruments is made evident in the revision of the ESG held in 2015. On the basis of an assumed "consensus among all the organisations involved on how to take forward quality assurance in the European Higher Education Area" the revision takes on that the "engagement with quality assurance processes, particularly the external ones, allows European higher education systems to demonstrate quality and increase transparency, thus helping to build mutual trust and better recognition of their qualifications, programmes and other provision" (ENQA, 2015, p. 4).

On the one hand, higher education institutions are supplied with a more efficient framework for evaluating quality and, on the other hand, the EQAR can use it to register the quality assurance agencies as they comply with the ESG.

On the basis of the revision was the definition of the problem related to the need of enhancing 'innovation', 'economic growth and global competitiveness', 'skills and competences', 'flexible learning paths and recognizing competences', 'diversification of modes of educational provision', 'development of national and institutional quality assurance systems' (ENQA, 2015). Quality is introduced as an objective to be dealt with and these instruments appear simultaneously as the problem definition and solution. The legitimacy of the end (quality) is provided by the means to achieve it. The instrument, then, becomes the policy itself.

Interestingly enough the revision assumes the normative purpose as an ultimate legitimacy instance as it is "an opportunity to reinforce the institutional response to challenges such as widening participation, reducing dropout, improving employability etc., and to ensure that QA encourages the development of a strong quality culture and the genuine engagement of the academic community" (European Commission, 2014, p. 5).

However, given the context within which the politics of quality has evolved in and the paraphernalia of instruments enacted for its implementation, the context restricts the room for manoeuvre for actors and higher education institutions to focus on the normative goals envisaged by the political endeavour of quality.

3. Conclusion

In analysing European quality in higher education the distinction between politics and policies made evident the power imbalance between institutions and actors dealing with quality issues. By convening the role of normative and cognitive ideas the shift from the centrality of political values as worthy by themselves, such as 'trust', 'mobility', 'cooperation' to instrumental ideas reflecting *proceduralism*, was identified. Both the ESG definition in 2005 and their revision in 2015 reflect this shift in the legitimation of policies to their justification by cognitive approaches to policy-making. In line with Schmidt one might argue that the ESG are assuming the role of "recipes, guidelines, and maps for political action and serve to justify policies and programs" (Schmidt, 2008, p. 306) providing taken-for-granted assumptions on political procedures that justify evaluation of quality. By overlapping the definition of the problem of quality with its solution "the evaluation of quality is worthwhile but its justification is not that it is worthwhile in itself. It gains its points from the benefits that flow from it" (Barnett, 1994, p. 178).

The ends/means reversal represents a configuration of political coordination where the nature of the policy is shaped by the nature of its instruments. As important as quality are the tools for its measurement and monitorisation because it is easier to take political action and furthering integration on the basis of procedures than on the basis of shared principles, values, and purposes. The analysis pointed to the fact that quality standards for EHEA are pragmatically oriented. While it is difficult to identify institutional practices indicating either the institutionalisation and/or the enactment of ESG (European University Association, 2005; Sarrico, Veiga, & Amaral, 2013), there doubts that agencies' membership in ENQA and their registration in the EQAR might generate the level of mutual trust needed for the credibility within the EHEA. Actually, research has been pointing out that when higher education institutions deal with quality processes oriented by the ESG (Manatos, Sarrico, & Rosa, 2014) the extent to which there are interdependencies between the intrinsic improvement of the learning experience of students and the adoption of the ESG remains to be seen.

References

Amaral, A., Tavares, O., & Cardoso, S. (2011). *Regaining Trust. Is it possible?* Paper presented at the Paper presented at the VI European Quality Assurance Forum, Antwerp, 17-19 November.

Barnett, R. (1994). Power, Enlightenment and Quality Evaluation. *European Journal of Education,, 29* (2), 165–179. doi:http://doi.org/10.2307/1561639

ENQA. (2005). *European Standards and Guidelines*. Helsinki, Finland: European Quality Association.

ENQA. (2006). Report by an ENQA review panel: Quality Assurance of Higher Education in Portugal: An Assessment of the Existing System and

Recommendations for a Future System. Occasional Paper 10. Helsinki, Finland.

ENQA. (2015). *Standards and guidelines for quality assurance in the European Higher Education Area (ESG)*. Yerevan.

European Commission. (2001). *European Governance - a White Paper*. Brussels.

European Commission. (2004). *Report from the Commission to the European Parliament, the Council, the European Economic and Social Committee and the Committee of the Regions on the Implementation of Council Recommendation 98/561/EC of 24 September 1998 on European cooperation in quality assurance in higher education*. Brussels.

European Commission. (2009). *Report from the Commission to the Council, the European Parliament, the European Economic and Social Committee and the Committee of the Regions - Report on progress in quality assurance in higher education*. Brussels.

European Commission. (2014). *Report from the Commission to the European Parliament, the Council, the European Economic and Social Committe and the Committe of the Regions - Report on Progress in Quality Assurance in Higher Education*. Brussels.

European Commission of the European Communities. (1991). *Memorandum on Higher Education in the European Community*. Brussels.

European University Association. (2005). *Developing an internal quality culture in European universities*. Brussels.

Glynos, J., & Howarth, D. (2007). *Logics of Critical Explanation in Social and Political Theory*. Oxon: Routledge.

Hall, P. A., & Taylor, R. C. R. (1996). Political Science and the Three New Institutionalisms. *Political Studies, 44*(5), 936-957. doi:10.1111/j.1467-9248.1996.tb00343.x

Hood, C. (2000). *The art of the state - Culture, Rhetoric, and Public Management*. Oxford: Oxford University Press.

Kingdom, J. (1984). *Agendas, Alternatives and Public Policies*. New York: Longman.

Kjaer, A. (2010). *Governance*. Cambridge: Polity.

Kjaer, P. (2010). *Between Governing and Governance: on the Emergence, function and form of Europe's Post-national constellation*. Oxford: Hart Publishing.

Laclau, E., & Mouffe, C. (1985). *Hegemony and Socialist Strategy: Towards a Radical Democratic Politics*. London: Verso.

Lascoumes, P., & Galès, P. L. (2007). Introduction: Understanding Public Policy through Its Instruments - From the Nature of Instruments to Sociologiy of Public Policy Instrumentation. *Governance: An International Journal of Policy, Administration and Institutions, 20*(1), 1-21.

Magalhães, A., Veiga, A., Ribeiro, F., Sousa, S., & Santiago, R. (2013). Creating a common grammar for European higher education governance. *Higher Education, 65*(1), 95-112. doi:10.1007/s10734-012-9583-7

Manatos, M. J., Sarrico, C., & Rosa, M. J. (2014). *Perceptions of academics on ESG implementation in Portuguese universities*. Paper presented at the EAIR 36th Annual Forum in Essen, Germany, Essen.

Mehta, J. (2011). The Varied Roles of Ideas in Politics: From "Whether" to "How". In D. Béland & R. H. Cox (Eds.), *Ideas and Politics in Social Science Research* (pp. 23-46). Oxford: Oxford University Press.

Neave, G. (1994). The Politics of Quality: Developments in Higher Education in Western Europe 1992-1994. *European Journal of Education, 29*(2), 115-134. doi:http://doi.org/10.2307/1561636

Neave, G. (2012). *The Evaluative State, Institutional Autonomy and Re-engineering Higher Education in Western Europe: The Prince and His Pleasure Institutional Autonomy, the* Basingstoke: Palgrave.

Phillips, L., & Jørgensen, M. W. (2004). *Discourse Analysis as Theory and Method*. London: Sage.

Sarrico, C., Rosa, M. J., Teixeira, P., & Cardoso, M. F. (2010). Assessing Quality and Evaluating Performance in Higher Education: Worlds Apart or Complementary Views? *Minerva, 48*, 35-54.

Sarrico, C., Veiga, A., & Amaral, A. (2013). Quality, management and Governance in European Higher Education Institutions. *Journal of European Higher Education Area, 4*, 47-69.

Schmidt, V. A. (2008). Discursive Institutionalism: The Explanatory Power of Ideas and Discourse. *Annual Review of Political Science, 11*(1), 303-326. doi:10.1146/annurev.polisci.11.060606.135342

Somers, M., & Gibson, G. D. (1996). Reclaiming the Epistemological "Other": Narrative and the Social Construction of Identity. In C. Calhoun (Ed.), *Social Theory and the Politics of Identity* (pp. 37-99). Oxford: Blackwell Publishers.

Stoker, G., & Marsh, D. (2010). Introduction. In D. Marsh & G. Stoker (Eds.), *Theory and Methods in Political Science* (pp. 1-12). New York: Palgrave.

DOI | https://doi.org/10.14195/978-989-26-1620-9_3

CHAPTER 3

THE CONCEPT OF QUALITY WITHIN THE EUROPEAN HIGHER EDUCATION AREA (EHEA).
Dimensions and discourses

Sandra Milena Díaz López

Faculty of Psychology and Educational Science, Coimbra University, Portugal,

Faculty of Educational Science, Universidad de La Salle, Bogotá (Colombia).

Email: samidilo@gmail.com

Maria do Rosário Pinheiro

Faculty of Psychology and Educational Science, Coimbra University, Portugal,

Email: pinheiro@fpce.uc.pt

Carlos Folgado Barreira

Faculty of Psychology and Educational Science, Coimbra University, Portugal,

Email: cabarreira@fpce.uc.pt

According to national concerns, since the signing of the Bologna Declaration, the search for quality guarantee has been one focus of attention of the European Higher Education Area (EHEA). This concern, shared by different stakeholders

involved in higher education improvement, has been reinforced by several communiqués on the advances made in these processes, as well as the challenges still to be faced. In this sense, from the conceptualization of what quality implies and taking into account the important role of discourse in the implementation of ways to view reality, and consequently, in social transformation processes, this chapter offers an analysis of these different dimensions of quality underlying EHEA discourses. This analysis has enabled us to notice that within the framework of the two main tendencies of quality, discourses promote an excision between quality and equity, and that the latter, though present in the different communiqués resulting from ministerial meetings, is still listed within the framework of social responsibility and that little progress towards it can be verified. This calls for a revision of this conception based on understanding education not as a product but as a right.

Introduction

Even though several publications have been made concerning the Bologna process, most of them aim at reporting back on advancements of the process rather than offering scenarios for the discussion of the conceptions which support the proposed reforms and their implications on higher education. As claimed by Oliveira and Wilewiki (2010), most available works on Bologna are accounts of the process, rather than debates centred around the concepts, ideas and rationalities which uphold it.

In this sense, and bearing in mind that this transnational endeavour is based on the search for quality, we deem it important to create a space to reflect on the definition of this concept and the dimensions revealed by discourse in the construction of the European Higher Education Area (EHEA). For this purpose, this chapter begins by highlighting the deep concern for quality shared by actors, institutions and in general, current society, as a demand to national educational systems

Having sketched this overview of the search and longing for quality in higher education, we shall move on to a thorny and unclear ground, that of the definition of quality. Here, as well as in many other aspects related to education, different opinions, perceptions and tendencies which shape a varied scenario determined by multiple interests and ways of understanding arise. Hence, in this section we will approach different conceptions and, specially, different factors or dimensions associated to this construct.

This framing allows us to establish the conceptions of quality underlying the discourses that have arisen at different ministerial meetings in which a follow-up of the progress achieved in the development of the Bologna plan is conducted, as well as in other discursive constructions that emerge from this space of harmonization and are shaped by the aims pursued by the agents of this transformation in education.

As colophon, we offer a few closing remarkswhich give rise to a reflection on everything which had been discussed. Apart from reinforcing the findings of the analysis, they serve as an invitation to carry out future research which will contribute to the questioning and permanent follow-up of the proposals made by this transnational education project in which higher education postulates are put to a test. Despite being basically a European affair, beyond its borders, the whole world has laid its eyes on the scopes and limitations of this huge effort and is affected by it.

1. Concern for quality, myth or reality?

Undoubtedly, at this time of important challenges and new social demands, search for quality becomes a concern shared by all higher education stakeholders, since it is acknowledged that this level of education affects, immediately and significantly, not only the individual but also the whole society, its development and wellbeing. In this line, addressing the needs of the current world demands the individual to achieve a high development of their social, ethical and political dimensions. However, such integration is hindered by a stagnant quality model which prioritizes products and results over processes, thus revealing the need for a constant review of what is understood by quality, the paradigms which support it and its scopes.

In the last decades, the attempts to improve the quality of university institutions have become more and more evident, so that concern for coverage has paved the way for direct attention regarding quality. According to Buendía and García (2000), while in the 1960s the main goal was coverage, and thus the admission of an increasing number of students, in the 1970s the tendency was to install a management system of the university process in order to guarantee effectiveness and efficiency; but it was in the 1980s that the improvement of the quality of the service became a priority.

In fact, the effort for coverage was the first to be addressed by many education policies which aimed at ensuring schooling for everyone. However, extending the possibilities to enjoy this legal right is not sufficient if the quality of the service is not good. Thus, it becomes essential to go beyond this and many organizations have drawn attention to the importance of being conscious of the fact that 'efforts should not only be invested on coverage extension itself, but also on the creation of conditions that ensure children and youngsters access to quality, inclusive and multicultural education that fosters diversity and democracy' (OEI, 2010, p. 36).

In this sense, Mendoza (2007) rightly points out that all those involved in the university community demand the university to offer a high quality service and that it takes into account individual, group and social needs. In fact, today's society's demand to this sphere of training goes well beyond command of knowledge and information and communication technologies. It aims at training autonomous and participative citizens that lead socio-economic transformation processes. Under the circumstances, the higher education system is expected to manage to combine high levels of self-regulations with significant rates of accountability, in order to ensure the fulfilment of such long yearned quality.

As Petruta y Cantemir (2012) claim, concern over quality in higher education is not recent. Throughout the years, different positions have been assumed regarding assessment, follow-up and improvement of the several components that make up the higher education system, that is to say, its forms of government and management, its curricular configuration, its pedagogical commitment, among others. However, what has in fact been constant in the political agenda of recent decades is the concern for assuring this quality on a permanent basis.

That said, this challenge of establishing factors that point out what a quality system is, as well as identifying strategies to reach it, is bigger when such aspiration is not solely concerned with a national education system but also addresses a transnational sphere as the European Higher Education Area(EHEA), into which not only different forms of organization converge, but alsodifferent interests and management styles. Therefore, quality analysis within this frame of possibilities of coordination, which poses common elements of reference, becomes not only relevant but necessary.

1.1. The concept of quality and its dimensions

Once evinced the common interest of ensuring quality education, the first expected step is determining its definition and associated factors and dimensions with the purpose of establishing shared criteria to reach it. Nevertheless, it is impossible to guarantee a uniform treatment of quality and many times the very same leaders foster ambiguous landscapes which demand an analysis of the ideological choices and policies behind the constant changes which have taken place in the context of higher education and that reveal some inconsistencies between discourse and practice. Just as confirmed by Rue (2007, p.29):

In political statements on higher education, a series of references can be found which far from clarifying the university which way to go, often bring about confusion. Thus, when in different official statements regarding changes in the EHEA arguments are based on 'efficiency', 'employability', 'market', 'competence' or 'mobility', it is not clear (or perhaps it is) what is ideological and what seem to be instructions for the university, nor is what basically should be assumed separated from what is arguable.

Faced to this reality, also applicable to the concept of quality, and taking into account that discourse, beyond being a meaningful construction, is a social practice which supports social transformation, it becomes relevant to analyse which concept of quality lies behind discourses produced by EHEA, bearing in mind that political processes, including those involved in teaching, are discursive by nature (Saarinem, 2005). In fact, within the framework of EHEA, quality ranks so highly that it reflects both this concept and the visions of higher education implications, scope and challenges, which has become a model for education policies in other places, such as in Latin America.

Providing a precise definition of quality is in itself a complex task. Within the frame of market and mercantilism, quality is probably much more demarcated, but in education it has a polysemic nature, since its comprehension depends on the context of elaboration and the consensus it may generate within academic community. In this sense, it is quite difficult to find a single definition, taking into account that it is associated to different aims and political, social and even economic interests, all of which requires understanding it in its context if the aim is to unveil the elements that shape it and also a thoughtful analysis which allows establishing both its scope and limits. Indeed, some authors claim that it is a contextual and comprehensive concept, as well as dynamic and ongoing(Gallego& Rodríguez, 2014; González, 2000).

In fact, is assumed that "from an etymological conception with absolute value it has moved on to be regarded as an emerging, contextual, polysemic and comprehensive concept" (González, 2000, p. 50). Other research reinforce this by characterising quality as a term which is dynamic (it changes with time), polysemic and lacking univocality, since diverse personal and professional perceptions coalesce into it (Gallego& Rodríguez, 2014). Seen in this light, quality is also regarded as tendency, path and a continuous construction process (Valdés, 2008).

In this attempt to understand the concept of quality, especially within the frame of higher education, several approximations associated to interests and purposes subjected to organisation logics have arisen. It is not claimed in vain that "debates centred around 'inside' understanding of this notion have given way to others related to its utility and especially to those who participate in its definition and accomplishment" (Perellon, 2005, p.53).

It is precisely within the frame of these debates that some insights which enable us to come near to a definition based on its intentionality arise. One of these taxonomies is put forth by Schindler, Welzant, Puls-Elvidgeand Crawford (2015), who claim that quality may be understood according to purpose (institutions and services which comply to a series of standards and requirements, usually established by regulatory agencies), excellence and prestige (goods and servicesthat achieve excellence by complying with high standards and thus stand out over others), transformation (goods and services that achieve a positive effect on students' learning) and finally, accountability (institutions and services which render account to those interested in the optimal use of services and the offer of proper education goods and services).

In accordance to this classification, these authors propose a conceptual model which offers a series of indicators associated to the different nuances quality may have in relation to its purpose. From this perspective, quality as purpose is associated to fulfilment of mission, transparency of the processes and attainment of specific goals. Regarding quality as a transformation endeavour, it includes indicators such as critical thinking and strengthening of reading-comprehension skills.Quality aimed at excellency includes categories such as prestige, credibility, rankings and all those factors that show the system or institution occupies a higher place than others. In this sense, it is associated to the academic and social reputation of some institutions. Finally, quality regarded as accountability is focused on continuous improvement and preparing students for employment, among other factors. Figure 1 illustrates the described model.

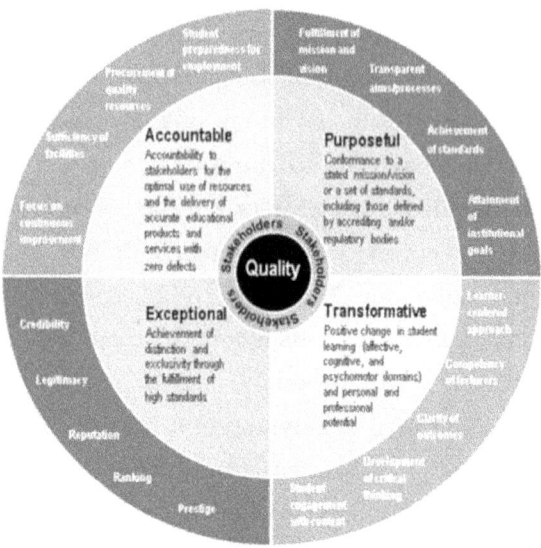

Figure 1. Conceptual model of quality depicting broad and specific strategies for defining quality.

(Source: Schindler, Welzant, Puls-Elvidge & Crawford, 2015, p.7)

Now, these portions could be seen from the two big trends encompassed by quality: accountable and exceptional would be on efficiency's side while purposeful and transformative would be seen from the need of change and equity. According to Canon and Levin (cited by Afonso, 1998), there is a permanent struggle between forces which put pressure on higher efficiency related to the reproduction of skills required by the system, and others which campaign for more democracy and equality in education. This dual perspective is correlated with formal quality, meaning skills to develop methods to deal with challenges faced by society, and on the other hand, political quality, understood as active participation of individuals as historical subjects in collective construction (Davok, 2007).

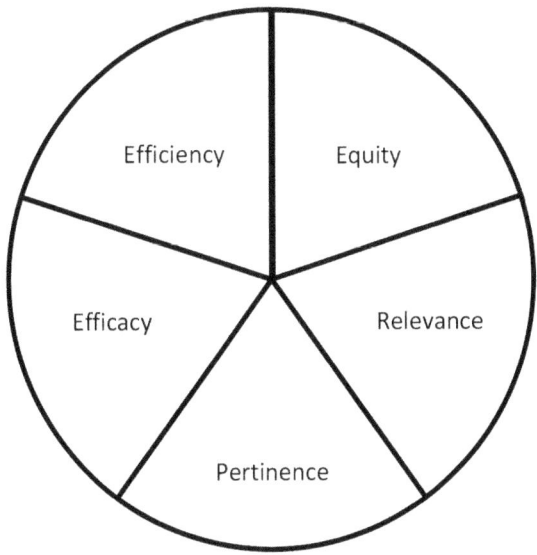

Figure 2.Dimensions of quality according to UNESCO

Within the framework of political and social quality, and consequently from its transforming purpose, problems such as the need to acknowledge the characteristics associated to the social and economic environment of the students arise. Thus, quality education "promotes full development of each person's manifold potentialities through socially relevant learning and education experiences appropriate to the needs and characteristics of individuals and the contexts in which they find themselves" (Regional Bureau of Education for Latin America and the Caribbean – OREALC-UNESCO, 2007, p.5). On this basis, the understanding of quality from five interdependent dimensions, though so highly interrelated that absence of one of them may alter the whole concept, is promoted. These dimensions are: equity, relevance, pertinence, efficacy and efficiency (see Figure 2).

In respect of *equity*, education should offer "the resources and necessary aids so that every student, according to their skills, reach the highest possible levels of development and learning" (*ibid*, p.12).*Education for all* thus becomes a principle of quality. Some authors even associate this characteristic to the notion of justice (Seibold, 2000) and some highlight that this stance leads to a more humane interpretation of the technical rationalization of quality (Braslavsky, 2006). This implies not only equity of access, but also of resources and processes so that everyone reaches results in accordance to their possibilities.

For its part, *relevance* is associated to coherence between educational purposes and current and future demands of society, which in the case of higher education, are related to such processes as globalization and knowledge society. According to OREALC-UNESCO (2007), education is relevant "as long as it fosters meaningful learning from the point of view of social demands and personal development" (p.14). In this sense, educational purposes determine processes and consequently, results, and should be coherent with current, and even future, demands of society and humankind.

In close relation to the previous dimension, we find *pertinence*, understood as respect and consideration for personal and social characteristics and needs in specific contexts. This means guaranteeing processes which, emanating from specific contexts and cultures, manage to converse with that immediate experience of subject and community. Researchers such as Barret et al (2006) associate this dimension to external effectiveness and social and individual development. In the same vein, Buendía and García (2000) reinforce the importance of this dimension in higher education by asserting that "pertinence is defined as congruence between context expectations and institutional offers (external dimension) and congruence between the institution's teleological platform and the resources and procedures employed for their attainment" (p. 210).

Lastly, we find the *efficacy* and *efficiency* dimensions, related to the attainment of goals and responsibility in the use of resources respectively. These aims are supported by an obligation derived from respect to citizen's conditions and rights, not from an economic imperative (OREALC-UNESCO, 2007). In effect, they do not aim at valuing quality exclusively according to academic results, since it may prove excessively restrictive or simplistic, but rather try to account for a phenomenon not as linear and predictable as a production system, within the traditional concept of "total quality", although thanks to it some advance has been made towards the comprehension of education as a system.

Sayed, taken up by Barret, Duggan, Lowe, NikelandUkpo (2006), is one of its most staunch critics and claims that through this perspective, only a partial definition of quality can be attained, both because its result is incomplete and because it emanates from the judgement of just a part of society. Likewise, it is claimed that educational achievement is assumed one dimensionally and is associated only to results and therefore, does not adapt itself to the particularities of the different educational systems

For their part, Barrett et al (2006) agree with these dimensions and also include another key one: *sustainability*, which turns out being the least highlighted in the pertinent literature. It implies that all considerations made in relation to the other dimensions should not be only about the present, but also the future. From this perspective "Quality education emerges in the context of the obligation to establish and sustain the conditions for each and every individual, irrespective of gender, ethnicity, race, or regional location, to achieve valued outcomes" (p. 15). Furthermore, these authors point out that these dimensions may be the basis to analyse innovation in education.

Facing this diverse scenario of understandings and topics to prioritise, we could confirm Estevão's conclusion (2012), who claims that the question of quality is above all, a matter of choosing a certain kind of quality over others which could be considered. Thus, "ela justifica-se, por exemplo, pelo apelo ora ao mundo cívico para salientar a promoção da igualdade diante do ensino, ou então, ao mundo doméstico em nome da maior proximidade relacional dos actores escolares" (p. 103). To sum up, and going back to our initial postulate, quality is historically and socially conditioned, therefore, it is determined by philosophical, sociological and pedagogical ideologies (Valdés, 2008).

2. Dimensions of quality underlying EHEA discourse

European higher education systems have gone through great changes in accordance to the different national and international needs. Among them, as stated by the Euricyde report (2008)"More recently, the impact of the Bologna Process on curricular reform, quality assurance, and mobility has become one of the key propellers of change" (p. 11).

Since the formalisation of the Bologna Declaration, it has been established on three main pillars: transparency, mobility and quality (Perellon, 2005). In fact, the main purpose of this declaration was the creation of a higher education area in order to ensure comparability, compatibility and coherence among higher education systems, with the aim of guaranteeing their coordination. It seems that quality is the backbone upon which the other rest, as confirmed by González (2006), who explicitly state that at the Convention of European Higher Education Institutions (2011), quality was regarded as an indispensable condition for trust, pertinence and mobility in the EHEA.

Thus, quality being one of the pillars for transformation, it becomes suitable to identify from which point of view this concept is understood and the factors or dimensions that explain it within the framework of this integrating purpose. This will allow us to understand the interests that justify this integrating and coordination seeking initiative.

In the different communiqués that inform about the follow-up of the successive agreements on the Bologna declaration, mainly those from ministerial meetings, all the quality dimensions mentioned above frequently appear. However, the efficiency, efficacy and relevance dimensions are highlighted as essential components of quality, while equity is taken as an additional factor linked to social responsibility. Just as Seixas (2010) points out:

> As políticas de ensino superior partilham hoje uma agenda global assente num discurso salientando a importância dos sistemas de ensino superior nas sociedades e economias mundiais do conhecimento, e privilegiando o desenvolvimento de sistemas de ensino superior orientados pelo e para o mercado. A lógica económica subjacente a este discurso, sublinhando as questões da competitividade, relevância e eficiência, incentiva a mercadorização da educação e o desenvolvimento da "indústria" do ensino superior. (p.67)

In effect, in the first communiqués that revealed the aims of the EHEA, quality was oriented towards management efficiency and accountability logic and great importance was given to meeting market needs. This is why it was necessary to develop programmes "combining academic quality with relevance to lasting employability" (EHEA, 2001, p.3). Evidently, in the light of the conceptual model proposed by Schindler, Welzant, Puls-Elvidgeand Crawford (2015), quality was seen mainly from the conceptualization of accountability and associated to all the indicators mentioned to assess that concept: student preparedness for employment, procurement of quality resources, sufficiency of facilities, and focus on continuous improvement.

Later on, in the Berlin communiqué (2003), emphasis was placed on achieving quality education, "The quality of higher education has proven to be at the heart of the setting up of a European Higher Education Area" (EHEA, 2003, p. 3). Already in this communiqué, a two-sided line is highlighted, which despite being far from considering equity as a key dimension of quality, regards it nonetheless as an independent factor which along quality, will strengthen the social dimension of the Bologna process. In this sense, according to this communiqué, the need to improve competiveness should be balanced with the aim to improve EHEA's social characteristics, "aiming at strengthening social cohesion and reducing social and gender inequalities both at national and at European level" (EHEA, 2003, p. 1). Furthermore, education is seen as a public asset, and so, as a social responsibility factor.

Though not developed as much as in the previous communiqué, in Bergen (2005) the social dimension of the Bologna Process is slighted mentioned and the need to guarantee proper conditions so that students manage to finish their studies regardless of their social or economic background is highlighted. According to this communiqué: "The social dimension includes measures taken by governments to help students, especially from socially disadvantaged groups, in financial and economic aspects and to provide them with guidance and counselling services with a view to widening access" (EHEA, 2005, p. 4).

During this same year, 2005, Standards and Guidelines for Quality Assurance were set up, which do not refer explicitly to equity. On the contrary, they promote the principles of efficacy and efficiency as key aspects of quality.

The quality of academic programmes need to be developed and improved for students and other beneficiaries of higher education across the EHEA; there need to be efficient and effective organisational structures within which those academic programmes can be provided and supported (European Association for Quality Assurance in Higher Education, 2009, p.14).

In the revision of these standards published in 2015, it is also possible to identify reference to relevance, since it is stated that"institutions should monitor and periodically review their programmes to ensure that they achieve the objectives set for them and respond to the needs of students and society" (European Association for Quality Assurance in Higher Education, 2015, p.12).

The London communiqué (2007) highlights some of the main achievements attained in the development of the Bologna plan since its initial signing. Reference is made on the one hand to the advance in ensuring quality and on the other to the social dimension of quality. In relation to the latter, direct reference is made to the importance of higher education in the reduction of inequity and promotion of knowledge. Based on this principle, it is emphasised how important it is that students are able finish their studies without being restricted by their socio-economic conditions. "We therefore continue our efforts to provide adequate student services, create more flexible learning pathways into and within higher education, and to widen participation at all levels on the basis of equal opportunity" (EHEA, 2007, p. 5)

Nevertheless, it is in the Leuven communiqué (2009) where we find the highest development of equity, mainly in reference to the groups mentioned infra:

Access into higher education should be widened by fostering the potential of students from underrepresented groups and by providing adequate conditions for the completion of their studies. This involves improving the learning environment, removing all barriers to study, and creating the appropriate economic conditions for students to be able to benefit from the study opportunities at all levels. Each participating country will set measurable targets for widening overall participation and increasing participation of underrepresented groups in higher education, to be reached by the end of the next decade. Efforts to achieve equity in higher education should be complemented by actions in other parts of the educational system. (EHEA, 2009, p.2)

With these words, the calls reinforced to guarantee permanence conditions, not just admission, for all students, including those belonging to the referred groups. Moreover, it is explicitly stated that attainment of this purpose should be a commitment made by all members and components of the education system.

A principle that leads us directly to the equity dimension appears in the Bucharest communiqué (2012), since one of the goals is "to provide quality higher education for all" (EHEA, 2012, p.1). As can be seen so far, some concern to consider equity as a key element to guarantee education is discernedin every report. However, our initial idea is reinforced, despite its importance, equity fails to be regarded as a structural part of quality, therefore inherent to it, but is rather seen as belonging to the parallel line of social responsibility.

Lastly, the follow-up reports evince that there are two different lines, with higher emphasis put on quality. Regarding quality, advance is evident "This report provides strong evidence that quality assurance continues to be an area of dynamic evolution that has been spurred on through the Bologna process and the development of the EHEA"(European Commission/EACEA/ Eurydice, 2015, p.18). In relation to equity, great challenges are still to be faced, "while some progress can be noted, the analysis clearly shows that the goal of to providing equal opportunities to quality higher education is far from being reached" (ibid, p.19).

Surely in some countries where difficult social conditions are present, this questioning about quality will make more sense, taking into consideration, for example, that in some countries public expenditure on education increased considerably, while in others, especially those that entered into crisis, it decreased significantly.

3. Final Considerations

The configuration of a coherent and relevant higher education system is in itself a difficult challenge to attend to, and the degree of complexity increases if it is a project that goes beyond the national borders, so that a proposal such as the Bologna Plan, by its integrating nature of such diversity, requires the establishment of common criteria that guide the course of the processes, and clear guidelines so as not to lose sight of the central objective: the pursuit of quality.

In this endeavor, one of the fundamental tasks will be the delimitation of what is meant by quality, and although there is no single definition, the starting point to measure it, and to improve it, will always be the determination of its dimensions and factors. In this way questions as basic as those posed by Grady and Bingham (2003) will always guide the first decisions we can make both for the design of a quality management system, and for the analysis of everything that is associated with it, from practices to discourses. Such questions fluctuate between: is it to be found in reputation or results? Is it carried in the perception of our academic colleagues or our students, or does it exist independently of their opinion? (P.2)

To answer these different questions, some models have emerged that from different perspectives try to explain the concept in question, and although the starting point of this understanding turns out to be different, it is possible to establish a dialogue between them that allows an integrative and therefore complementary view, rather than an exclusive one. In this holistic view of the models, what has become clear is that there are two trends from which quality is understood. On the one hand, from the attention to results, and therefore related to the effectiveness, efficiency and conception of education as a service; and on the other hand, from the processes, and consequently focused on pertinence and equity, which shows a more social alternative that leads to the understanding of quality as a right that as such should be guaranteed.

A holistic view of the system will allow quality not to be confined only to academic results, but to be determined by the way each component is interwoven with the others, so that within a contextual framework recognized for its potentialities and limitations, a balance is achieved between pertinence, efficacy, efficiency, functionality, sustainability, and beyond that, equity. In other words, it is necessary to review quality based on factors associated with results, but also based on causal factors (Murillo & Román, 2010; Sarramona, 2004).

A multidimensional view of quality, as we have previously projected, implies the conception of education as a right, and not as an asset; which does not seem to coincide with the understanding of this concept in the Bologna process. This is supported by Wielewicki and Oliveira (2010), for whom the intentions of the Bologna plan lead to interpret the process as a commoditization of higher education, with all the implications that this entails.

Indeed, in the framework of the EHEA, despite the attempt to balance all the characteristics that structure quality, it is not enough to treat the dimensions from different perspectives.

Instead, it is necessary to integrate them into a construction in which the threat of failure in one of them, especially equity, has consequences on the quality of education, and this also applies to social concepts, discourses, and practices. It is not enough to emphasize the importance of guaranteeing the same conditions for students regardless of their cultural background, it is necessary that this concern passes from being a matter of social responsibility, and is incorporated into quality. That is, equity, rather than being an added value, becomes the pillar of quality education.

The constitution of a European area of higher education has to be aligned with the logic of services and rights, because the responsibility of the university is twofold, in terms of the concept of quality: responding to the demands of producing knowledge that is applied, and economically useful, and realizing its social and cultural responsibility. In this respect, UNESCO stresses that "quality must pass the test of equity, since a system of education that discriminates against a specific group, whatever it may be, does not fulfill its mission." In addition, it is assumed that the Bologna plan corresponds to a commitment between countries ready to tackle the reforms necessary to achieve the construction of a more social Europe. (Garmendía, 2009)

It is important to emphasize that social and economic efforts to achieve inclusion will never be too excessive. Consequently, the process of democratization of higher education must continue in order to guarantee equity, both in access and success, thus contributing to strengthening both the individual and collective role in building more cohesive societies, with higher levels of social justice.

Ultimately, it will be necessary to rethink the issue of quality, so that it involves different dimensions, and ensure that this resignification is consolidated within the social and political budgets, which when oriented towards social progress, give direction to this great proposal. In the words of Wielewicki and Oliveira (2010):

Se compararmos os comunicados iniciais com os mais recentes, pelo menos dois factos se salientam: 1) um processo de unificação de tamanha envergadura e complexidade, mesmo conduzido a partir de uma nítida visão hierárquica – na qual os interesses da Europa devem prevalecer sobre aqueles de cada país membro – demanda tempo e arranjos sociopolíticos de igual complexidade; e 2) os impactos desse processo podem ser maiores do que os inicialmente esperados ou explicitados (p. 226).

This will involve the active participation of educational actors and all those who, considering education as a right, can audit the different actions, and based on a clear and solid standpoint, can question the foundations and intentions, both social and political, of new endeavors and big proposals.

Undoubtedly, it will be necessary for the reflection to be based on what for, and even more on for whom, rather than on how, in this way transcending the functional and instrumental. For Marcelo (1998, p. 431), "talking about quality in education is a debate not exclusively technical but also political and ideological" and Moratalla (2002), for his part, takes the question further by affirming that "quality in education has to be considered not only as a technical, legal, political or administrative challenge, but as an ethical and cultural challenge "(p.5). The challenge is then posed so that as actors of the education system, we can understand what quality implies and, consequently, contribute to its achievement, and also participate as observers of its scope and permanence.

In this extension of quality from the recognition of its ideological, political and even ethical scope, it is valuable to recover some of the principles emphasized by Gobantes (2000) as evidence that the educational paradigm is increasingly oriented towards the needs of demand, and not necessarily towards the intentions of what is on offer: quality has become a requirement of today's society, it is a factor of change, flexibility and personalization. Quality leads us to quality (the more information is available, the greater the demand for it will be), quality implies commitment, and quality involves many agents(it is not only attributed to teachers), quality in its final state is projected in a culture of quality (it makes sense with the change of attitudes within the institution itself).

References

Afonso, A. (1998). *Políticas Educativas e Avaliação Educacional*. Braga: Centro de Estudos em Educação e Psicologia, Instituto de Educação e Psicologia, Universidade do Minho.

Barrett, A., Duggan, R., Lowe, J., Nikel, J.,& Ukpo, E. (2006). The concept of Quality in Education: A review of the international literature on the concept of quality in education. *EdQualWorkingPaper, 3,*2-18, University of Bristol,

Bralavsky, C. (2006). Diez factores para una educación de calidad para todos en el siglo XXI. *Revista electrónica iberoamericana sobre calidad, eficiencia y cambio en educación.4*(2e), 84-101. Consulted in August, 2014,athttp://www.rinace.net/arts/vol4num2e/art5.pdf.

Buendia, L. & García, B. (2000). Evaluación institucional y mejoramiento de la calidad en la enseñanza superior. In T. González (Coord), *Evaluación y gestión de la calidad educativa: Un enfoque metodológico*(pp. 203-226). Málaga: Ediciones Aljibe.

Davok, D. (2007). Qualidade em educação. *Revista da Avaliação da Educação Superior, 13*(1), 505-513.

European Higher Education Area (EHEA), (2001). *Communiqué of the Conference of European Minister Responsible for Higher Education.* Prague, 18-19 May. Consulted in August, 2015, at http//www.ehea.info.

European Higher Education Area (EHEA), (2003).*Communiqué of the Conference of European Minister Responsible for Higher Education.* Berlin, 18-19 September. Consulted onAugust11, 2015, at http//www.ehea.info

European Higher Education Area (EHEA), (2005). *Communiqué of the Conference of European Minister Responsible for Higher Education.* Bergen, 19-20 May. Consulted onAugust20, 2015, at http//www.ehea.info

European Higher Education Area (EHEA), (2007). *Communiqué of the Conference of European Minister Responsible for Higher Education.* London, 18-19 May. Consulted onAugust12, 2015, at http//www.ehea.info

European Higher Education Area (EHEA), (2009). *Communiqué of the Conference of European Minister Responsible for Higher Education.* Leuven and Louvain-la- Neuve, 28-29 April. Consulted on August 12, 2015, at http//www.ehea.info

European Higher Education Area (EHEA), (2012). *Communiqué of the Conference of European Minister Responsible for Higher Education.* Bucharest, 26-27 April. Consulted on August 12, 2015, at http//www.ehea.info

European Association for Quality Assurance in Higher Education (2009). *Standards and Guidelines for Quality Assurance in the European Higher Education Area* (3ª.ed). Helsinki. Finland.Consultedathttp://www.ehea.info/Uploads/Documents/Standards-and-Guidelines-for-QA.pdf

European Commission/EACEA/Eurydice (2015). *The European Higher Education Area in 2015: Bologna Process Implementation Report.* Luxembourg: Publications Office of the European Union

Eurydice European Unit, (2008). *Higher Education Governance in Europe, Policies, structures funding and academic staff* Belgium.

Gallego, J.,& Rodríguez, A. (2014). El reto de una Educación de Calidad en la Escuela Inclusiva. *Revista Portuguesa de Pedagogia, 48*(1), 39-54.

Garmendía, C. (2009). De la construcción del Espacio Europeo de Educación Superior, "Bolonia" y otros demonios. La Cuestión Universitaria. 5, 3-8.

Gobantes, J. (2000). Calidad y evaluación de programas: Usos y diseño de la evaluación. In T.González (Org.), *Evaluación y gestión de la calidad educativa, un enfoque metodológico (pp 83-125)*. Málaga: Ediciones Aljibe.

González, T. (2000). *Evaluación y gestión de la calidad educativa, un enfoque metodológico*. Málaga: Ediciones Aljibe

González, I. (2006). Dimensiones de evaluación de la calidad universitaria en el Espacio Europeo de Educación Superior. *Revista Electrónica de Investigación Psicoeducativa.10*(4), 445-468.

Grady, B. & Bighgman, K. (2003).Quality and accountability in higher Education. Greenwood publishing Group. Inc.

Marcelo, C. (1998). Calidad y eficiencia de los profesores. In OEI, *Una educación con calidad y equidad* (pp.429-458). Madrid: FotoJAE, S.A.

Mendoça, M. (2007). *A qualidade e as percepções de qualidade no ensino universitário*. (Tese de Mestrado). Coimbra: Universidade de Coimbra.

Moratalla, A. (2002). Calidad educativa y justicia social. Madrid: Imprenta SM.

Murillo, J., & Román, M. (2010). Retos en la evaluación de la calidad de la educación en América Latina. Revista Iberoamericana de Educación, 53, 97-120.

Oficina Regional de Educação para a América Latine e Caribe – UnitedNationsEducational, Scientific and Cultural Organization [OREALC-UNESCO]. (2007). El derecho a una educación de calidad para todos en AméricaLatina y el Caribe. Revista electrónica Iberoamericana sobre calidad,Eficiencia y Cambio en Educación, 5(3), 1-21.

Organización de Estados Iberoamericanos para la Educación, la Ciencia y la Cultura. (OEI) (2010). *Metas educativas 2021. La educación que queremos para la generación de los Bicentenarios*. Madrid: Autor.

Perellon, J. (2005). Nuevas tendencias en políticas de garantía de calidad en la educación superior. *Papers,* 76, 47-65.Petruta, A. &Cantemir, D. (2012). The importance of quality in higher Education in an increasingly- knowledge- driven society.*International Journal of Academic Research in Accounting, Finance and Management Sciences,2*(1), 120-127

Rue, J. (2007). *Enseñar en la Universidad. El EEES como reto para la educación superior*. Madrid: NarceaEdiciones.

Saarinem, T. (2005). Quality in the Bologna Process: from competitive edge to quality assurance techniques. *EuropeanJournal of Education, 40*(2),189-204.

Sarramona, J. (2004). *Factores e indicadores de calidad en la educación.* Barcelona: Octaedro

Schindler, L., Welzant, H., Puls-Elvidge, S. & Crawford, L. (2015). Definitions of Quality in Higher Education: A synthesis of the literature. *HigherLearningResearchCommunications,* 5(3), 3-15.

Seibold, J. (2000). La calidad integral en educación: reflexiones sobre un nuevo concepto de calidad educativa que integre valores y equidad educativa. *Revista Iberoamericana de Educación, 23,* 215-231.

Seixas, A. (2010). Globalização, Regulação Supranacional e Políticas de Ensino Superior em Portugal. InE. Brutten, G. Pires & M. Ferreira. (Orgs), *Políticas Educacionais e Práticas Educativas* (pp. 67-82). Natal: Editora da UFRN.

United Nations Educational, Scientific and Cultural Organization (2004). Educación para todos, el imperativo de la calidad. Informe de seguimiento de la EPT en el mundo. Paris: Graphoprint.

Wielewicki, H.,& Oliveira, M. (2010). Internacionalização da Educação Superior: Processo de Bolonha. *Evaluación de Políticas Públicas en Educação,18*(67), 215-234.

DOI | https://doi.org/10.14195/978-989-26-1620-9_4

CHAPTER 4

THE HUMAN FACTOR AS A DIFFERENTIAL IN THE TEACHING LEARNING RELATIONSHIP:
Sense built on the Bologna Process
in higher education

Eliana Nubia Moreira

Centro Universitário Unirg /Brasil

Email: enubiamoreira@gmail.com

> *The implementation of that Bologna Process dictates the development levels of social, human and economic growth, in order to respond to the crisis and the growing increase in youth unemployment, resulting in graduate employability. The need for changes in the educational paradigm is emerging, in dimensions of educational processes quality in higher education, in the scientific, pedagogical and human dimensions, taking into account the current social challenges. In this sense, this chapter offers a current reflection on the search for a new meaning in the act of teaching, learning and research, in an attitude that transforms, learning from living experience, reflecting on the paths that the phenomenological method points to didactic- pedagogic in higher education and contributing to the*

understanding of subjectivity, from which emerge aspects of the human being singularity and its essence as a possibility of reading the reality, the phenomenon and the lived experience, without forgetting the objectivity that permeates it.

Introduction

"*Know all the theories and master all the techniques, but as you touch a human soul, be just another human soul.*" (Carl Gustav Jung)

The reform on the European Higher Education Area has been a target, over the last few years of innumerous debates, many times with little consensual registers, about the substantiality and pertinence of the effectively operationalized changes.

To reflect on the transformations that occur in the higher system is not an easy task, given the multiple analysis perspectives that can be adopted, in face of the complexity of the set of actions of the reformulation and organization of the higher education systems, proposed in the Bologna Declaration, with the objective of European cohesion through the graduates' knowledge, mobility and employability. It is a challenge for higher education institutions, through globalization and the strong influence of political power, considering the existing economic dependence, to develop in students, in cultural and scientific terms, the capacity to learn and reflect critically on the knowledge and abundant information provided by the globalization of our contemporary society.

According to Ferreira (as quoted in Lopes & Menezes, 2016):

> Influence of the so-called globalization (economy) followed by a (re) emergence of the market economy and neoliberal policies, higher education institutions (IES) are now under imperatives and duties of economic competitiveness, rather than the satisfaction of social needs, and they will be asked to present and justify their expenses in relation to the activities they carry out. (p. 96)

Diversity is and must be sustained by countries and citizens, so it is necessary to establish bridges of contact that allow citizens to live without borders, are increasingly open to diversity and multiculturalism, education and training being a growing sharing mode among citizens, benefiting and finding a common course of action, which will address the strong pressure of the European guidelines for higher education, resulted from the Bologna Process, so that they can be put into operation in the national education system.

Education is a very rich and multifaceted phenomenon, and its concept is not easy to delimit, because it is facing a diverse unfinished reality, articulated with everyday practices, institutionalized processes and norms, objectives and purposes, which cover several aspects of human existence.

Even when there is professional pedagogical training, teachers are eventually socialized in the work context in which they are inserted and suffer the influence of the prevailing rules. But when such training is not required (or available) as a condition for professional practice at this level of education, so far it has been understood that teachers also base their action on their personal and professional experience, intuition and convenience, rather than on any conceptual or Pedagogical knowledge.

Guenther (2009) reports that the educational process starts from the understanding in the internal phenomenal field, emphasizing that relevant learning usually happens when people interact with each other and with the world, in the dynamic process of living. It also emphasizes that:

> An educational environment includes a teacher, didactic material, a meeting place with the students ... Everything that helps to draw appropriate directions to the moment when the student is able to capture personal meaning in facts, information, phenomena, experiences and therefore, take greater control over what is important to his life. It is at this very moment that education happens ... or ceases to happen. (p.21)

Santos (2006), and Amado & Boavida (2006) consider that the educational process is complex, profound and inevitable in regards to being constitutive from both individuals and societies, therefore, education can be considered a vital necessity, being a factor of cohesion and responsibility of social and personal dimensions. Thus, education has its own specificity and cannot be dissociated from its deep insertion in the cultural and social dimensions. In its broadest and most essential meaning, education consists in a movement by which the individual becomes a person.

To conceive education as a battlefront in the construction of a more humane society should be the main direction of educational action. In this author's view, pedagogical work at any level of education and especially in higher education should be directly related to the needs of human life in its relationship with the world. The production and use of knowledge should contribute to the evolution of the human being in all its dimensions.

The authors, Amado & Boavida (2006) also consider that education is a phenomenon so complex that "it needs, not a schematic and reductive thinking, that was as we have seen, on the basis of experimental science, but a new rationality based in the paradigm of complexity" (p.187), considering that the articulation of a greater number of factors allows us to understand the educational system as part of the broader set of social systems.

According to Kuenzer & Moraes (2005), it is usually stated that one of the biggest difficulties the research in the area of education faces is the fact that the claim to a more defined epistemological status is hampered by the complexity of the educational phenomena and the confluence nature of various disciplines that characterizes it.

A study carried out by Morgado (2009) on the *"Bologna process and higher education in a globalized world"* found that the educational system must create conditions that allow young people to develop skills both scientific and professional as well as communicational, affective and moral content.

> It's considered that educational mediation structured on the basis of critical reflexivity and ethical questioning contributes to the development of the human personality and to facilitate personal interactions, mediation emerges as a core element in the development of critical thinking and in the assumption of individual and collective responsibilities, in favor of a more just and egalitarian society (Amado, Freire, & Caetano, 2005, as quoted in Morgado, 2009, p.17).

According to the same author, education should focus on a teaching that promotes debate and reflection, where the students as the protagonists of their own learning, producing knowledge that focuses above all their applications to real situations in daily life, without gaps between real and school life, valuing communicative action in detriment of instrumental rationality, where a flexible curriculum, in a global world, is based in solving local problems (Morgado, 2009). Because it is essential to build new knowledge and its connection with social situations, this chapter intends to modestly emphasize "the human factor as a differential in the teaching-learning relationship: building a phenomenological path", articulating the understanding of education and university training in a humanistic aspect.

Thus, according to this author, there is a need to promote tighter bonds between the higher education field and scientific research, discussing the values and social relevance of research meaning and its contributions to understanding human nature through questioning which corresponds to a complete act involving rational argumentation as well as subjective experiences.

It begins here by invoking the role of research as a teaching strategy and as a competence that is expected to be acquired by the trainees, a requirement that meets the Bologna Process, despite being present in the spirit of university education for a long time. What is questioned here is if the pedagogical practice of teachers in higher education is based on their conceptions of science, their own vision of the world, society and the human person, and whether or not this vision, which should be complex, is combining theory and practice, if is it able to lead to the necessary transformations, through a pedagogical *praxis* that contemplates learning for life: knowing, doing, coexisting and being.

The author agrees that in order to improve the teaching and learning quality, it is necessary to think of strategies and approaches that encourage students not to be passive in the classroom, promoting a true spirit of questioning, which helps to build ideas.

Therefore, this text refers to the process of thinking, presupposing a work in education anchored in the inner life, encompassing behavior, actions and manner, noticeable by the way of acting, reacting, interacting with others and with the world. There is a conviction that a deep transformation of the contemporary educational paradigm is possible on the basis of a change of mentalities, in a conception of practice with an emphasis on action and immediate positioning, understanding the phenomena in the present, emphasizing the essence of humanistic thinking as being the concern with the human being. This text also aims to make some considerations about the contribution and applicability of phenomenology as a favoring method of teaching in the university context.

1. Higher education: critical reflection

1.1. Thought autonomy and critical reflection

It is agreed by several researchers that is the university's function to promote thought autonomy and critical reflection, and it is no longer possible to accept a teaching practice that reinforces passivity instead of awakening the student's spontaneity and creativity. In this context, the university becomes the focus of attention, by questioning the quality of the knowledge produced in it and the educational processes for which it is responsible, aiming the dissemination of scientific knowledge and the training of professionals from different areas of activity.

To train university students implies understanding the importance of the teaching role and, in this way, deepening their scientific-pedagogical capacities, making them able to face fundamental questions of the university seen as a social institution, since teaching as a social practice implies ideas of formation, reflection and criticism.

Here we value the idea that a competent university teacher is one who teaches the student to think, question and seek solutions to a problem, which stimulates the student to look for knowledge that involves him in the teaching process, valuing an education that is in service of human promotion.

It is worth mentioning that the purpose of the university is to create new knowledge and disseminate it through teaching, research and extension, according to the demands of society and the transformations of the world, forming reflective and critical citizens capable of acting in the workplace and to promote improvements in the context they are inserted.

It is a challenge for higher education the need to "train people with levels of cognitive and psychosocial development that allow creative, innovative, autonomous and cooperative problem solving" (Figueiredo, 2012, s/p), contributing to "the promotion of Autonomy in learning and that are related to the development of the student's self-direction and its epistemological complexity ˝.It is understood that effective and lasting learning implies a "personal commitment in the attribution of meaning to the knowledge produced" (Figueiredo, 2012, s/p).

According to Garcia (as quoted in Ferreira, 2011), "critical thinking arises associated with reflexive thinking ... and metacognition is then an important aspect of critical thinking, as it presents itself as a self-dialogue of which we reflect on what, how and why we think and act " (p.14). Critical thinking can be considered to have a practical value in protecting us from mistakes and influences from others and promoting autonomy and responsible citizenship.

The studies carried out by Figueiredo (2012) emphasize that in order to have a high technical and scientific level of training, one has to rethink the strategies of work with the students and in the concepts of knowledge and research, and that the epistemological change has to occur in the way that the students attribute meaning to the knowledge and how they reflect the issues, positioning themselves in the decisions and the commitments assumed.

Oliveira (2005), in a cross-sectional study, evaluated the extent to which university students notice to have attitudes and aptitudes that predispose them to self-directed learning, identifying those epistemological beliefs (somehow linked to reflexive thinking), along with other factors, revealed to significantly influence the development of self-directed learning, recognizing the need for pedagogical processes to move away from the transmissive approach and to promote critical thinking.

It is considered that a critical attitude demands a skillful application of knowledge and ability to make discriminatory judgments and evaluations, and also implies decision making and autonomy in the face of the need to choose an option mediated by the context. The individual chooses what to believe in or not to believe. Thinking critically requires overcoming the surface structure of a situation, requires curiosity, open-mindedness, flexibility, honesty, good sense, and other qualities.

In order to facilitate such teachers as a paradigm shift in education, many may need to undergo personal paradigm shifts in their own beliefs about knowledge, teaching, and learning. These beliefs can also be described as personal, epistemological beliefs that reflect a person's views about what knowledge is, how it can be acquired, and its degree of certainty, and the limits and criteria for the determination of knowledge (Perry, 1981).

Investigations of the Avena Project carried out by several authors from universities in Portugal and Brazil have resulted in articles about curricular practices of teachers and the perception of students and teachers regarding these same practices, compiled in a book (Fernandes *et al.,* 2014). The results showed subtle changes in Pedagogy in Higher Education.

The studies carried out by Borralho, Fialho, Cid, Alves & Morgado, (2014), a comprehension of the relation between teaching, learning and evaluating practices in higher education, and the improvement of the students' academic success, is directly related to the possibility of the evaluation being done, preferably, as a space of intersubjectivity, negotiation and communication, proposing that the effectiveness of this paradigmatic change, is only possible in an interactive logic which allows to transform the learning-teaching-evaluation process in a dialogical space, critical and emancipating, where the main function is the development of knowledge, abilities, competences and procedures of (self) regulation of the formative processes by the students (p.31), creating an effective flexibility and articulation of their resume, with resource and a systematic feedback use.

In the same Avena project, the studies carried out in the Portuguese universities showed that in relation to teaching

> In all scientific areas, teachers and students have the perception that teaching practices are essentially transmissive (traditional or masterful) and without significant changes, that is, on the one hand, teachers exposing the contents provided in the programs while the students are listening and/or taking notes. (Borralho, Fialho, Cid, Alves & Morgado, 2014, p.180)

As part of the Bologna Process, higher education institutions have had to adapt one of their missions to lifelong learning, in particular methodologies focused on student learning.

1.2. Ways of conceiving science

Scientists, in their investigations, seek various means to achieve the true meaning of the reality researched. Most of the researchers make use of the experimental scientific method in research, considering the human being as one among other objects of nature, which can be observed through the external aspects of his psyche. In this way, the behaviors objectively observable are valued.

Other researchers acknowledge that the human psyche is very broad and complex and therefore the aspects related to the lived experience have a meaning that can only become conscious, when achieved by the subject himself in the face of the events of his existence. In this case, the intimate experience is valued, and the researcher collects information about the events of the subject's existence to unravel the lived experience.

There is a variety of ways to research, but all of them are guided by a certain method. Method is the live act revealed in actions when the researchers seek to organize and develop a research work, where beyond the logic is the researcher's experience with the researched. "It is not only a routine question of steps and stages, of income, but of experience, with pertinence and consistency in terms of perspectives and goals" (Gatti, 2010, p.10), and there is a tradition of methodological bases in the area of physical and biological sciences, having been more restricted in the area of human and social sciences, due to non-specific training in empirical research.

Gatti (1999) in his studies finds that it is common in these areas to carry methodological theories of the most consistent traditions, occurring problems in the work field because there is no adequate domain of the transplanted theories, having an inadequate appropriation, superficial and impoverishing and even misleading, leaving to desire the necessary consistency of the knowledge produced.

> In this absence of dense tradition in dealing with theory and research, we initially saw in the areas of human-social sciences an attachment to certain models that predominated in the areas of physical and biological sciences. This absorption was made under the aegis of the principle that the procedures that define science are unique, that is, from the perspective that science is one, and therefore its method as well. (Gatti, 1999, p. 3)

Under these conditions, the methodological model consolidated in the experimental sciences of the late 19th century, beginning of the 20th century, starts from a logical-empirical perspective, in the use of methodological standards, and in the production of objective-scientific knowledge repeated by the peers, in the search of validation, conceiving that the phenomena can be directly measured, observable and quantifiable, and thus have the recognition as an area of science and be considered valid by the circles of power that form it, however bringing problems to the human-social sciences.

> Not that the quantification and the experimental methodology are not in any case applicable to the areas of socio-human studies, that is, an evil in itself or dispensable. But it is the ideology within which this appropriation was made, the dogmatic perspective with which one began to construct instruments of measurement, to believe in measures in an absolutized way, to believe in the neutrality of research interventions and data. The very way in which we proceeded to

> measure and describe phenomena as if measurements were accurate and linear relations of cause and effect were directly detectable and could explain everything from human and social phenomena without further inquiries about the nature of measures and property or reality validity of the concepts that underlie them. (Gatti, 1999, p. 6-7)

Due to the impasses revealed by the investigations themselves, paradigm shifts have changed perspectives, adhering to qualitative procedures, which is a type of research that does not dispense accuracy and theoretical methodological consistency. This procedure requires the researcher to have solid theoretical knowledge in their area, so that they develop research skills where the construction of the method offers basic guidelines that guarantee the consistency and validity of the research.

The qualitative research provided a significant advance for the human and social sciences, since it allowed the search of subjectivity in its investigations, being that there is flexibility in the process that establishes the research path, being that in this context, researcher and researched are influenced by the research, due to the active participation of the researcher.

In qualitative research, one seeks the understanding of what is specific in the study, focusing on aspects of the subject's reality.

Studies on quantitative and qualitative method, report that unlike the quantitative researcher, the qualitative researcher "(...) does not want to explain occurrences with people, individually or collectively, by listing and measuring their behaviors or quantitatively correlating events in their lives. However, he intends to know in depth his experiences, and what representations these people have of these life experiences". (Turato, 2005, p.509)

It is characteristic of the qualitative method, the researcher seeks the understanding of the meanings that phenomena, ideas, feelings, experiences, and events have in the lives of the people participating in the research.

Qualitative research is epistemological and theoretical, being that the researcher distinguishes the quantitative and qualitative on the plane of the techniques and when researching "seeks to maintain a constant relationship between four guidelines: theory, the empirical moment, the instruments and the process of construction and interpretation of information with the production of knowledge, in a continuous development established by both the researcher and the researched (Andrade & Holanda, 2010, p. 261).

The myth of neutral science, produced by exempt scientists, has long fallen, at least among researchers in the social and human sciences. The definition of what to research is often influenced (and often defined) by the availability of funding and by the researcher's belonging to a specific academic community.

Even so, higher education maintains the influence of the positivist conception, organizing in a linear way the academic knowledge, being that the idea that supports this conception:

> Requires that the apprentice first master the theory to later understand the practice and the reality. It has defined practice as proof of theory and not as its challenging source, often finding itself at the end of courses, in the form of internships. In addition, we work with the knowledge of the past, with information that science has legitimized, never with the challenges of the present or with the empirical knowledge that can lead to the future (Cunha, 1996, p.86).

In addition, it can be assumed that if knowledge is constructed in interaction with the activity of science, it is necessary to know if the conception of science that higher education teachers have can be an epistemological obstacle to pedagogical transformations, since it is this context of educational practices that critical knowledge happens .... or fails to happen. It is questioned the purpose of the research, interested in knowing for whom or to whom the knowledge should be produced, and if the knowledge produced has ethical concerns regarding the quality of the collaboration and the effective changes.

Some of the many questions that can be put right at the outset is the relationship between teaching and research as an extension of the work of the teacher/researcher, who according to Cunha (1996), bring results of the studies themselves is important, but not enough for the student to develop scientific skills and attitudes. This type of teaching continues to be of results, and often the researcher professor may be more dogmatic in defending "his truth", the fruit of his own process of discovery.

The demands on academic production have generated a real productivist outburst in which it is no matter which reissued version of a product or several makeup versions of a new product counts. The quality of production – the truly relevant one – can hardly be measured, since a reasonable and rapid formula for assessing quality in terms of the social and scientific impact of products on quality of life, social and economic democratization, preservation of the environment, and so on (Kuenzer & Moraes, 2005).

In order to reach a scientific knowledge beyond restricted experimentalism, established by logical relations, empirical generalizations derived from hypotheses, formulating general laws, which enabled science to achieve knowledge considered as safe, absolute and predictable based on Positivism, it is necessary to evolve in understanding the problem of epistemology of doing science, or the construction of scientific knowledge (Baxter Magolda 2004; Beers, 1988; Felder & Brent 2004; Fredericks & Miller 1993; Hofer 2004).

Epistemology today applies to the problems of scientific knowledge, requirements, possibilities, in short, to the conditions of knowledge to be considered scientific, debating problems related to the questions about what is scientific knowledge, how it is defined, what methodological conditions (Amado & Boavida, 2006). In this paper, we present the results of the research, which is based on the results obtained by the researcher.

The need for epistemological ruptures with the barriers to knowledge, that is, against tradition, against common sense, against prejudice, against habit is also evidenced in contemporary studies. However, Santos (as quoted in Amado & Boavida, 2006, p.126) proposes an epistemological rupture, in the sense of the reunion of science with common sense. In fact, common sense, left to itself "may legitimize prepotencies, but interpenetrated by scientific knowledge may be the source of a new rationality˝. It is evident here that common sense is an important way of capturing reality, although it needs to be crossed with criteria for the using acquired systematic knowledge.

According to this idea, Arriscado Nunes (as quoted in Amado & Boavida, 2006) reports that there are nowadays multiple and recognized initiatives of approximation between science and common sense, and one of the most relevant aspects of this movement is

The recognition that scientific knowledge cannot be written in people's minds as if it was a blank sheet. All human beings acquire competences throughout their lives that are the starting point - whether as a resource or as an obstacle to the acquisition of new skills and knowledge, and which are invariably linked to localized forms of activity (p.128).

According to several experts (e.g.Bohm & Peat, 1989; Amado & Boavida, 2006), scientific knowledge may involve the confluence of different points of view, and there are specific subjective determinants of the human phenomenon, which require investigations from the experiences of their historical and social values, and these reveal facts of the realities internal to the subject, requiring an epistemological thought freed from the positivist jargon. That is, it is appropriate to give voice to those who are studied, valuing their subjectivities and their ways of understanding the real and this is not in line with the nomothetic vision defended by the perspective that values the establishment of universal laws, based on the ideal of generalization of results.

Qualitative research represents the process of subjectivation rescue in the scope of science, and phenomenology a process of construction of this new way of researching the subjective reality, understanding the human phenomenon in the sense of the discovery of reality.

2. Reflecting on doing human science

The choice of the humanist ideology and the open system of thought to base the work on education occurs because it offers more effective orientation for human beings to live and relate to one another, being a referential framework for thinking about the problems of our time. Thus, it is evident that the task of education is to enable people to achieve adequacy as human beings within their physical and social space. Adequate in a democratic society, it is the desire to build people capable of thinking for themselves, examining each situation and making appropriate and efficient decisions (Guenther, 2009).

The ransom of the human in education matches a vision of man as one who is and becomes, becoming and becoming, a basic conception of the democratic principle that, when they are free, men are able to find the best solution for your problems. Thus, "the task of education, at any stage of life, is to stimulate and facilitate the human being's own development and continuous improvement, in the search for adaptation to ever higher levels, in terms of self-realization and transcendence" (Guenther, 2009, p.200).

Guided by Guenther's (2009) studies, there can be an enlightening understanding of the two types of systems models to deal with human problems, each of which has its own way of looking at phenomena and having its own theoretical and practice. They are methodological approaches that seek ways to arrive at a better understanding of what is important and central to life and to be human. The author refers to the Closed System of Thought (SFP) and Open Thought System (SAP), here briefly explained.

The closed system of thinking has a sequential and linear way of thinking, where the final product is predetermined and established mechanisms to achieve them. It is an objective way of dealing with situations, in a logic of beginning, middle and end. The purposes are set in advance and the objectives accurately.

The open system of thought is a non-linear divergent way of thinking, which can begin a process by a visual direction, without having an objective defined as the end result. They operate subjectively, exploring the unknown, guided by discovery and creativity, trying to understand and not prove.

The researcher is the one who chooses the system for the analysis of human events and this result in different implications for the action. There are several avenues for the investigation of the human.

Studies involving the humanist position are carried out by professionals who in some practice impose an emphasis on action and immediate positioning, understanding the phenomena from the present, because the essence of humanistic thinking is the concern with the human being. Humanistic education answers the questions of today's demands by dealing with human needs that are constantly changing.

The humanist position brings a new reference to the process of thinking, indicating the open system of thought as the most appropriate to deal with situations of education, presupposing a work anchored in the inner life, encompassing behavior, attitudes and way of being and what can be observable by their way of acting, reacting, interacting with others and with the world.

Amatuzzi (2001b, p. 47) defends the originality movement of the human, affirming that what belongs to the human belongs to another type of science, since it has to deal with self-determination, with freedom, with subjectivity. It emphasizes that the relation presupposed by the investigation of the human sciences is of the type subject-subject, because the object is the other subject. It also emphasizes that "objectivity arises from an understanding between subjects; it is an objectivity that springs from an inter-subjectivity. The world of the human sciences is not the world itself, but the world as experienced by man, and therefore carried of meanings ".

It is relevant that the scientific investigations seek to deepen in what is characteristic of the human, thus contributing to a fruitful dialogue in search of true exits to the educational, social and health problems. It is proposed to value and rescue the investigation of lived as a study and practice of understanding and developing the sense that has to be a researcher who seeks to have a comprehensive understanding of the daily, in the process as critical and constitutive historicity.

It is a change of relationship with the object of research, where in the search for understanding of human phenomena, it has to deal with questions of meaning that define its actuality. "The deciphering of meaning will only be a discourse in the present if it is experiential, experiential, an experience of one's own meaning creating meaning. It is facing the challenges that I am deciphering the senses and creating new senses" (Amatuzzi, 2001b, p.13).

It is believed that science cannot be just a set of technical knowledge serving any purpose, no matter how real it may be. The concrete scientific act is never neutral, although scientific claims may be true, they do not usually characterize what is specifically human. "A scientific discourse, or even philosophical, correct from the formal point of view, may be irrelevant, not significant, directly inoperative, secondary. Even science itself can say nothing" (Amatuzzi, 2001b, p.13).

The search for clearer and more complete explanations of the nature of human beings as people and apprentices is an alternative that facilitates life-learning in a context of human formation and the theoretical construct of the Customer-Centric Approach by Carl R. Rogers (1977), brings significant contributions to rescuing people in spontaneous feeling, thinking and acting. Educational intervention in this humanistic approach aims at establishing a relationship that favors and promotes growth and personal maturity through the functional use of latent internal resources, trusting in the development of the potential of the person, and recognizing that there are inherent growth forces The tendency for self-actualization, enabling the revaluation of being through intellectual, social and practical learning (Rogers, 1977).

Research based on humanist approaches finds that through rational knowledge and sensitive understanding, people can manifest their own realizing tendency, transforming their potential into capabilities, becoming autonomous people and making constructive choices. The transformation of an ordinary person into a highly qualified person by the improvement of their quality of relationship takes place, in a privileged way, in the frank and confident encounter of person to person. The true encounter fosters personal growth at all levels and this means personal liberation from ignorance and fears that embarrass creative spontaneity (Moreira, 2002).

The definition of humanism, according to the conception of the Dutch studies:

> Is an idea whose basic guideline is the reaction to the concepts and attitudes that leave the human being relegated to a lower plane; It is, therefore, a reframing of this human, where it is prized for its dignity and freedom; Is a consideration of the totality of the human being, since there is no humanism that resorts to a compartmentalized man; Is the resumption of the sense of integration to the environment in which he lives, since it is not possible to be considered humanistic the conception that emphasizes the man of his environment, or that highlights the middle of man; And thus, as a corollary of the first guideline, it is an idea that places man in the foreground, not the secondary one. (Holland, 1998, p. 21-22)

One of the contributions of the humanist approach to learning is the recognition that learning is an active process that results from efforts in the search for needs resolutions, and learning is the discovery of what events mean to the person. "The closer the perceived relationship between an event, information, experience ... and the phenomenal self, the greater will be the influence on the person's behavior and way of being and acting, and the greater will he learn that situation" (Guenther, 2009, p. 169). The possibility of learning is inherent in every human being, so it must be recognized that education is a deeply human experience.

The sense of the act of research: building a phenomenological path - has been observed throughout history that the scientificity of knowledge is also dependent on the dominant ideas that constitute networks of evidence, acceptances or rejections, called Paradigms, and that these evolve on the basis of revision, change or replacement (Santos, 2006). Each historical epoch is marked peculiarly by the different ways of responding and relating to reality. Paradigm stands for model, standard. The paradigm "designates accepted general and theoretical principles, which provide a standard of investigation of a scientific community and which are taught as necessary for the advancement of science. Scientific revolutions happen by exhausting a paradigm and by the emergence of a new paradigm" (Josgriberg, as quoted in Pokladek,2004, p. 31).

It is a fact that both the explanatory paradigm that seeks to establish causal relations between the objects of the external world and the understanding paradigm that seeks to understand historical and social facts through the experiences of the internal realities of individuals has its advantages and limitations. The researcher must be aware that one cannot reduce a theory to a glossary of the concepts with which it works, for the very meaning of concepts depends on the relations between them in the scope of theory, and any reductionist stance Isolate and privilege only one aspect of reality, perceiving it in a static and unchanging way.

Science, like objective and public knowledge, is necessary and indispensable and can be obtained by verifying facts demonstrated through logic. These facts can, from a systematic observation and with rules of precision, be measured objectively and indisputably.

> As a result of a linear development, whose objectives were guided by the needs of a production-oriented society for a technical conception such as 'effectiveness and profitability', objectivity was gradually being valued, to the detriment of the subjective character of human reality. In this technical consideration of thought, of the act of thinking and rethinking reality, one forgets or forsakes the meaning of one's thinking being (Hollanda, 1998, p.30).

Scientists, in their investigations, seek various means to achieve the true meaning of the reality researched. Most of the researchers make use of the experimental scientific method in psychological research and education, considering the human being as one among other objects of nature, which can be observed through the external aspects of his psyche. In this way, the behaviors objectively observable are valued.

Other researchers (Moreira, 2002) acknowledge that the human psyche is very broad and complex and therefore the aspects related to life experience have a meaning that can only become conscious when reached by the subject himself, in the face of the events of his existence. In this case, the intimate experience is valued and the researcher collects information about the events of the subject's existence in order to unravel the lived experience.

To know better the ways of investigating the human, is to open the possibility of, from the subjective experience, to study the human-world relation. The relation presupposed by the investigation of the human sciences is of the type subject-subject, because the object is the other subject. "The knowledge produced is concretely another, the subject researched is another, the possessor of knowledge is another. It is a difference in the way of conceiving human relation and knowledge "(Amatuzzi, 2001a, p.21), because it is in human interaction with the world that one has true knowledge.

What belongs to the human belongs to another type of science, because it has to deal with self-determination, with freedom, with subjectivity, because it is believed that science cannot be just a set of technical knowledge in the service of any purpose, even if you have a real value. Science in Education, with its cognitive knowledge, has to have a transforming action, "objectivity arises from an understanding between the subjects, and it is an objectivity that springs from an inter-subjectivity" (Amatuzzi, 2001b, p.47). Science does not become and does not form as science if there is no genesis and a direction in human thought.

According to Josgrilberg (as quoted in Pokladek,2004), phenomenology in the understanding of living has its starting point in the assertion that every human being carries with him the basic element of all knowledge and must examine it in order to substantiate the meaning of things and to substantiate the Sense of things. It asserts that every science that deals with human reality as a whole need to see the subject-object correlation as a true starting point.

The phenomenologist is based on the premise that man is the subject and object of knowledge and that he intentionally experiences his existence, giving it meaning and meaning. In this type of phenomenological investigation, the conscious experience is perceived by the person, because it is their own attitude towards the life that lives, and this causes the subject-object-world relation to be prioritized, overcoming the subject-object dichotomy, as something separate from an intentional consciousness and the world (Moreira, 2002).

There has been a significant increase in the application of the phenomenological method to empirical research in several areas, including education and health. The starting point of phenomenological inquiry is the understanding of living. The course of the research depends on the context in which it is inserted, and there is always an active participation of the researcher in the search for an understanding of what is being studied.

The autonomization of research in education and the solution of epistemological problems has been revealed in phenomenological research, "which is interpretive, hermeneutic and qualitative; And a critical investigation, capable of revealing the game of forces and powers that determines the course of human and social things" (Amado & Boavida, 2006, p. 222).

The phenomenological movement is bringing significant contributions to the advancement of science that seeks to understand what is human, through lived experience and its meanings in real life. Giorgi (as quoted in Bruns, 2001), "corroborating this expressed view that meaning is the result of the encounter between man and the world, an encounter where both are essentially involved" (p. 60).

When the immediate experience was studied, researchers Bruns and Holland (2001) of the "Center for Advanced Studies in Phenomenology" in Campinas / SP, made a collection of psychological studies with other authors that use phenomenology as a method of approaching the human, aiming to serve as a theoretical and methodological support to the researchers in formation.

The phenomenological researcher is based on the premise that man is the subject and object of knowledge and that he intentionally experiences his existence by giving it meaning and meaning. In this type of phenomenological investigation, the conscious experience is perceived by the person, because it is their own attitude towards the life that lives, and this causes the subject-object-world relation to be prioritized, overcoming the subject-object dichotomy, as something separate from an intentional consciousness and the world.

Amatuzzi (2001) makes the distinction between two types of research, which may be of a nature, when the interest is in knowing "what is certain thing", in an attempt to construct an understanding of what happens with the phenomenon investigated, in another direction, the research may be of extension, in which the interest is in knowing how to distribute a certain phenomenon, mediating the extension of what has already been defined. The movement of the research process is thus defined: "In one, the process of researching is the process of constructing theory or concept from the facts. In others, the process of research is to verify whether what is already constructed in the plane of possible theories or concepts can be found in the facts and to what extent" (Amatuzzi, 2001a, p.17).

According to this same author, the phenomenological research, which is qualitative and of a nature, seeks to be based on a systematic analysis of records of experiences, reported and collected in a personal relationship, in which the researcher facilitates to the collaborator the access to his lived experience.

The experience lived for phenomenology is the possibility of looking at things as they are manifested, describing the phenomenon without explanation or interpretative analysis, as faithful as possible to the collaborating subject, and investigator in the attempt to reach the essence of the phenomenon, without conceptual assumptions.

3. Final comments

The rescue of the human in the educational system: Implications of the Bologna Process

Following this perspective of critical reflection on the educational process in a humanitarian perspective, it reiterates the need to continue the promotion and reflection of the Bologna Process combined with a profound pedagogical reorganization that prevents education from being a common good and transform into a factor of production, directed to a utilitarian logic that reduces it to a merely marketable product. As long as the State conducts educational destinations, since it is the only actor with the power to institutionalize and legally standardize the solutions found through the Bologna process dynamics, the other actors involved must persistently continue the interaction through investigations, meetings, seminars and conferences as a way of accessing public and private interactions and interests, national and international, although the reduction of funding for higher education is notable, implying financial obstacles that allow mobility and student participation in the evaluation processes while maintaining the fragile reports. It is not denied that the Bologna Process has brought benefits in the national educational policy, aiming at quality higher education, however, it is necessary to better articulate education, research and innovation by promoting the evolution of the early career of researchers in a more attractive, autonomous and critical. If, in fact, following the Bologna Process, education in higher education is aimed at the professional training of graduates, there should be a greater incentive for a more flexible and open teaching and learning with the aim of making the student the active agent of their learning and the teacher the mediator who supports them learns to learn with a student-centered approach, encouraging critical reasoning and flexibility in solving problems, and thus acting intelligently in real situations. The reflection and research on the reality arising from the implications of the Bologna Process should continue to analyze more closely, what has changed and what still needs to be changed in relation to teacher training, since these are the main agents of a possible education transformative in practical terms. What is presented is that there has not yet been a paradigm shift.

The considerations presented here are final in relation to this chapter, but they are far from conclusive. As a researcher one must therefore be open to multiple options for understanding and intervention in the real, and the one presented here is one of them, which contrasts in some way with others.

The way education knowledge is constructed and organized in higher education is being rethought, since the use of the closed system of thought has resulted in a large part in the fragmentation and distancing of relevant issues related to the problems of the human being.

As a field of human sciences, education is seen as the focus of discussion about scientificity, about the absence of an identity of the field of knowledge production, about the epistemological and methodological fragility, that is, absence of scientific rigor, because its investigations do not fit the molds of what would be proper of the so-called (natural) sciences.

Thinking about higher education and teacher training based on a human-centered interest is a desire to be a well-informed and motivated citizen capable of analyzing and thinking critically about social problems, seeking solutions to problems, and assuming commitments and social responsibility, consolidating ideals, based on a comprehensive, meaningful education, presenting for this purpose an interdisciplinary stance for the collective construction of programs of solidarity service to the community, as has demanded the current social demand.

To those who have invested in research on education, it is not unknown that the focus of the investigation of much of the work on the teaching activity falls on "how to teach", on "teaching" or on "relationships" invested in this process. It does not fall, in general, on the contents and the theoretical source that legitimates such contents.

Science as objective and public knowledge is necessary and indispensable, and can be obtained by verifying facts demonstrated through logic. These facts can be measured objectively and indisputably from a systematic observation and with rules of precision. However, to know better the ways of investigating the human, through the human sciences, is to open the possibility of starting from subjective experience, to study the human-world relationship. For some professionals in the area of human sciences, science with its cognitive knowledge has to have a transforming action, and so called dialectic or pragmatic.

Nor is it not unknown the feeling of being "uncomfortable" with the purpose of acting in search of knowledge that allows the educator to be aware of his actions, in the complex of relations of the economic, political, and historical organization of society. To understand, in this context, the connections between theory and individual and collective practical experience is precisely to understand the material reality of the objective structures of the creation of meanings of the real.

Effectively, education must be thought and done between action and thought, with high levels of coherence. Therefore, the whole educational practice has the goal of building students' knowledge. A complex approach to educational behavior requires a particular educational practice that corresponds to a theory in such a way that thought and action and practice are consequences of one and

/ or another. In fact, knowledge must be extracted from practice, and practice should be a source of knowledge, in which aspects of the singularity of the human being and its essence emerge as a possibility of reading reality, of the phenomenon and of lived experience, without forgetting the objectivity which permeates it.

It is argued here that this is one of the epistemological postulates on which knowledge and education are based, in order to discover the true reality of education.

The use of epistemology to say what Education is, perhaps is an effort to define the object of Education from a theoretical construction that, not being neutral, will influence the result of this search, to the point of making objects different according to Theoretical perspective by which they are seen.

In the movement of the discourse on the knowledge legitimized and conveyed by the institution, mediated by the discourse of the method, the knowledge is fragmented. The state of knowledge in education requires an alliance with concrete reality. Higher education in its pedagogical practices, still centered on transmissivity teaching, contributes to the slow evolution of autonomy in learning, even though it is a function of the university to create new knowledge and its Dissemination through teaching, research and extension.

It is in this educational process that the training should be able to analyze and think critically the social problems, assuming a commitment that promotes improvements in the inserted context, with a motivated knowledge to investigate, being able to analyze and to think critically the educational, social, human issues, with a real, critical, transformative investigative stance.

The research of the phenomena in their natural contexts, respecting the rigor of the research procedures, the commitment to build scientific knowledge, the ethics of professional practice and social responsibility, requires a process of creation and adaptation of an appropriate research methodology.

Reflecting on the paths that phenomenology points to research on human nature is to contribute to understanding subjectivity, opening up an immense range of possibilities to think the real, opening spaces for other knowledge.

The development of this type of research indicates a fertile exchange between research and practice, as well as the theoretical contribution that may bring greater clarity of criteria in judging the pertinence of the path taken by qualitativist researchers from the research plan through data collection to interpretation of results in the expected rigor for any generation of knowledge in science.

Science needs to change the discourse of explanation of why to an attitude of how to do, and thus the application of knowledge may respond to the meaning of the act of searching and the truth sought will be the interaction between objectivity and subjectivity.

To recognize this problematic and based on it to objectify a humanizing formation assured in scientific bases is the goal of a science with ways and forms for education - an education committed to the social history of the Country. If the content does not correspond with the lived world, this will tend to be innocuous.

References

Amado, J. & Boavida, J. (2006). *Ciências da Educação: Epistemologia, Identidade e Perspectivas*. Coimbra: Imprensa da Universidade.

Amado, J. (2013). *Manual de Investigação Qualitativa em Educação*. Coimbra: Imprensa da Universidade.

Amado, J. & Ferreira, S. (2013). A entrevista na investigação educacional. In J. Amado (Coord.), *Manual de Investigação Qualitativa em Educação*, 207-232. Coimbra: Imprensa da Universidade.

Amatuzzi, M.M. (2001a). Pesquisa Fenomenológica em Psicologia. In: Bruns. M.A.T., Holanda, A.F. (Org.) *Psicologia e Pesquisa Fenomenológica: Reflexões e Perspectivas* (pp.15-22). São Paulo: Ômega Editora.

Amatuzzi, M.M. (2001b). *Por uma Psicologia Humana*. Campinas. São Paulo: Editora Alínea.

Amatuzzi, M.M. (2009). Psicologia fenomenológica: uma aproximação teórica humanista. *Estudos de Psicologia* (Campinas), 26 (1), 93-100.

Andrade, C.C. & Holanda, A.F. (2010). Apontamentos sobre pesquisa qualitativa e pesquisa empírico-fenomenológica. *Estudos de Psicologia* (Campinas), 27(2), 259-268.

Baxter Magolda, M. B. (2004). Evolution of a constructivist conceptualization of epistemological reflection. *Educational Psychologist*, 39(1), 31-42.

Beers, S. E. (1988). Epistemological assumptions and college teaching: Interactions in the college classroom. *Journal of Research and Development in Education*, 21, 87-93.

Borralho, A, Fialho, I., Cid, M., Alves, P., & Morgado, J. (2014). Práticas Curriculares nas universidades portuguesas: estudo comparativo para as diferentes áreas do conhecimento. In: Fernandes, D., Borralho, A., Barreira, C., Monteiro, A., Catani, D., Cunha, E., & Alves, M. P. *Avaliação, Ensino e Aprendizagem no Ensino Superior em Portugal e no Brasil: Realidades e Perspectivas,* (p.137-184) Lisboa: Educa.

Bruns, M.A.T. & Holanda, A.F. (2001). *Psicologia e Pesquisa Fenomenológica: Reflexões e Perspectivas*. São Paulo: Ômega Editora.

Cunha, M.I. (1996). Relações ensino pesquisa. In: Veiga, I.P.A. (Org.). *Didática: o ensino e suas relações*. (pp. 86-126). Campinas: Papirus.

Felder, R. M., & Brent, R. (2004). The intellectual development of science and engineering students. Part 2: Teaching to promote growth. *Journal of Engineering Education*, 93(4), 279-291.

Fernandes, D., Borralho, A., Barreira, C., Monteiro, A., Catani, D., Cunha, E., & Alves, M. P. *Avaliação, Ensino e Aprendizagem no Ensino Superior em Portugal e no Brasil: Realidades e Perspectivas,* (p.137-184) Lisboa: Educa.

Ferreira, M.C.L. (2011). *Pensamento crítico: um imperativo educacional para o século XXI*. School Project for completion of the specialized training course in School Administration (not published). Alcobaça: Centro de Estudos Superiores da Universidade de Coimbra.

Figueiredo, C. (2012). O sentido da autonomia e a construção da complexidade epistemológica do estudante do ensino superior. In: Leite. C & Zabalza. M.(Coords.), *Inovação e Qualidade, Actas VII Congresso Ibero Americano de Docência Universitária do Ensino Superior*. Universidade do Porto, Faculdade Psicologia e Ciências Educação.

Fredericks, M., & Miller, S.I. (1993). Truth in packaging: Teaching controversial topics to undergraduates in the human sciences. *Teaching Sociology*, 160-165.

Gatti, B. A. (1999). Algumas considerações sobre procedimentos metodológicos nas pesquisas educacionais. *Eccos Revista Científica*, Uninove, São Paulo,(1), 63-79.

Guenther, Z. C. (2009). *Nova Psicologia para Educação: educando o ser humano*. Bauru, São Paulo: Canal 6 Editora.

Hofer, B. K. (2004). Introduction: Paradigmatic approaches to personal epistemology. *Educational Psychologist*, 39(1), 1-3.

Holanda, A. F. (1998). *Diálogo e Psicoterapia: Correlações entre Carl Rogers e Martin Buber*. São Paulo: Lemos-Editorial.

Josgrilberg, R. S.(2004) A fenomenologia como novo paradigma de uma ciência do existir.In Pokladek. D. D. (Org.). *A Fenomenologia do Cuidar: práticas dos horizontes vividos nas áreas da saúde, educacional e organizacional*. São Paulo: Vetor.

Kuenzer, A. Z. & Moraes, M. C. M.(2005). Temas e tramas na pós-graduação em educação, *Educação e Sociedade*, Campinas, 26(93),1341-1362.

Lopes, H., & Menezes, I. (2016). Transição para o processo de Bolonha: Significações de docentes e estudantes da Universidade do Porto. *Educação: Sociedade e Culturas*. 93-125

Moreira, E. N. (2002). *Plantão Psicológico no Ambulatório de Saúde Mental: um estudo fenomenológico*. (Unpublished Master's Dissertation). Pontifícia Universidade Católica de Campinas, Campinas, São Paulo.

Morgado, J. C. (2009). Processo de Bolonha e ensino superior num mundo globalizado. *Educação & Sociedade – Revista de Ciência da Educação*, 30 (106), 37-62.

Oliveira, A. L. (2005). *Aprendizagem autodirigida: Um contributo para a qualidade do ensino superior*. Unpublished PhD dissertation. Universidade de Coimbra: Faculdade de Psicologia e de Ciências da Educação.

Perry, W. G. J. (1981). Crescimento cognitivo e ético: A fabricação de significado. In: AW Chickering (Ed.). *A faculdade americana moderna* (pp. 76-116). San Francisco: Jossey-Boss.

Rogers, C. R. (1977). *Sobre o Poder Pessoal*, São Paulo: Martins Fontes.

Santos, B. (2006). *Um discurso sobre as ciências* (4ªed.). São Paulo: Cortez.

Turato, E. R. (2005). Métodos qualitativos e quantitativos na área da saúde: definições, diferenças e seus objetos de pesquisa. *Revista de Saúde Pública*, *39*(3), 507-514.

DOI | https://doi.org/10.14195/978-989-26-1620-9_5

CHAPTER 5

THE INFLUENCE OF BOLOGNA PROCESS AND LISBON STRATEGY ON THE RHETORIC CHANGE IN GOVERNMENT' PROGRAMS IN PORTUGAL

Jorge Lameiras

University of Aveiro (Portugal)

Email: jorge.lameiras@ua.pt

In 1974 a military Revolution changed the political regime, and opened the Portuguese society to new social, economic and cultural challenges. A reform launched by the old regime in 1973 as a response to a social and economic need to modernize Portuguese society, was adjusted but continued until the full creation of the binary system. This organizational option was adopted for the higher education system to enhance its ability to produce knowledge, to deliver teaching and to give the expected contribution to improve the economy and to raise culture and qualification in society. During all the time, economic issues have been present in discourse about higher education: as the essential issue of funding to assure the sustainability of institutions; as a contributor agent through knowledge transfer to increase productivity and economy. At European

level the willingness and decision to introduce changes at higher education systems became merged with a European initiative to increase the potential of European economy. In Portugal the Bologna Process triggered a reform of the higher education system, from legal framework to pedagogical methodologies in the classroom, and so is an opportunity to improve quality and deepen the identity of institutions and sectors.

Introduction

Huntington (1991) describes the evolution of democracy in the modern world through an idea of waves of democratization. The first wave started in 1820 with the widening of suffrage to a large proportion of the male population in the United States of America, and continues until circa 1926. However in 1922 there was a reverse wave associated to the raising of fascist regimes in Europe. The second wave appeared after the World War II until mid-sixties of the XX.th century. A new reverse wave occurred until mid-seventies. But between 1974 and 1990 approximately, a third wave of change brought a new hope and an increase in the number of democratic countries. This wave includes different processes, as external imposition of a regime after a military conflict (Germany and Japan), negotiated changes (Spain) and revolutionary processes (Portugal) (Fernandes, 2014; Huntington, 1991). Reasons for revolutionary change are diverse, including change in political institutions, the quest for better life conditions, and the more equitable distribution of social and economic resources as education (Fernandes, 2014).

The uprising of a neoliberal influence in European political regimes, since the 80's produced an increasing pressure over higher education institutions to be more effective in providing educational services and research, in more volume, more competitive in international grounds and capable to attract funding intended to reduce their dependence from public funding. The idea of a self-regulated and diversified system appeared as a means to make institutions accountable, more innovative, easier to manage, and more efficient in managing the available resources (Zha, 2009).

This chapter presents a perspective about the relation between the changing European context in higher education following the Bologna Declaration (1999) and the Lisbon Strategy (2000), seemingly merged in the form of the Bologna Process, and the change in rhetoric of Portuguese Government Programs. The objective is to assess the match between the rhetoric associated to the Bologna Process and to the Portuguese' Government Programs in matter of higher education. For that, several issues were identified in international documents that represent the origin and monitoring of the Bologna Process, and 27 Government Programs were assessed, from before and after the implementation of the Bologna Process in Portugal.

1. A brief context in recent political history of Portugal

In 1910 Portuguese monarchic regime fall giving way to the First Republic. Later, a military coup in 1926 ended the First Republic (Carvalho, 2008) and gave rise to a corporative regime since 1933 with the approval of a new Constitution. Until 1974, Portugal was under a conservative, corporative and authoritarian regime called 'Estado Novo'. This regime was based in ideas as a national union and a social democracy inspired in principles of the Christian social doctrine, a strong but not totalitarian regime and a corporative option as an alternative to capitalism and socialism, stating a difference to fascist regimes that share the corporative option (Torgal, 1999).

Under 'Estado Novo' and until the Revolution occurred in 1974 the Portuguese higher education system was a 'university dominated system'. As Scott (1995, p. 37) defines, it was a system «in which any other institutions are seen as part of the secondary, or at the most, technical education sector, and in which the universities and these embryonic post-secondary institutions are regarded as separate sectors». In fact, the Portuguese system could hardly be considered a system at least in the sense of a network of institutions following a diversity of social interests. Instead, there were a few universities pursuing their vision of academic functions of teaching and research.

In the Portuguese Constitution adopted in 1933, University was considered as a corporative entity responsible for scientific, cultural, artistic or physical education objectives. Universities were seen with a corporate rationale of a community of scholars under a common legal framework limiting their general autonomy and submitting their mission to an ideologically driven vision of society (Torgal, 1999). The regime had put university inside the regime as an instrument for culture and to raise the nation leaders (Garrido, 2008).

By 1974 there were only 4 public Universities (Coimbra, created in the XIII.th century, Porto and Lisbon 'classic' in 1911, and Lisbon 'technical' in 1930), 1 public higher education institute (ISCTE, created in 1972) and the Catholic University (formally created in 1967). Beyond those institutions there were some other non-University institutions with a status of high level education, 2 in arts, 1 in physical education, 1 in economic and social studies and 2 military academies. A kind of general alternative to the University was the 'Ensino Médio' a vocational and professionally driven path of education. It was formally created by two legal diplomas in 1931 and later considered as a third level after elementary and complimentary professional training (1947, and 1948).

By the beginning of 2016, Portugal had 48 Universities and Polytechnic Institutes, not including delegations, almost three hundred units for teaching and research ('Faculdades' or 'Escolas Superiores'), and another 75 Higher Education Schools not integrated in a University or in a Polytechnic Institute, mainly in the Private sector.

1.1. Pressure for change and emergence of the binary system

In the past century, during the sixties, several papers from Portuguese researchers have shown some changes in the society landscape and university internal environment in Portugal. It is important to know how Portuguese research at that time read the social and academic reality.

In a context of high level of illiteracy, between early 50's and middle 60's there was a growth of approximately 68% in general student population, mostly at elementary level, while the demographic growth were less than 8% (Martins, 1968). University student population has also grown between middle 50's and late 60's (Cruzeiro, 1970) but university students were a very few percentage of the total student population. In 1978 even after a sudden growth in access following the Revolution of 1974 they represent only 4.4% of total student population (Pordata, 2016).

Sedas Nunes (1968) consider that University was a promoting factor of entrenchment of social inequality in Portugal. He points three problems. First, the high level of dropout during elementary and secondary level generates an underrepresentation of lower social classes among university' students. Marcelo Caetano (1974) the last Prime Minister of the pre-revolution conservative regime in his defense manifesto book mentioned that there were no obstacle to a son of a blue collar man to study at 'liceu' (the post-elementary school) nor to the son of bourgeois to enter at a technical school. And because the elementary technical education give access to 'ensino médio' and this give access to higher education every student in an industrial technical school could continue its studies to become an engineer. This liberal principle of access is recognized by Torgal (1999). Even so, the reality was the advantage of children of upper social classes to reach to the university, comparing to children from lower social classes. There was also an advantage of men comparing to women (Cruzeiro, 1970). The reality reported by Gomes (1964) is a precocious option between middle and technical education resulting later in difficulty to achieve conditions for mobility between academic and professional education. Other suggested explanation is a 'intra-projection' by individuals of the social structures, relations and institutions, strongly enough to condition educational and professional choices (Nunes, 1970).

The second problem is the inadequacy of the structure and functional organization of the university to the demand. It included structural insufficiency, programs too long without intermediate degrees, the excessive theoretical character of courses lacking pedagogical innovation, and high dropout level. Beyond the pre-access selectivity or scholarly aptitudes many students face insufficient economic resources to cope with the duration and cost-benefit of programs (Nunes, 1968). The mention to inadequacy of some pedagogical methods is a curious discourse also found thirty years later in several documents about the Bologna Process.

Finally, the third problem is the apparent insufficiency of the whole system to respond to changes in the social and professional requirements (Nunes, 1968). The existence of a technological and organizational gap between the most and the less industrial and economic developed countries could be seen as an incitement to the building of a united Europe and to the modernization of activities (Sousa, 1968). Democratization of the access to University could be seen as a route to broad the qualified human resources Portugal needed to face economic, technological and social challenges (Sousa, 1968). Technological changes in production systems and changes in the work and employment structures suggest for policies to remove obstacles in the access to graduate education and to lifelong education (Nunes, 1966; Rocha, 1968; Sousa, 1968). The expectation about the rising number and diversity of candidates generated a great concern on the system capacity to accommodate that expansion. From that, the concern is the risk that a desirable and essential process to the Portuguese society, the democratization of access, turn on a paradoxical effect of jamming in the access and overcrowding of institutions because of the structural, functional and pedagogical incapacity of institution to deliver education for all the candidates and with an acceptable level of quality (Guerra & Nunes, 1969). As Nunes say (1966, p. 686) «if the university have to transform is because around it the own society is transforming and want to transform».

Later, in 1971, the World Bank produced a Sector Working Paper that identifies several trends in educational development including topics related to quantitative expansion, efficiency and productivity of education systems, and the contribution of education for the labor market (WB, 1971). An OECD meeting in 1973 made clear that a simple increase in dimension of the institutions or their replication, 'more of the same' strategies, would not be the best solution to cope with all the problems of higher education, as the increasing numbers, a more diversified student body and the rapidly changing manpower needs of highly industrialized societies (OECD, 1974). A problem identified in early 70's was a discrepancy between the supply of and demand for skills adjusted to the labor market, generated by a response given by the education systems to increasing demand based on those solutions (OECD, 1974; WB, 1974). As so, OECD considered that Universities should undergo major changes. An envisaged strategy was a diversification of post-secondary systems, through the development of a variety of extra or non-university institutions and programs originally created to provide terminal and, for the most part, vocationally oriented post-secondary education (OECD, 1974). From the assessment about the expansion of world education systems and the suggestions produced, these documents became important to support the idea of change in Portugal.

Caetano (1974) declares that when he was appointed for Prime Minister, in 1968, he assumed the urgent need to make a broad reform of the education system. About higher education two problems seemed especially relevant for the Government: the pressure to expand the system, broadening the access and increasing the institutional capacity to accommodate students; and the political mobilization and pre-revolutionary environment in academic institutions. From 1968 onwards the new Prime Minister Marcelo Caetano, gave opportunity for regime openness to some development challenges, namely a reform of higher education under supervision of Veiga Simão, the Ministry of Education. In 1973, the Government produce two legal diplomas that translate the reformist idea. Law n. 5/73, 25/07/1973, established the basis for the organization of the whole education system. The Decree-Law n. 402/73, 11/08/1973, created new Universities, but the most innovative issue was the creation of Polytechnic Institutes and other non-University institutions. This is the fundamental legal diploma to convert the institutions and programs of 'Ensino Médio' into the new short-cycle institutions and short-cycle higher education institutions as recommended by OECD. After the 1974' Revolution but still under that juridical scheme, several institutions of 'Ensino Médio' change their statutes and became included in higher education system.

The 1973' reform became an important opportunity for systemic diversification generating a binary system. In fact, an additional merit of that reform is that the idea survived the change of the regime and the whole revolutionary aftermath, and it has never been repealed. More than that, even with adjustments it became the basis for the change of the national higher education system.

In the 1973' reform and even during the Provisional Governments (1974-1976, until the approval of the new Constitution) the Government Programs and legislation refers to 'University', with a university component and a non-university component. On the first two Constitutional Governments (1976-1978) the idea of system deepens and emerges the designation of 'Higher Education'. At the same time there seems to be a concern to create an identity to the non-university sector, and it became to be called as 'Short-Term Higher Education'. The V.th Constitutional Government [CG] Programme introduces the term of 'Polytechnic Higher Education'. A legal diploma (Decree-Law n. 513-L1/79, 27/12/1979) from that Government determines definitely the binary character of the system, lately confirmed through the approval of the specific academic career (Decree-Law n.185/81, 01/07/1981 – VII.th CG)

The concession of the final designation (V.th CG), the creation of the academic career (VII.th CG), the concession of autonomy (XI.th CG), and changes in the educational structure in the context of Bologna Process (XVII.th CG) became fundamental for the consolidation of the Polytechnic Higher Education subsystem. However, although the equal formal statute clearly established in the Juridical Regime for Higher Education (Law n. 62/2007, 10/09/2007) still include some differences, being the most symbolic the fact that Polytechnics cannot grant the third cycle degree.

The participation of Portugal in the Declaration of Bologna (1999) and full adoption of the Bologna Process turn to be the opportunity to make a reform in the national higher education system and to modernize it, in the sense of making it more suitable to academic mobility and evaluation in the international arena. The reform imposed the need to update the juridical framework for higher education. The binary option became confirmed on the revision of the legal and normative framework for higher education made in the first decade of XXI.th century.

2. A new agenda for higher education in Europe

There is a difference between the Bologna Declaration (1999) and documents that precede it such as the *Magna Charta Universitatum* (1988) and the Sorbonne Declaration (1998), on one hand, and the monitoring reports about the implementation of the Bologna Process, on the other hand.

Especially in documents previous to Bologna Declaration there is an emphasis in arguments of internal benefits for the system of higher education, even if there is a transfer from particular national interest to a set of common interests for the whole European system. On those documents the discourse in centered in issues of the system and the autonomy of institutions seeking for the progress of knowledge, with some mentions to the contribution of the higher education for society. Sorbonne Declaration (1998) states clearly that facing some steps in European process of political development «they should not make one forget that Europe is not only that of the Euro, of the banks and the economy: it must be a Europe of knowledge as well». And for that «we must strengthen and build upon the intellectual, cultural, social and technical dimensions of our continent» (Sorbonne Declaration, 1998). This doesn't mean blindness for economic issues. In fact even in 1988 the *Magna Charta Universitatum* stated that «universities' task of spreading knowledge among the younger generations implies that, in today's world, they must also serve society as a whole; and that the cultural, social and economic future of society requires, in particular, a considerable investment in continuing education».

Bologna Declaration marks a pivotal point in the quest for a change because it spells out clearly a set of objectives intended to raise international competitiveness of the European higher education as a whole. This Declaration recognizes the 'Europe of Knowledge' as an «irreplaceable factor for social and human growth and as an indispensable component to consolidate and enrich the European citizenship». The idea comprises the capacity of «giving its citizens the necessary competences to face the challenges of the new millennium, together with an awareness of shared values and belonging to a common social and cultural space» (Bologna Declaration, 1999). This change seems to have got some momentum from the conclusions of the European Council meeting held on 23-24 March 2000 in Lisbon. The document presents a «quantum shift resulting from globalization and the challenges of a new knowledge-driven economy» affecting every aspect of people's lives and requiring a radical transformation of the European economy. Also the need to «set a clear strategic goal and agree a challenging Programme for building knowledge infrastructures, enhancing innovation and economic reform, and modernizing social welfare and education systems» (European Council, 2000, p.1). From that, it raises a "new strategic goal for the next decade: to become the most competitive and dynamic knowledge-based economy in the world, capable of sustainable economic growth with more and better jobs and greater social cohesion" (Lisbon European Council, 2000, p.2). To European Union, Europe only would achieve that major goal if education and training work as growth factors for the economy, research, innovation, competitiveness, sustainable employment and social inclusion, and active citizenship. Later, in the monitoring reports of the implementation of the Bologna Process, pointing to the creation of the European Higher Education Area, there are several ideas that are gradually imposing their presence and direction to the Bologna Process. Considering the contribution to economic and social development and social cohesion we find ideas as: lifelong learning, employability, modernization and a new structure for higher education systems; emphasis on quality assurance, adequacy to diverse social and economic environments and accountability; innovation as a competitiveness factor for institutions and for economy at large.

 The change in discourse strongly suggests a mutual influence to leverage changes envisaged by both interest areas: the higher education (Bologna Declaration, 1999) and the economy (Lisbon European Council, 2000). It is the coalition of an academically seductive discourse about modernization and quality assurance with the agenda for competitiveness and economic growth from the Lisbon Strategy. The connection between the reform of the higher education systems in Europe, in the context of the Bologna Process, and the economic arguments whatever its interests, can be seen in some concepts we can identify in several documents. The economic arguments may have a direct interest to the system of higher education, as the efficiency of the system, or they may have an external interest, in the sense of relevance of transferable knowledge for companies or community.

3. Higher education and economic rhetoric

Jean Monnet and Robert Shuman had the federalist idea and belief on an integrated Europe where international organizations would embody a moral authority higher than that of Nation-States, as a path to heal the World War II wounds and to prevent or overcome deep and irremediable contradictions between States. Instead, the project of European integration assumed a pragmatic and functionalist character and "tended to focus on the means of promoting economic cooperation, seen by states as the least controversial but most necessary form of integration" (Heywood, 2007, p. 152).

In 1955, during negotiations to build the European Economic Community (EEC), there was a proposal for a European University as a contribution to build a community of knowledge and to share a European cultural dimension. It was considered as a way to override differences to USA and, through research, contribute to innovation and the cultural, social and economic dimensions of that community (Corbett, 2005). The perspective of a relation between higher education and economy becomes quite interesting when analyzing the relation between Europeanist rhetoric about higher education and the development of structures and projects on economic development for countries gathered in a European community. There is a linkage between a process of economic character as the Lisbon Strategy (Lisbon European Council, 2000) and a process of organizational and educational character seen in the Bologna Process.

As Meyer and Rowan (1977, p. 343) say "in modern societies, the elements of rationalized formal structure are deeply ingrained in, and reflect, widespread understandings of social reality". It means that some elements of formal structure of organizations became expressions of powerful institutional rules which function as highly rationalized myths that are binding on such organizations. Those rules are enforced by public opinion, by the views of important constituents, by knowledge legitimated through the educational system, by social prestige or by the laws (Meyer, & Rowan, 1977). The idea of globalization used in politics, economy, culture and even in everyday life to give sense to several social transformations and to undertake some action in accordance with that, bring together some other myths associated with it: a minimalist State, a feature that emphasizes a reduction of the central regulative and intervening role of State in favor of a mediating role; the value of entrepreneurialism and managerialism as management paradigms; and the idea of knowledge society, linked to technological development, to its effect over social relations, and to the rhetoric of competitive advantage (Vaira, 2004).

Myths have consequences over organizational arrangements and social legitimacy of higher education institutions. Supranational agencies and actions, such as the Bologna Process, set political orientations about higher education that define models of institutional arrangement and operation. These models operate as archetypes or templates that States are impelled to embed in their national contexts for political legitimization and as a positive signal of social development. A general and common framework on structure and performance are set in motion based on ideas of effectiveness, efficiency and success, contributing to legitimize, objectify and reproduce those institutional myths. That model may arise in the form of a kind of 'reform packages', very similar in contents, means, orientations and goals, and a common rhetoric shared by different political parties breaking through ideological boundaries (Vaira, 2004).

In the last few decades, terms as 'internationalization' and 'globalization' have increased their importance in rhetoric about higher education. The concept of internationalization has an underlying meaning of increase in cross-border activities between national higher education systems that still retains their own autonomy and decision power while the concept of globalization suggests blurred national limits relating the activity of national systems (Guri-Rosenblit, Sebková, & Teichler, 2007; Teichler, 2004; Zha, 2009). As so, the creation of a European Higher Education Area seems a kind of regional version at world dimension of the globalisation process (Teichler, 2004). On the other hand, Teichler (2008) also points that the term 'globalization' "is used to underscore that higher education is increasingly affected by worldwide economic developments which weaken national regulation, put a stronger emphasis on market mechanisms" (p. 364), and the use of that concept shows a stronger emphasis on market mechanisms challenging the institutional units to strengthen their position in the reputational hierarchy to compete globally (Teichler, 2004, 2008). At the same time, the use of this concept suggests relatively steep vertical diversification of the institutional pattern of higher education is acceptable or even desirable without advocating certain formal dimensions of vertical diversity (Teichler, 2004, 2008) that may be politically sensitive in national context. So, the argument for vertical diversity is diverted to the idea to reinforce country prestige through the position of national institutions in a worldwide competition. As Teichler (2008) points, "at the apex of the system, the institutions do not play anymore in national leagues, but rather (...) in a champions' league" (p. 366).

By the ending of XX.th century the Bologna Declaration and some previous documents translate the hope to create a kind of architectural blueprint to higher education, a contribution to create a new idea of Europe in social, cultural, intellectual and technical dimensions. The European Union has appropriated and turned it an instrument, seeking to strengthen the economy as a way to reach social objectives. Amaral (2002) highlights a significant change in discourse about higher education: from the 'harmonization' in the first documents (as the Sorbonne Declaration, 1998), to 'convergence' and later to 'tuning' in documents of the Bologna Process. Even the Bologna Declaration (1999) does not use 'harmonization' but instead there are several mentions to 'cooperation' in actions (educational cooperation, cooperation in quality assurance) and levels (inter-institutional cooperation and inter-governmental cooperation). But these are not the only changes in discourse. Along the Reports from the meetings of European Union Ministers responsible for higher education, attaining goals and priorities to accomplish the European Higher Education Area, terms as 'qualification' and 'employability' got more importance as they carry a sense of preparedness, of applicability and relevancy of knowledge, instead the traditional terms of education and employment (Table 1). Especially in a market driven or even more liberal discourse, employment is no longer a granted right.

Table 1. Some concepts present in European documents

	Document	Year	Qualification	Employability	Innovation	Competitiveness	Attractiveness
	Sorbonne Declaration	1998	X	X			X S
	Bologna Declaration	1999	X	X		X S	X S
EU	Lisbon Strategy	2000	X	X	XR/XE	X E	X R
Bologna Process (under EU)	Prague Communiqué	2001	X	X		XS/XE	X S
	Berlin Communiqué	2003	X	X	XE	X S	X S
	Bergen Communiqué	2005	X	X	XS / XR	X S	X S
	London Communiqué	2007	X	X	XS /XR	X S	X S
	Leuven Communiqué	2009	X	X	XR/ XRE	X S	X S
	Budapest-Vienna Declaration	2010	X	X	XE	X	XS
	Bucharest Communiqué	2012	X	X	XS/XE		X S
	Yerevan Communiqué	2015	X	X	X		

Notes: S – for the higher education system; R – for research; E – for economy.

The 'Communication from the Commission – The role of the universities in the Europe of knowledge' (CEC, 2003) points three economic challenges to higher education institutions and systems. First, to consolidate excellence in research and teaching and to increase the international attractiveness of European higher education institutions and, as so, to achieve enough and sustainable resources and use them efficiently. Second, their contribution to an useful knowledge and qualification allowing a better response to local and regional needs and strategies, and the emergence of an open European labor market without the problems concerning the recognition of qualifications country by country. Third, to establish closer cooperation between universities and enterprises geared more effectively towards innovation, the startup of new companies and, more generally, to ensure the transfer and exploitation of new knowledge in the economy and society at large.

4. Changes in the rhetoric of Portuguese government Programs

After the revolutionary phase (1974-1976) and implementation of the new political regime brought by the 1974' Revolution, two political parties emerged as the main representatives of the majority of voters and key players in the process of democratization in Portugal: the Socialist Party (PS) and the Social-Democrat Party (PSD) (Lobo, 2000). Solely or as distinct coalition leaders, these parties have been responsible for most of the Governments since 1976. So, although the electoral plurality, there is a kind of bipartisanism in Constitutional Governments (Jalali, 2003).

Merkel and Petring (2007) consider the existence of three general types of social-democrat parties: traditional parties emphasize redistributive regime, with a highly regulated labour market; the modernized social-democratic parties do not liberalize existing structures of the welfare state and the labour market, and do not replace the welfare state but do some adjustments to cope with a changing context of global competitiveness; finally, the liberal social-democratic parties do partially replace state regulations with market solutions converging towards liberal ideas of a provision of social-political minimum standards and the inclusion into the markets due to economic pressure (Merkel &

Petring, 2007). From the classification of welfare regimes made by Esping-Andersen (1996), Pennings (1999) presents three welfare state responses to economic and social change: the continental route, clearly more conservative; the Scandinavian or Nordic route of social investment; and the Anglo-Saxon route of neo-liberal inspiration. These welfare regimes keep some proximity to the previous contexts of social-democracy.

It is important to not confound the name of the parties and their political advocacy. Parties can do slight ideological adjustments, they can change their discourse and the effect of their political initiatives may produce different results for different countries, and even for different circumstances of politics in the same country. The 'Scandinavian' social-democracy in the last decades of XX.th century in Nordic countries is more approximated to the political space that in Portugal have been occupied by the socialist party since late 90's. In fact, Portuguese socialist party, considering its Government Programs, has changed its position from the left-wing to central-left, while the Portuguese social-democrat party has moved to the right-wing. Meanwhile, these two parties have been acting as a big political block moving together and dominating the spectrum from centre-left to centre-right. This condition represents the domination of political discourse by mainstream parties, older democratic parties (Busemeyer, Franzmann, & Garritzmann, 2013) and a steady increase in consensus around a desirable issue for society and for political propaganda especially for electoral campaigns (Jakobi, 2011). In fact, the logic behind party action is not just sociologic representing a population sector but also political in the sense of dealing with electoral power to attain social and economic objectives (Busemeyer, 2009). So the result was a trend to narrow the gap between mainstream traditional parties and a general move of those political families to the right in the political spectrum, including socialists in the place previously occupied by social-democrats (Knutsen, 1998).

The political-parties discourse tends to assign to the higher education a status as essential sector for the efforts of national development, from the education in specialized areas of knowledge to the culture. The higher education system is considered relevant to solve problems and to meet several issues of national interest, of social, economic or technological character (Clark, 1983). Nowadays higher education, through learning, research and knowledge transfer to industry and other production sectors, is accepted as an important source of innovation and economic development and an instrument to promote social cohesion (Triventi, 2014). Education is considered able to compensate for differences and educational gaps arising in early childhood, and equal access to education therefore helps to secure equality of opportunities (Sauer & Zagler, 2014).

Ansell (2008) considers that higher education policy, as he studied in OECD countries, is driven by a set of partisan choices within what he calls a 'trilemma' between the level of enrollment, the degree of subsidization, and the overall public cost of higher education (Ansell, 2008).

In an elite system left-wing parties have limited gains from public funding for higher education, since their electorate do not profit from it (Jungblut, 2014). So, while right-wing parties favor greater public spending on higher education and expansion of enrollment, protecting the interest of its traditional electorate, left-wing parties are more reluctant to expand public funding and enrollment until enrollment has already reached mass levels. Accordingly, initial moves towards the mass public model are made by right-wing governments (Ansell, 2008). In Portugal this process was initiated by a conservative Government prior to the 1974' Revolution. Once a mass enrollment system has been attained, those partisan preferences switch, with left-wing parties more sensitive to the expansion and quality of higher education through increased public funding and right-wing parties seeking to limit further expansion (Ansell, 2008). Later, there seems to be a convergence of large centre parties, being the strongest proponents of educational expansion while parties on the more extreme ends of the political spectrum are less supportive of expanding education (Jungblut, 2014).

In fact, it seems that current partisan composition of the Government may not be the sole explanatory factor, but several other factors such as the level of economic development, the institutional and systemic structure and the whole level of public social spending are determinants of public education spending in OECD democracies (Busemeyer, 2007). These features show how the political position of parties about higher education might be conditioned by the structure of the existing higher education system (Ansell, 2008). Ansell (2008) also notes that Bologna Process may generate unlikely political alliances across left-right boundaries.

Until 1999 there is a rotation between two visions about the relation of social and economic issues but always with the assumption that higher education has an important role to accomplish policies. One vision emphasizes the economic component, which means that vision relies on the rationale that education and training are essential to create employment, work is essential to produce, and the enrichment allows for better living conditions (PSD' Government Programs). Other vision emphasizes the social component instead. The rationale is based on the idea of public investment to generate employment and new opportunities of inclusion (PS' Government Programs). From primacy of economy to generate a social profit there is a change to the primacy of solidarity to assure economic capacity.

Several Government Programs of PSD also adopted the discourse of reducing the weight of State in economy, increase efficiency of public institutions, adoption of organizational models based on flexibility, autonomy and responsibility, and competitiveness of production and economic structures. Qualification of human resources is seen mostly as a production factor.

Until the 70's prevail an idea of the university as foundational for the democratic society, capable to provide citizens with the resources to take advantage of the best social opportunities emerging from the economic development and a place of intellectual independence and resistance to a corporative society (Zomer & Benneworth, 2011). The analysis of Portuguese Government Programs since the 1974' Revolution until 1999, when Bologna Declaration was signed, reveals an evolution in the societal functions of higher education. In particular, there is a change from a utilitarian function to the ideological and cultural reform of society, to new ideas about the State organization and the social and economic transformation reinforced by the desire to modernize the society and economy, introduce technological innovation and to bring Portuguese economy closer to the other countries of the European Union.

In the beginning of 80's, economic crisis seemed to have an effect of reducing the willingness of State to keep the full independence of academy. That is, by a steady adoption by State of market mechanisms and a promotion of international relations, university become more and more in comparison with other institutions from other countries and competing for transnational resources. This condition forces a strategic appreciation of their 'third mission', the relation with community and industry because of its social and economic relevance (Zomer & Benneworth, 2011). This is precisely what happens in Portugal during that period under social-democratic parties in the Government. As a result of that there are changes in Government Programs about the relevance of higher education for the national economy and a stronger emphasis in professional training and vocational higher education. It is also interesting to note that in the whole evolution of the binary system in Portugal, the economic relevance was a strong issue for the development of polytechnic higher education subsystem. This issue adopts the form of three arguments: the education and training for technical jobs and careers (qualification argument); the willingness to engage in applied research and transferable knowledge (the innovation argument); and as instrument for regionalization of higher education through a closer response to local and regional needs from the predominant industry (the expansion/regionalization argument).

In late 90's there is a political drift of the discourse of Socialist Party in the Government (XIII.th CG, 1995-1999; followed by XIV.th CG, 1999-2002) to the centre. In fact more and more the mainstream parties adopt a pragmatic and utilitarian perspective. There is still a difference in the ideological basis and political priorities, but pragmatic measures bring PS and PSD closer each other. Ideas about the structure of State and economic planning seen in previous PS' Government Programs to induce social and economic transformation are changed after full integration in European Community. The pragmatic position of socialists means that matter is no longer an egalitarian solidarity from a Marxist inspiration but instead is a solidarity based on the opportunity of economic benefit. It is a change from a revolutionary socialism to a democratic socialism, more pragmatic, reformist and closer to social-democracy, accepting capitalist instruments like markets. At the same time, socialists start to step back from economy by doing some steady transfer of responsibility and acceptance of a model of management based on accountability and evaluation, and a regulatory State.

With the beginning of XXI.st century we can identify three major periods in the discourse of Government Programmes. First period comprises a Government (XIV.th CG, 1999-2002) lead by PS and a brief PSD' Government (XV.th CG, 2002-2004). It is the time to fully apprehend the new paradigm of higher education objectively generated by the Bologna Declaration (1999). The PSD Government represents already a turn to the vision of strengthening the economy to generate resources and then accomplish social objectives. The challenges of quality assurance, competitiveness and technological innovation are assumed as strong arguments to reinforce continuous professional training, post-secondary training and vocational higher education, and also a close link to industry.

A second step started in 2004 with the XVI.th Government supported by PSD and was followed by two socialist Governments (XVI.th CG, 2005-2009; XVII.th CG, 2009-2011). It is the period of implementation of the Bologna Process. Initiated slightly in 2003 by some involvement of social and professional partners, the full completion would come with the directives from the meetings of European Union Ministers responsible for higher education, attaining goals and priorities to accomplish the European Higher Education Area. That is precisely the moment of the most intense change in the political discourse of socialists. There is wider acceptance of arrangements and interests of an Europeanized/globalized market and it is adopted a new strategic vision for Portugal trying to conciliate the idea of Welfare-State, traditionally linked to socialist' discourse, to acceptance of markets as instruments of economic policy, as accepted by social-democrats, and benefits from ideas of modernization, qualification, innovation and competitiveness. It is also a discourse of political opportunity at European level as a means to share from the social and economic models and be side-by-side with other countries of European Union and also a relevant position in international context. Especially since 2005 (XVII.th CG) there is a broad revision of the legal structure for higher education. Beyond that, in 2007 is created a national Agency for Evaluation and Accreditation of Higher Education (Decree-Law n.369/2007, 05/11/2007) directed to reinforce the implementation of the revised legal and normative framework for higher education. It sets a new challenge to all institutions.

From 2011 onwards there is a third period, starting with PSD' Governments (XIX.th CG and the very brief XX.th CG) followed by a socialist Government (XXI.st CG) since 2015, supported by a parliamentary arrangement with left-wing parties. The period started under a deep economic crisis that affected financial support and sustainability of the system. This is a period of a stabilization in the number of institutions. The PSD' Governments emphasize continuous training to provide transverse and multifunctional skills to promote entrepreneurship, independent and innovative jobs.

5. Bologna Process and ideas of higher education and economy

The terms we have identified from the European documents were not yet central in the discourse of Provisional Governments in Portugal (1974-1976). These Governments were constrained in time and range of political and social intervention by the necessity to make changes in Constitution, and to establish new philosophical and legal basis for governance. They were also constrained by ideology because they were grounded in a document of the revolutionary Movement, advocating a socialist reform of the State. So, the Government Programs are quite limited in range and policies they advocate. In fact, they emphasise general principles and social and economic actions intended to improve the quality of life and the building of a 'more equal and fair society'. State is the major agent to implement the 'transition to socialism' but there is still a space to include private and cooperative sectors in economy. Education as a whole and higher education in particular are considered to have a fundamental role in the reform of the society. Before the Revolution, University was considered a political indoctrination and opposition centre against the regime. Now it became an instrumental agent to develop the democratic culture of the new generations of students and the country.

From 1976 onwards, with the Constitutional Governments, there is in fact an adjustment in Government Programs rhetoric. Although the IX.th Government (coalition government of socialists and social-democrats, even so, for no longer than two years, 1983-1985) education/training and employment are the terms usually found. A concept linked to economy is productivity, since there is a recurrent concern about the economical crisis in the country, partially due to a legacy of structural problems coming from before the Revolution and also to some disruption of the industrial fabric after the Revolution. At almost every Government Program we can find explicitly that concern. The block made by X.th– XII.th Governments (1985-1995) organized by social-democrats deepens the linkage between education/training and economy. Terms as 'qualification', 'innovation' in research and its interest to industry and technological sectors, to enhance 'competitiveness' and economic 'productivity' become important issues in those Programs, namely in the discourse about higher education. These three Programs make clear a difference of social-democrats (PSD) to socialist' Programs: on PSD Programs the discourse about State organizations is much directed to the reduction in State intervention in economy, while reinforcing the private sector participation. Professional training and vocational higher education are quite valuated as a mean to support qualification and to reconvert and upgrade professional skills. A full utilitarian value of education and training emerges to enhance what later will be termed 'employability' and economic development.

The XIII.th Government (1995-1999) and the XIV.th Government (1999-2002) of Socialist Party (PS) mark the new time of Bologna Declaration. From now on, every Government Program includes the ideas of 'qualification', 'employability', innovation' in the sense of innovative, transferable technological innovation and in the sense of new forms of administrative organization of State and organizations intended to reduce costs and increase efficiency. Other important terms recurrently found are 'productivity' and 'competitiveness', concepts applied both to economy and to the research and higher education system.

6. Concluding remarks

The evolution of the higher education system in Portugal, since 1973, can be characterized by a cluster of issues in interaction: access, expansion, diversification and regionalisation or territorial dispersion. The overall expansion in access, expansion in number of institutions, and diversification of the higher education system in Portugal is a reality and continuous process along the last forty years, but it is not a homogenous process. There are differences in the rhythm in time and between regions with periods of growth, stabilization or even some reduction. In the whole process the economic relevance of higher education has been an important argument. As mentioned before, Portuguese research in the sixties have shown how much the societal change has introduced not only cultural but also economic arguments as drivers for change in the University.

The system is formally binary but it is not exactly equal. It means that there is some imbalance as a birth mark of the Polytechnic subsystem. It has not been born from the traditional and prestigious University by a process of differentiation generated from the will of autonomy of some academic disciplinary sector trying to state its difference. On the contrary, it is a top-down process confronting the university monopoly of a higher education statute. Institutions and programs were promoted to higher education by law. It had major consequences. During some decades, occurred a process of academic drift, an isomorphic process (DiMaggio & Powell, 1991) to emulate some characteristics of the University, the academic reference. The Bologna Process brought the opportunity of a challenge to Polytechnics to consolidate its own identity and prestige. We have to make clear that the issues here are solely differences at social-academic statute, not the quality of management, teaching, research or knowledge transfer.

The major organizational reform of higher education in Europe launched in the nineties of XX.th century became an opportunity to merge interests of the system, the society and the State. It was the opportunity to generate a wide higher education area, a 'Europe of Knowledge' as a condition to promote human and social growth, to consolidate the European citizenship and to develop and strengthen stable, peaceful and democratic societies. This reform was intended around a new organizational structure, academic mobility and exchange of knowledge but there is a consciousness about the need of an objective and a bridge between the academy and the society with mutual benefits for mutual sustainability. The Bologna Process by European Union is the result of a convergence of the Bologna Declaration (1999) and the Lisbon Strategy (2000).

Portugal has completely adopted the advocated higher education reform. Whatever it be considered a harmonization process or a full convergence process, it can be seen as an allomorphic process because to a common level of strategic decision and political declaration match several forms to operationalise it (Machado, Ferreira, Santiago, & Taylor, 2008; Faber & Westerheijden, 2011). As a concept it means that a model for a broad landscape may and is effectively adjusted to national or local contexts according to political, social or cultural features (Vaira, 2004). Although the pressure to share a model, institutions may not become more homogenous. They retain capability to do at least some strategic choices and their own organizational culture but, at the same time, without a cultural retrenchment or refusal of influences from society (Zha, 2009). Faber e Westerheijden (2011) point the idea of operationalization levels which mean that there might be an upper political level of acceptance for major organizational features and a lower level at institutions that hold the ability to maintain diversity in the system. As so, Bologna process may be considered a soft policy because prescriptions are followed in a voluntary basis. The 'framing effect' persuades domestic policy-makers to reflect on external prescriptions and then construct their proposals within the limits of these frameworks. The result is compatibility at high level of political organization between States, while prescriptions are fitted to national interests (Faber & Westerheijden, 2011; López-Santana, 2006).

At the political level clear changes have been made in the rhetoric of Portuguese Governments' Programs. These documents go far beyond parties electoral manifestos because Programs are the basis for the assessment and political judgement over the performance of Governments. The macro-structural adjustment has been made and the binary system reaffirmed. All of this happened at the same time that mainstream parties adjusted their discourse. Government Programs lead by Social-Democratic Party always had a more market-friendly discourse but along the first decade of XXI.th century it came closer to a neoliberal position. Socialist Party has traditionally emphasized the social primacy over the economy but the rhetoric in Government Programs reveals a steady closeness to the centre. It is 'the owner' of the central-left of the political spectrum.

The merge of the goals of Bologna Declaration and Lisbon Strategy provided Governments with an opportunity to ideological change and to infuse a structural reform of the public administration alleging modernization and efficiency arguments.

At higher education system level, facing a European political wave of acceptance of a common market for employment and funding resources for higher education and applied research Portuguese Governments grabbed the opportunity. For the system to be attractive, high quality teaching and research is essential and graduates competence must be fully recognized in employment market. At the same time Portuguese Governments avoided political costs of non-adhesion to the Bologna Process. This way Portuguese Governments revealed a real pragmatism in their choices about higher education.

At institutional level, the Bologna Process and the quality assurance and accreditation system implemented create an opportunity to social legitimization and prestige, to attract new candidates and to stimulate research and the quest for funding.

Even before the Bologna Process, Amaral e Teixeira (2000) pointed how the expansion and diversification of the higher education system in Portugal had been impaired by some uncontrolled proliferation of private sector, by the academic drift of Polytechnics that delayed the building of the subsystem identity and the State that had not fully undertake its responsibility and competence for monitoring and regulate the system. Several studies have been made showing the insufficient contribution of sectors to diversification (Almeida & Vieira, 2012; Amaral & Teixeira, 2000; Amaral et al., 2000; Correia, Amaral, & Magalhães, 2002; Teixeira, Rocha, Biscaia, & Cardoso, 2012). A consequence of that seemed to be stratification in the system (Amaral & Teixeira, 2000; Fonseca, Encarnação, & Justino, 2014).

Kogan (1997) presents the stratification process in higher education as a consequence of the massification in terms of the diversity of students and interests, and increased pressure from the employment market. Gumport (2005) underlines how development of economy based on knowledge and the economic value of research and technology generates a competition for resources needed to sustain the knowledge production.

Competitive conditions between institutions, their differences in strategic options and scientific potential contributes inevitably to differences in quality. Even in a legal frame of formal equality the absence or malfunction of a regulatory element in the system contribute to deep the vertical difference in quality of the institutions. But we think that in conditions of unavoidable competition between institutions, if institutions, the regulatory element, and the State adopt a 'race to the top' position, the system and each sector may not loose entirely from stratification. It does not mean stratification is desirable or not. The pragmatist view is the challenge to adopt procedures directed to improve quality and sustainability of each institution, reducing the effective differences in quality (even if they are equal in legal statute), and raising the quality of the system as a whole. Acceptance and implementation of the Bologna Process in a country cannot be seen as a straight condition to make the system more competitive and attractive for students and to guarantee more employability to its graduates. In Portugal, the existence of a real evaluation and accreditation system and agency for higher education is an opportunity for institutional investment in quality and to deepen the identity of sectors in the binary system.

References

Almeida, A. N., & Vieira, M. M. (2012). From university to diversity: the making of Portuguese higher education. In G. Neave, A. Amaral (Eds.) *Higher education in Portugal 1974-2009 – A nation, a generation* (pp. 137-159). Dordrecht: Springer. ISBN 978-94-007-2134-0

Amaral, A. (2002). *O Processo de Bolonha. Da harmonização à sintonização, passando pela convergência.* Porto: CIPES e Universidade do Porto.

Amaral, A., & Teixeira, P. (2000). The rise and fall of the private sector in Portuguese higher education. *Higher Education Policy*, 13(3), 245-266.

Amaral, A., Correia, F., Magalhães, A., Rosa, M. J., Santiago, R., & Teixeira, P. (2000). O ensino superior pela mão da economia. Matosinhos: CIPES – Fundação das Universidades Portuguesas.

Ansell, B.W. (2008). University challenges: Explaining institutional change in higher education. *World politics*, 60(2), 189-230.

Bergen Communiqué (2005). Bologna Follow-Up Group. Available at: http://www.ehea.info/pid34363/ministerial-declarations-and-communiques.html

Berlin Communiqué (2003). Bologna Follow-Up Group. Available at: http://www.ehea.info/pid34363/ministerial-declarations-and-communiques.html

Bologna Declaration (1999). Joint declaration of the European Ministers of Education. Available at: http://www.ehea.info/pid34363/ministerial-declarations-and-communiques.html

Bucharest Communiqué (2012). Bologna Follow-Up Group. Available at: http://www.ehea.info/pid34363/ministerial-declarations-and-communiques.html

Budapest-Vienna Declaration (2010). Bologna Follow-Up Group. Available at: http://www.ehea.info/pid34363/ministerial-declarations-and-communiques.html

Busemeyer, M. R. (2007) Determinants of public education spending in 21 OECD democracies, 1980-2001. *Journal of European Public Policy*, 14(4),582-610.

Busemeyer, M. R. (2009). Social democrats and the new partisan politics of public investment in education. *Journal of European Public Policy*, 16(1), 107-126.

Busemeyer, M. R., Franzmann, S. T., & Garritzmann, J. L. (2013). Who owns education? Cleavage structures in the partisan competition over educational expansion. *West European Politics*, 36(3), 521-546.

Caetano, M. (1974). Depoimento. Rio de Janeiro: Record.

Carvalho, R. (2008). *História do Ensino em Portugal*. Lisboa: Fundação Calouste Gulbenkian. ISBN 978-972-31-0173-7

CEC – Commission of the European Communities (2003). Communication from the Commission – The role of the universities in the Europe of knowledge. COM(2003) 58 final (05.02.2003). Brussels: European Commission.

Clark, B.R. (1983). *The higher education system – Academic organization in cross-national perspective*. Berkeley: University of California Press. ISBN 0-520-04841-5.

Corbett, A. (2005). *Universities and the Europe of knowledge: ideas, institutions, and policy entrepeneurship in European Union higher education policy, 1955-2005*. Basingstoke: Palgrave MacMillan. ISBN-13 978-1-4039-3245-7 ISBN-10 1-4039-3245-X

Correia, F., Amaral, A., & Magalhães, A. (2002). *Diversificação e diversidade dos sistemas de ensino superior: o caso português*. Lisboa: CNE. ISBN 972-8360-16-9

Cruzeiro, M. E. (1970). A população universitária portuguesa: uma nota estatística. *Análise Social*, VIII(32), 721-740.

DiMaggio, P. J. & Powell W. W. (1991). The iron cage revisited: institutional isomorphism and collective rationality in organizational fields. In W. W. Powell, & P. J. DiMaggio (Eds.), *The new institutionalism in organizational analysis* (pp. 63-82). Chicago: The University of Chicago Press.

Esping-Andersen, G. (1996). After the Golden Age? Welfare state dilemmas in a global economy. In G. Esping-Andersen (Ed.), *Welfare states in transition: national adaptations in global economies* (pp.1-31). London: Sage. ISBN 9780761950486

European Council (2000). Lisbon European Council 23 and 24 march 2000 – Presidency conclusions. Available at: http://www.europarl.europa.eu/summits/lis1_en.htm

Faber, M. & Westerheijden, D. (2011). European degree structure and national reform – Constitutive Dynamics of the Bologna Process. In J. Enders, H. F. De Boer, & D. F. Westerheijden (Eds.). *Reform of higher education in Europe* (pp. 11-28). Rotterdam: Sense. ISBN 978-94-6091-553-6

Fernandes, T. (2014). Rethinking pathways to democracy: civil society in Portugal and Spain, 1960s-2000s. *Democratization*, 1-31.

Fonseca, M., Encarnação, S., & Justino, E. (2014). Shrinking Higher Education Systems. In G. Goastellec, & F. Picard (Eds.). *Higher Education in Societies. A multi scale perspective* (pp. 127-147). Rotterdam: Sense. ISBN 978-94-6209-744-5

Garrido, A. (2008). A Universidade e o Estado Novo: de "corporação orgânica" do regime a território de dissidência social. *Revista Crítica de Ciências Sociais*, 81, 133-153.

Gomes, A. S. (1964). O desenvolvimento socio-económico e a Educação. *Análise Social*, II(7-8), 652-670.

Governo de Portugal (1974-2015). Programas dos Governos Provisórios e Programas dos Governos Constitucionais. (26 Programas).

Guerra, J. P. M., & Nunes, A. S. (1969). A crise da Universidade em Portugal: reflexões e sugestões. *Análise Social*, VII(25-26), 5-49.

Gumport, P. (2005). The organization of knowledge: imperatives for continuity and change in higher education. In I. Bleiklie, & M. Henkel (Eds.), *Governing Knowledge* (pp. 113-132). Dordrecht: Springer. ISBN-10 1-4020-3489-X / ISBN-13 978-1-4020-3489-3

Guri-Rosenblit, S., Sebková, H., & Teichler, U. (2007). Massification and diversity of higher education systems: interplay of complex dimensions. *Higher Education Policy*, 20, 373-389.

Heywood, A. (2007). *Politics*. Basingstoke: Palgrave MacMillan. ISBN 978-0-230-52497-2

Huntington, S. P. (1991). Democracy's third wave. *Journal of Democracy*, 2(2), 12-34.

Jakobi, A. P. (2011). Political parties and the institutionalization of education: a comparative analysis of party manifestos. *Comparative Education Review*, 55(2), 189-209.

Jalali, C. (2003). A Investigação do Comportamento Eleitoral em Portugal: História e Perspectivas Futuras. *Análise Social*, XXXVIII(167), 545-572.

Jungblut, J. (2014). Partisan Politics in higher education policy. In Gaële Goastellec & France Picard (Ed.s). *Higher education in societies. A multi scale perspective*. (pp. 87-111). Rotterdam: Sense Publishers. ISBN 978-94-6209-746-9

Knutsen, O. R. (1998). Expert Judgements of The Left-Right Location of Political Parties: A Comparative Longitudinal Study. *West European Politics*, 21(2), 63-94.

Kogan, M. (1997). Diversification in higher education: differences and commonalities. *Minerva*, 35, 47-62.

Leuven / Lovain-la-Neuve Communiqué (2009). Bologna Follow-Up Group. Available at: http://www.ehea.info/pid34363/ministerial-declarations-and-communiques.html

Lisbon European Council – Presidency Conclusions (2000). Lisbon Strategy. European Council.

Lobo, M. C. (2000). Governos Partidários numa Democracia Recente: Portugal, 1976-1995. Análise Social, XXXV, 147-174.

London Communiqué (2007). Bologna Follow-Up Group. Available at: http://www.ehea.info/pid34363/ministerial-declarations-and-communiques.html

López-Santana, M. (2006). The domestic implications of European soft law framing and transmitting change in employment policy. *Journal of European Public Policy*, 13(4), 481-499.

Machado, M. L., Ferreira, J. B., Santiago, R., & Taylor, J.S. (2008). Reframing the Non-University Sector in Europe: Convergence or Diversity? In J. S.

Taylor, J. B. Ferreira, M. L. Machado, & R. Santiago (Eds.), *Non-University higher education in Europe* (pp. 245-260). Dordrecht: Springer. ISBN 978-1- 4020-8334-1

Magna Charta Universitatum (1988). Available at: http://www.magnacharta.org/resources/files/the-magna-charta/english

Martins, C. M. A. (1968). Alguns aspectos do Ensino em Portugal. *Análise Social*, VI(20-21), 57-80.

Merkel, W., & Petring, A. (2007). Social democracy in power: explaining the capacity to reform. *Zeitschrift für Vergleichende Politikwissenschaft*, 1(1),125-145.

Meyer, J. W., Rowan, B. (1977). Formal Structure as Myth and Ceremony. *American Journal of Sociology*, 83(2), 340-363.

Nunes, A. S. (1966). Para a reforma da universidade: um importante debate em frança. *Análise Social*, IV(16), 684-696.

Nunes, A. S. (1968). O sistema universitário em Portugal: alguns mecanismos, efeitos e perspectivas do seu funcionamento. *Análise Social*, VI(22-23-24), 386-474.

Nunes, A. S. (1970). A universidade no sistema social português – uma primeira abordagem. *Análise Social*, VIII(32), 646-707.

Organisation for Economic Cooperation and Development (1974). Towards mass higher education – Issues and dilemmas. Conference on Future Structures of Post-Secondary Education. Paris: OECD.

Pennings, P. (1999). European social democracy between planning and market: a comparative exploration of trends and variations. *Journal of European Public Policy*, December, 743-756.

Pordata – Base de Dados Portugal Contemporâneo. Fundação Francisco Manuel dos Santos. Available at: http://www.pordata.pt/

Prague Communiqué (2001). Bologna Follow-Up Group. Available at: http://www.ehea.info/pid34363/ministerial-declarations-and-communiques.html

Rocha, M. (1968). A Educação Permanente. *Análise Social*, VI(20-21), 43-56.

Sauer, P., & Zagler, M. (2014) (In)equality in education and economic development. *Review of Income and Wealth*. 60(S2), S353-379. Doi: 10.1111/roiw.12142

Scott, P. (1995). *The meanings of mass higher education*. Buckingham: SRHE and Open University Press. ISBN 0-335-19443-5

Sorbonne Declaration (1998). Joint Declaration on harmonisation of the architecture of the European higher education system. Available at: http://www.ehea.info/pid34363/ministerial-declarations-and-communiques.html

Sousa, A. (1968). Algumas reflexões sobre a democratização do Ensino Superior. *Análise Social*, VI (20-21), 248-253.

Teichler, U. (2004). The changing debate on internationalization of higher education. *Higher Education*, 48, 5-26.

Teichler, U. (2008). Diversification? Trends and explanations of the shape and size of higher education. *Higher Education*, 56, 349-379. DOI 10.1007/s10734-008-9122-8

Teixeira, P. N., Rocha, V., Biscaia, R., & Cardoso, M. F. (2012). Competition and diversity in higher education: an empirical approach to specialization patterns of Portuguese institutions. *Higher Education*, 63, 337-352. DOI 10.1007/s10734-011-9444-9

Torgal, L. R. (1999). *A Universidade e o Estado Novo. O Caso de Coimbra. 1926-1961*. Coimbra: Minerva. ISBN 972-8318-59-6

Triventi, M. (2014). Higher education regimes: an empirical classification of higher education systems and its relationship with student accessibility. *Quality & Quantity*, 48(3), 1685-1703.

União Europeia (2000). Conclusões da Presidência do Conselho Europeu de Lisboa. Lisboa. Available at: https://infoeuropa.eurocid.pt/registo/000003888/documento/0001/

Vaira, M (2004). Globalization and Higher Education Organizational Change: A Framework for Analysis. *Higher Education*, 48, 483-510.

World Bank (1971). *Education – Sector Working Paper*. Washigton D.C.: World Bank.

World Bank (1974). *Education – Sector Working Paper*. Washigton D.C.: World Bank.

Yerevan Communiqué (2015). Bologna Follow-Up Group. Available at: http://www.ehea.info/pid34363/ministerial-declarations-and-communiques.html

Zha, Q. (2009). Diversification or homogenization in higher education: a global allomorphism perspective. *Higher Education in Europe*, 34(3-4), 459-479.

Zomer, A., & Benneworth, P. (2011). The rise of the university's third mission. In J. Enders, H.F. de Boer, & D.F. Westerheijden (Eds.), *Reform of Higher Education in Europe* (pp. 81-101).

DOI | https://doi.org/10.14195/978-989-26-1620-9_6

CHAPTER 6

THE TRAINING OF EDUCATORS AND TEACHERS IN PORTUGAL IN THE FRAMEWORK OF THE EUROPEAN SPACE FOR EDUCATION AND TRAINING (2007-2018)

António Gomes Ferreira

Faculty of Psychology and Education Sciences, University of Coimbra | GRUPOEDE, CEIS20, UC

E-mail: antonio@fpce.uc.pt

Luís Mota

Polytechnic Institute of Coimbra, College of Education | GRUPOEDE, CEIS20, UC;

E-mail: mudamseostempos@gmail.com

> Our intention is to discuss the training of educators and teachers in Portugal, from pre-school education to the 2nd grade school teaching, as well as its evolution from the beginning of the new millennium, taking into account the processes of Europeanisation and its impact on the nation-state and its educational policies. Within this perspective, we will proceed with an analysis of documents taken from a broad range of sources in an attempt to cast a more intelligible light on the options of educational policy on the initial training of educators and teachers, namely with respect to recruitment, training structure and the professional profile.

INTRODUCTION

Within a context in which the nation-state has lost its centrality as "the privileged unit of economic, social, and political initiative" (Santos, 2001, p. 42), large regional economic and political supranational entities have emerged (for example, MERCOSUL, NAFTA, or the European Union), acting with state-like initiative, with their objective being the expansion of their influence in the dynamics of globalisation, translating into new forms of action for the State in certain aspects of social life where often individual nations have found themselves unable to maintain control (Jessop, 2005). The European Union, an example of an advanced form of "network State" (Castells, 2007), presents itself as a more developed institutional configuration and since the 1990s has been assuming an increasing role in the area of social policies, namely education and educational policies, a theme that is taken up less and less by the nation-state (Moutsios, 2009).

The process of Europeanisation of education and educational policies gained steam following the *Lisbon strategy* and the undertaking of a political agenda that strove to transform the European Union during the time-horizon 2000-2010 "into the most dynamic and competitive knowledge-based economy able to guarantee sustainable economic growth with more and better jobs and greater social cohesion" (Conselho Europeu, 2000, p.1), by executing the programme *Education and Training 2010* and the European Space for Education and Training. More recently, a new strategic framework for European cooperation in education and training (EF 2020) was approved (EF 2020) (Conselho da União Europeia, 2009a) which "calls for common strategic objectives for Member-States, including a set of principles to achieve these objectives as well as common work methods with priority domains for each work cycle in the period" (Conselho da União Europeia, 2009b).

The education and training programmes include the initiatives in the context of the inter-governmental platform for the *Bologna Process* (Conselho da União Europeia, 2009a) which dates back to the joint declaration of education ministers from 29 countries gathered in that Italian city in 1999, in which they expressed their will that within the time-horizon of one decade a European Space for Higher Education (ESHE) should be created.

The development of the process involved a set of courses of action for the creation and development of an attractive, cohesive, and competitive ESHE (Brito, 2012) as a response to contemporary societal transformations. Higher education distanced itself from the Humboldtian model, structuring itself with closer bonds to the market economy and a broader basis for competitiveness, as in the North American model (Neave, 1998).

As for higher education in Portugal, its ability to adapt to the commitment it assumed within the scope of the Bologna Process dates back to 2005, and this brought about a change in the paradigm of training, centred now "on the full scope of activity and on competences" (Decreto-lei n.º 42/2005, 2005a) to acquire along the different stages of adult life to be articulated with respect to the evolution of individual or collective knowledge and interests.

As a result, the Basic Law for the Educational System was revised for the second time since its passage in 1986 (Decreto-lei n.º 49/2005, 2005b). The model for organising higher education into three cycles was adopted. The objectives for higher education were redesigned, more clearly specifying the guidelines for the two subsystems: the universities and the polytechnic institutes. The universities and the polytechnic institutes confer Bachelor's and Master's degrees whereas the Doctorate degrees are reserved to the former; in both cases, qualified teaching faculty are required. Thus is established the transition from an educational system founded on the transmission of knowledge to a system based on the development of competences and the European Credit Transfer and Accumulation System – ECTS, based precisely on student work. Government made it possible for all citizens to have access to lifelong learning by defining the guidelines allowing access to higher education to persons 23 years of age and over with post-secondary qualifications (Decreto-lei n.º 49/2005, 2005b).

The following year meant new regulations would be implemented as a result of the changes made to the Basic Law for the Educational System (Decreto-Lei n.º 74/2006, 2006), later reviewed [Decreto-lei n.º 107/2008 (2008)]. Regulations governing the conferring of academic degrees and higher education diplomas established the framework for how each cycle would grant their respective degree, requiring 180 to 240 ECTS credits over six to eight semesters for degree courses in the first cycle (Bachelor's degree) and from 60 to 120 credits for the second cycle (Master's degree) over two to four semesters. The second cycle, in special situations common in the EU for access to a certain profession, an integrated format was established with 300 to 360 ECTS credits and lasting from 10 to 12 months. The government went on to clarify the competences required for the awarding of each degree, defined the general principles that underlie the process of accreditation, the rules to be applied for the reorganisation of degree courses currently being taught as well as the transitional norms to adopt for the creation of new study cycles leading to the creation and inauguration of the accreditation agency, and finally, issued rules for implementing any registry of alterations to the degree course's curriculum (Decreto-Lei n.º 74/2006, 2006).

Once the Legal Framework for Higher Education Institutions (RJIES) had been approved (Lei n.º 38/2007, 2007b), the Portuguese government created the Agency for Assessment and Accreditation of Higher Education (A3ES), whose objective was the assessment and accreditation of institutions of higher learning and their study cycles as well as the performance of those functions inherent to Portugal's inclusion within the European system that assures quality in higher education. A3ES exercises scientific and technical autonomy and is responsible for how Portugal stands within the framework of quality assurance. It is a permanently functioning entity whose work involves the issues of student learning, the performance of both the teaching faculty and nonteaching staff, as well as the performance of the schools and of the system itself (Decreto-lei n.º 362/2007, 2007a). Since 2009 the agency has been an associate member of ENQA (Rosa & Sarrico, 2012).

1. Teacher training in Portugal since 2007

It is natural that the previously noted modifications to higher learning in Portugal should spark the need for adjustment to the initial training afforded to educators and teachers. Months prior to the creation of the A3ES, the first legal framework was published for the professional qualification and training of the teaching profession on the pre-school, primary, and secondary level (Decreto-lei n.º 43/2007, 2007c), with legislative alterations made to be in compliance with the Bologna Process.

The legal framework for the professional qualification and training of non-higher education teachers is an innovative document. In fact, it was the first time that Portugal addressed the training of educators and teachers in an integrated and articulated way. However, it should be noted that this was an initiative that the government pursued of its own volition and not one stemming from any manifest appeal or expression coming from institutions of higher education.

The Portuguese government, taking into consideration the improvement of educational opportunities for its citizens and the consequent need for a teaching corps that is better trained, more qualified and stable, enacted a reformulation of the domains of professional qualifications and granted a broader scope for level and cycles of teaching, allowing for mobility of teachers amongst them. From the standpoint of the legislation, this mobility enables teachers to accompany students for a longer period of time and makes the management of human resources and career paths for teachers more flexible. The domains of qualification for the generalist teacher were extended to include qualification in the field of pre-school and primary school or qualification for the primary school and 2nd grade school teaching.

With higher education structured into three levels, professional qualification for all teachers has meant holding a Master's degree. To earn the professional qualification for generalist teaching on the pre-school, primary school and 2nd grade school teaching, a person must obtain a Bachelor's degree in Basic Education and a Master's in Teaching.

The new system for qualifying individuals for the teaching profession, from the position of the legislation, strives to place value on the dimensions of academic knowledge in the field, the substantiation of teaching practices founded on research, and professional development; in addition, it considers that mastery of oral and written Portuguese is a common dimension required for the qualification of future teachers.

The legal document further underscores that the exercise of the teaching profession demands that an individual possess mastery of the scientific, humanistic, technological or artistic knowledge of the relevant academic disciplines. The emphasis on research methodologies in education clearly indicates the commitment to establishing solid training for educators and teachers able to adapt to complex situations and respond to the specific nature of the students and the given academic and social contexts (Decreto-lei n.º 43/2007, 2007c).

The new legal framework for professional qualification once again took on a general profile (Decreto-lei n.º 239/2001, 2001a) – defined for early-childhood educators and teachers on the primary and secondary level, and the specific profiles (Decreto-lei n.º 241/2001, 2001b) of both early-childhood educators and teachers in the primary school – in the proposal of the general principles for organising the curriculum of training for those pursuing higher education qualifications in the teaching profession. Thus, to address the defined profiles and underpinned by the existing research, the legislation defined the five components for the degree programmes: i) General Educational Training; ii) Specific Teaching Practices; iii) Professional Development; iv) Cultural, Social and Ethical Training; v) Educational Methodologies and Research Practices (Decreto-lei n.º 43/2007, 2007c).

The structure of the study cycle leading to the Bachelor's degree in Basic Education is a six semester programme. The 180 credits are distributed amongst the fields of General Educational Training, Specific Teaching Practices, and Professional Development, with 15 to 20 credits each, and they include classes on Cultural, Social and Ethical Components in Education and Educational Methodologies and Research Practices. The component of Training in teaching area requires from 120 to 135 credits, with a minimum of 30 credits each in the track of 'Studies of the Social Environment,' which includes the Natural Sciences and Social and Human Sciences, and Expression Skills, which encompasses Mathematics and Portuguese, as can be seen in Table 1 (Decreto-lei n.º 43/2007, 2007c).

Table 1. Breakdown of Credits by Study Cycle and Training Components (2007)

ECTS	180	60	90	90 a 120
Study Cycle (SC) / Training component	Bachelor in basic education	Master's degree in preschool education **or** primary school training	Master's degree in preschool education **and** primary school training	Master's degree in primary school training and 2nd grade school teaching (b)
Specific Teaching Practices (STP)	15 a 20	15 a 20	25 a 30	20%
Cultural, Social and Ethical Training	(a)	0	0	0
General Educational Training (GET)	15 a 20	5 a 10	5 a 10	5%
Educational Methodologies and Research Practices	(a)	(a)	(a)	(a)
Training in the Teaching Area (TTA)	120 a 135	0	0 a 5	25%
Introduction to Professional Practice (IPP)	15 a 20	0	0	0
Supervised Teaching Practice (STP)	0	30 a 35	40 a 45	45%

(a) ECTS included in SIP, GET and IPP components.
(b) Minimum percentage to be calculated according to ECTS.

The study cycles leading to the Master's degree (*Mestrado*) are divided into four areas of specialisation in the field of teaching, with the options being: early-childhood educator, teacher at the primary school, both an early-childhood educator and teacher in the primary school, and a teacher in both the primary school and 2nd grade school, with this last specialisation covering all the areas of the primary school teaching as well as the subjects of Natural Sciences, Portuguese History and Geography, and Mathematics and Portuguese Language Skills for the 2nd grade school teaching. Thus, the Master's degree is granted with specialisations in either Pre-school Education, Primary school, Pre-school Education together with Primary school, or Primary school and 2nd grade school teaching (Decreto-lei n.º 43/2007, 2007c).

The Master's programmes (2nd cycle) which offer a degree for a single level of teaching – either Pre-school Education or Primary school – are given over two semesters, corresponding to 60 ECTS credits (one academic year) and divided into the components of General Educational Training, Specific Teaching Practices, and Supervised Teaching Practice. The degree which comprises these two professional qualifications, that is, the Master's in both Pre-school Education and Primary School (Table 1) is organised over three semesters and corresponds to 90 ECTS credits and covers four components of academic study – Training in the Teaching Area, Specific Teaching Practices, General Educational Training, and Supervised Teaching Practice.

The Master's degree with a specialisation in Primary school and 2nd grade school teaching incorporates professional qualification in the areas of Mathematics, Natural Sciences, Portuguese Language, and Portuguese History and Geography for the 2nd grade school and is six to eight semesters in length, which would correspond roughly to 90 to 120 ECTS, respectively. Naturally, a degree course which would confer a professional qualification of such scope would have to include different academic components, i.e. in the areas of Training in the Teaching Area, Specific Teaching Practices, the track of General Educational Training, and Supervised Teaching Practice. As explained in Table 1, given that the legislation establishes a range of ECTS credits, the legal norm establishes a percentage with respect to the number of ECTS credits in the degree course.

As a result of the modifications carried out, two aspects have emerged which have become the focus of analytical study in the literature: the degree of academic title of professional qualification and its attribution to all teachers, and the issue of the training model. With respect to the degree, there is, in effect, an elevation of the academic degree without this corresponding, however, to more time dedicated to "pedagogical-instructional training and contact with professional situations" (Mouraz, Leite, & Fernandes, 2012, p. 192). As for the granting of the same academic title of professional qualification to all non-higher education teachers, this option fell in line with the evolution of Portuguese education policy over the last two decades which has tended toward greater equality of status and title amongst teachers across the various levels of non-higher education.

As for the training model (Ferreira & Mota, 2013), its concept of two non-integrated study cycles is based on a sequential 2-cycle model, focusing first on academic training in the areas of Training in the Teaching Area, Specific Teaching Practices and General Educational Training, and later on Supervised Teaching Practice (Brito, 2012; Melo & Branco, 2013). However, careful observation enables one to examine this sequential nature of the components of the training more closely. Indeed, Table 1 shows that in the first cycle we note the integrated aspect of components in the syllabus areas of Training in the Teaching

Area, Specific Teaching Practices, General Educational Training, and Professional Development, which for certain institutions are distributed over three years of study, which points to a certain degree of integrated approach (Agência Avaliação e Acreditação Ensino Superior, 2014; Despacho n.º 4793/2015, 2015). This analysis may, generally speaking, be extended to the different degree courses in the 2nd cycle which tend to be organised in a more integrated fashion.

The Master's degree in primary education and 2nd grade school teaching was an attempt to create a generalist teacher profile (Table 1) for 2nd grade school. Such an option breaks with tradition in Portuguese education, which is immediately visible in the present educational system that now offers a specialised Master's in 2nd grade school and is organised according to academic subjects, not to mention the fact that up to the mid-1990s the counterparts to today's teachers would have been required to hold only a simple, non-specialist university degree. Due to either lack of political will or political capacity, the gap felt between basic teacher training and the reality of the educational system was an issue that was never fully resolved.

In 2011, the global financial crisis, combined with the country's sovereign debt crisis, profoundly altered Portugal's political and social fabric; as a result, the composition of the Portuguese Parliament was realigned and the government changed hands. Lack of consensus in terms of social policy, namely with regard to education, led to the issuance of a new legal framework for the initial training of teachers (Decreto-lei n.º 79/2014, 2014a).

It was in the name of initial training, one that is "more rigorous and which places greater value on the teaching profession," that the legislation justified the new legal framework, that is, a need that is underpinned by "multiple international studies" and by "analyses and syntheses" disseminated in unidentified "scientific publications" and by "independent organisations" such as the OECD and the Eurydice Network. According to the legislation, these studies give evidence that the overall level of quality of educator and teacher training "tends to have a measurable and very significant effect on the quality of the system of education" (Decreto-lei n.º 79/2014, 2014a, p. 2819). The National Education Council (CNE) considered that the project neither came with justification of its relevance and potential for opportunity nor with the information that might support a better understanding of the impact of its application (Despacho 4291/2014, 2014b, p. 7781).

The new legal framework – in addition to the Knowledge and Skills Assessment Test needed by teachers for admission to the selection and recruitment process, the changes made in continuing education and training for teachers, and the tighter requirements for admission to university degree courses in Primary Education – constituted a strengthening of instruments such that "in the medium and long term, we will have in our schools the best prepared, the best trained, the most skilled and most motivated to perform the noble and demanding task of teaching" (Decreto-lei n.º 79/2014, 2014a, p. 2820).

The 2-cycle structure (1st and 2nd cycle) and the integrated format of the training components in both cycles were kept. The 1st cycle diploma in Basic Education remained as an entry requirement of the Master's programmes although they were reorganised with a change in the number of credit hours. Table 2 (Decreto-lei n.º 79/2014, 2014a) synthesises the new legal framework for initial training of educators and teachers, whose alterations the CNE viewed as "specific and coherent, with a position of clarification and improvement introduced into the diploma" (Despacho 4291/2014, 2014b, p. 7781).

Table 2. Breakdown of Credits by Study Cycle and Training Components (2014)

Study Cycle (SC)	Bachelor in basic education	Master's degree in preschool education	Master's degree in primary school training	Master's degree in preschool education **and** primary school training	Master's degree in primary school training and 2nd grade school teaching in Mathematics and Experimental Sciences	Master's degree in primary school training and 2nd grade school teaching in Portuguese and History and Geography of Portugal
ECTS	180	90	90	120	120	120
Componente de formação (b)						
Specific Teaching Practices (STP)	15	24	21	36	30	30
Cultural, Social and Ethical Training	(a)	(a)	(a)	(a)	(a)	(a)
General Educational Training (GET)	15	6	6	6	6	6
Training in the Teaching Area (TTA)	125	6	18	18	27	27
Introduction to Professional Practice (IPP)	15	0	0	0	0	0
Supervised Teaching Practice (STP)	0	39	32	48	48	48

(a) ECTS included in STP, GET and IPP components.
(b) Minimum percentage to be calculated according to ECTS.

The legislation announced the changes considered relevant from the outset: the increase in the duration of the Master's programmes in Pre-school Education and in Teaching in Primary Education from two to three semesters, corresponding to 90 ECTS, and the joint Master's programme in Pre-School Education and Primary Education expanded from 90 to 120 ECTS credits with a duration of four semesters. The other Master's programmes were configured over four semesters, corresponding to 120 ECTS.

The reinforcement of qualification in the areas of Training in the Teaching Area, Specific Teaching Practices, and Supervised Teaching Practice took place when the study cycles were made longer and the relative weighting of these fields made greater. However, in the Bachelor's degree in Basic Education and in the Master's degree programmes which concentrate on teaching in the primary education and 2nd grade school, the relative weight of training in the Teaching Area has not increased. The same situation is observed for Supervised Teaching Practice for the Bachelor's in Basic Education and the Master's in Primary Education (Lopo, 2016). The CNE, adding to the small number of published comments reflecting on the new legal framework, considered these alterations to be "factors that can create the conditions for making the requirements more rigorous and raising the quality of training" (Despacho 4291/2014, 2014b, p. 7781).

The Master's degree in teaching in the primary education and 2nd grade school is divided into two, to reflect the subject areas taught in the 2nd grade school teaching – Mathematics and Natural Sciences, and Portuguese Language Skills and Portuguese History and Geography – and with recruitment groups from the 2nd grade school teaching. From the standpoint of the legislation, this alteration allowed for the reinforcement of training in the area of Training in the Teaching Area, but in fact, as a result of the 50% reduction in subject areas – from four to two – it represented an increase in the time spent on the areas of Specific Teaching Practices and Supervised Teaching Practice. If the CNE viewed this division within the Master's degree programme as a positive option "in that it makes the supply and demand relationship clearer" (Despacho 4291/2014, 2014b, p. 7781), it also reflects the abandonment of an attempt to introduce the generalist teacher into the 2nd grade school teaching, resulting in a substantive difference from the previous legal frameworks which we have analysed.

The suppression of the component of Research Methods seems to point toward a more technically-oriented perspective on teaching activity (Esteves, Rodrigues, Silva, & Carita, 2015) in a posture that is directed more toward the efficiency of actions and student results, to the detriment of a more critical and reflective attitude on teaching and its practices. (Pacheco, 2011).

2. Final remarks

As can be deduced, the process of Europeanisation has made its contribution to a certain convergence of education policies, namely the concretisation of the European Space for Higher Education (ESHE). We have underscored how higher education in Portugal has been visibly impacted by the changes introduced in the 21st century (recognised and comparable academic degrees, a system of three study cycles for higher education, the ECTS credit system, external assessment and certification, etc.) with impact on the level of initial training of educators and teachers.

Within this scope, it was the policy changes that led to alterations in the legal framework of the initial training for educators and teachers, thus illustrating the extent to which the Government remains the regulatory entity nationally, as opposed to transnational education regulation.

The change in legal framework in 2014, although lacking in empirical underpinnings, seems to substantiate the evolution of a perspective of the teacher as an autonomous professional endowed with a critical sense and able to assess his own performance, being one who is inquisitive and constructs his own professional knowledge in a reflective way for a keener technical vision of the tasks required of the teaching profession, and who is guided toward and by the results. However, it was via this new legal framework that the duration of the 2nd cycle degree courses were set at fewer than four semesters.

Training is based on a 2-cycle structure but with clear integration of the dimensions of the training. Nevertheless, and in line with Portuguese tradition, structural models prevail over conceptual ones, to the latter's detriment (Ferreira & Mota, 2013). It is precisely this 2-cycle structure, related to the adoption of the Anglo-Saxon model, which has contributed to the differentiation of the educational offer available, in contrast to its predecessor, and to the applicability envisioned for the second half of the 21st century.

In Portugal, the political context over the last six months has apparently changed in radical fashion. A wide variety of measures adopted in the last four years covering a broad range of fields, and most especially Education, have been reversed. Might this mean that the field of education's well-recognised susceptibility to changes in the political sphere on the national level will lead to a third legal framework for the initial training of educators and teachers in less than a decade?

References

Agência de Avaliação e Acreditação do Ensino Superior (11 de fevereiro de 2014). *ACEF/1213/10027 — Relatório final da CAE*. Obtido de A3ES: http://www.a3es.pt/sites/default/files/ACEF_1213_10027_acef_2012_2013_poli_aacef.pdf

Brito, E. B. (2012). *As implicações do Processo de Bolonha na formação de professores: um estudo nas Escolas Superiores de Educação em Portugal*. (tese de doutoramento não publicada). Covilhã: Universidade da Beira Interior.

Castells, M. (2007). *A sociedade em rede. Volume I: A era da informação: economia, sociedade e cultura*. Lisboa: Fundação Calouste Gulbenkian.

Conselho da União Europeia (2009a, 28 de maio). Conclusões do Conselho de 12 de Maio de 2009 sobre um quadro estratégico para a cooperação europeia no domínio da educação e da formação («EF 2020») (2009/C 119/02). *Jornal Oficial da União Europeia*, pp. C119/2-C119/10.

Conselho da União Europeia (2009b, 23 de outubro). *Educação e Formação (2020)*. Obtido de EUR Lex - Acesso ao direito da União Europeia: http://eur-lex.europa.eu/legal-content/PT/TXT/HTML/?uri=URISERV:ef0016&from=PT

Conselho Europeu (2000, 23 e 24 de março). *Conselho Europeu de Lisboa. 23 e 24 de março de 2000. Conclusões da Presidência*. Obtido de European Parliament: http://www.europarl.europa.eu/summits/lis1_pt.htm

Decreto-lei n.º 107/2008 (2008, 25 de junho). *Diário da República. 1ª Série*, *121*, 3835-3853.

Decreto-lei n.º 239/2001 (2001a, 30 de agosto). *Diário da República. I Série – A*, *201*, 5569-5572.

Decreto-lei n.º 241/2001 (2001b, 30 de agosto). *Diário da República. I Série – A*, *201*, 5572-5575.

Decreto-Lei n.º 289/98 (1998, 17 de setembro). *Diário da República. I Série – A*, *215*, 4805-4812.

Decreto-lei n.º 362/2007 (2007a, 5 de novembro). *Diário da República. 1ª Série*, *212*, 8032-8040.

Decreto-lei n.º 42/2005 (2005a, 22 de fevereiro). *Diário da República. I Série – A*, *37*, 1494-1499.

Decreto-lei n.º 43/2007 (2007c, 22 de fevereiro). *Diário da República. 1ª Série, 38*, 1320-1328.

Decreto-lei n.º 49/2005 (2005b, 30 de agosto). *Diário da República. I Série – A, 166*, 5122-5138.

Decreto-Lei n.º 74/2006 (2006, 24 de março). *Diário da República. I Série – A, 60*, 2242-2257.

Decreto-lei n.º 79/2014 (2014a, 14 de maio). *Diário da República. 1ª Série, 92*, 2819-2828.

Despacho n.º 4291/2014 (2014b, 24 de março). *Diário da República. 2ª Série, 58*, 7780-7781.

Despacho n.º 4793/2015 (2015, 8 de maio). *Diário da República. 2.ª série, 89*, 11347-11350.

Esteves, M., Rodrigues, A., Silva, M. L., & Carita, A. (2015). *Para pensar a educação em Portugal: A formação de professores.* Lisboa: Grupo Economia e Sociedade.

Ferreira, A. G., & Mota, L. (2013). A formação de professores do ensino secundário em Portugal no século XX. *Rev. educ. PUC-Camp, 18* (1), 107-114.

Jessop, B. (2005). *Globalização e o império da informação.* Viseu: Pretexto.

Lei n.º 38/2007 (2007b, 16 de agosto). *Diário da República. 1.ª série, 157*, 5310-5313.

Lopo, T. T. (2016). Entre Dois Regimes Jurídicos, o que Mudou no Currículo da Formação Inicial de Professores em Portugal? *arquivos analíticos de políticas educativas, 24* (7), 1-20.

Melo, A. S., & Branco, M. (2013). A formação inicial de professores no âmbito do processo de Bolonha: o caso da formação de professores de Educação Visual e Tecnológica. *Saber e Educar, 18*, 22-35.

Mouraz, A., Leite, C., & Fernandes, P. (2012). A Formação Inicial de Professores em Portugal decorrente do Processo de Bolonha: Uma Análise a Partir do "Olhar" de Professores e de Estudantes. *Revista Portuguesa de Pedagogia, 46* (2), 189-209.

Moutsios, S. (2009). International organisations and transnational education policy. *Compare, 39* (4), 467–478.

Neave, G. (1998). Modelos de éxito. Los sistemas de cuatro países han influído en la educación superior del mundo entero? Qué han aportado? *El Correo UNESCO. La Educación Superior. Y después qué?* LI, 21-23.

Pacheco, J. (2011). Currículo, Aprendizagem e Avaliação. Uma abordagem face à agenda globalizada. *Revista Lusófona de Educação,* 17 (17), 75-90.

Rosa, M. J., & Sarrico, C. S. (2012). Quality, Evaluation and Accreditation: from Steering, Through Compliance, on to Enhancement and Innovation? In G. Neave, & A. Amaral (Eds.), *Higher Education in Portugal 1974-2009* (pp. 249-264). London/New York: Springer/Cipes - Centro de Investigação de Políticas do Ensino Superior.

Santos, B. S. (2001). Os processos de globalização. In B. S. Santos, *Globalização: Fatalidade ou Utopia?* (pp. 31-106). Porto: Edições Afrontamento.

DOI | https://doi.org/10.14195/978-989-26-1620-9_7

CHAPTER 7

THE ANTINOMIES OF POST BOLOGNA HIGHER EDUCATION CRITICAL APPRAISALS ON THE "SOCIAL DIMENSION" OF THE REFORM

Cristina Pinto Albuquerque

University of Coimbra, Faculty of Psychology and Educational Sciences, Portugal.

E-mail: crisalbuquerque@fpce.uc.pt

Ana Cristina Brito Arcoverde

Federal University of Pernambuco, Brazil / Department of Social Work.

E-mail: ana.arcoverde@gmail.com

This chapter seeks to reflect critically on the (indirect) effects of Bologna's Process namely associated with the teleological orientation of what is taught and researched in high education institutions, as well as the impact of these debates in extra European countries like Brazil. Additionally it is discussed the presupposition of equality in the access and attendance of high education in the European higher education area and the issues associated with the so-called social dimension of the Bologna Process, either in a historical, or substantive perspective.

Introduction

Higher Education Institutions, especially Universities, have been playing and consolidating, throughout History, a crucial role in defining guidelines and models of social and scientific progress. The axiological pillars of modern societies, in particular, and the possibility they opened for the universalization of knowledge found, in universities, the essential mainstay for the promotion of Reason as the basic principle of social, political, scientific and economic organization, notably in the last three centuries.

Similarly, social transformations, *lato sensu*, have over time, in a more or less explicit or implicit way, determined a wide range of adaptations and changes in higher education institutions. These changes, however, did not call into question, at least until the last decade, the core values and organizational principles, which have historically legitimized the scientific and social role of higher education institutions, and, as such, have contributed to the consolidation of their identity. In fact, not neglecting the enormous diversity and pluralism that always existed between higher education institutions, in terms of organizational and structuring models of their teaching and research – diversity which is the translator of the heterogeneity of their own socio-political contexts and founding ideologies -, the University constituted itself as the bulwark of freedom (and, consequently, of pluralism) and of the supremacy of knowledge and science in the face of the determinants and needs of the market and politics. Knowledge held, therefore, a value in itself and not a utilitarian and cyclical value associated to functionality and employability criteria. The search for knowledge, entailing time for reflection, consolidation of ideas and sharing, was assumed as a premise of quality and construction of a consistent, consequent and coherent science. A science dissociated from assumptions of "excellence" proven by: a) measuring what is produced, instead of the quality and importance of what is published and taught; b) the amounts of funding and "technification" of scientific research projects, instead of the prioritized appreciation of the relevance of their objectives and the effective impact they cause in terms of progression of knowledge and social relevance, and c) the publication of results, allegedly striking but quickly disseminated and quickly forgotten. Actually, results that only validate (in some cases) ratings and rankings (of higher education institutions and regions) based on impact criteria and rules that are, finally, defined by some organizations that wish to preserve their own favorable position on the rankings. Contemporary science seems to be, therefore, carried out in accordance with a kind of "contingent *poietics*", if we consider the Aristotelian categories of human activity, as Michel Messu underlines (2015, p.77).

In fact, over the course of the last decade, it has become clear that the challenges faced by higher education institutions, following the so-called Bologna Process, are not only a set of organizational and functional readjustments but also, and above all, an axiological and normative transformation that tends to produce impacts on the identity of the institutions themselves and, consequently, on the teaching they provide and the science they develop (Gumport, 2000).

Within this scope, new values and principles, substantially different from the founders, seem to emerge in the "Bologna's" context. Tapper & Palfreyman (2000) refer to the major challenges that higher education institutions face today, which cluster under what the authors designate by the three "M's": marketization, massification, and managerialism. In fact, at the heart of the Bologna process, the employability of graduates and the attractiveness and competitiveness of the European area are constituted as two of the basic and priority axes. To this end, higher education institutions have been invested in introducing faster training processes (in shorter and articulated cycles), more focused than before on the needs of the labor market. The evaluation of the performance of higher education institutions and, accordingly, their funding has even been associated, in some countries, with the employment performance indicators of their graduates (Smith, McKnight, & Naylor, 2000; Moreau & Leathwood, 2006). Higher education becomes thus hostage to a set of presuppositions that are alien to it and which determine, in a more or less reactive way, its formative and investigative options (in this sense, more tactical than strategic).

A profound epistemological (and even ontological) debate is therefore required, as it has already been acknowledged by several academic bodies, teachers and researchers from various scientific areas of knowledge (Crozier, Curvale, & Hénard, 2006), and even by the European Association for Quality Assurance in Higher Education (ENQA).

The need to redefine frameworks for analysis and reflection, which allow us to construct a critical view of the ongoing evolution and, therefore, to build and consolidate new perspectives on what should be the mission, vision and values of Higher Education Institutions today, acquires all the relevance and opportunity. In fact,

> [F]rom its medieval origins to its post-modern incarnation, universities are not mainly local organizations justified by specific economic and political functions or shaped by particular historical legacies or power struggles. A much broader cultural and civilizational mission has always informed higher education. Its legitimacy and development throughout history have been linked to enacting this broader mission, which today includes the

> idea that universities are sites for developments that lead to social progress (Meyer, Ramirez, Frank, & Schofer, 2007, p. 210).

The idea of social progress, emphasized by Meyer, Ramirez, Frank and Schofer (2007) among others, puts also in the first page of the discussion agenda the need of a deep reflection on the "social dimension" of the Bologna process. Since 2001, such dimension has been translated into a set of general guidelines and measures designed to ensure equal access to higher education by all students who can and wish to do so, regardless of their socio-economic background. Higher education should reflect, in this perspective, the socio-economic diversity of a given society (London Communiqué, 2007). But, as we will argue, such strategies seem to be clearly insufficient to guarantee effective equality among students. Higher education institutions have, in fact, in the last centuries, exerted a central influence on students' personal trajectories and on the possibilities of social mobility. This is truth also nowadays. As European data (Eurostat, 2009) show,

> In the EU-27, almost a third of the population aged between 25 and 34 has completed higher education. This share is increasing in younger generations in almost all Bologna countries. This increase in the number of higher education graduates particularly benefits women, who are closing the gap with men, which is often high among the oldest generation (45–64 year olds) (p. 115).

Even so, a more profound and critical reflection on the true conditions of equity in the current higher education, as well as on the paradoxes generated by the Bologna process on this matter is necessary. The mere legal, *a priori* and universal guarantee of equality in access to higher education, while extremely relevant and translating a significant civilizational advance, cannot effectively obscure in-depth reflection on persisting inequalities, whether in the access, or, above all, in the continuity of superior studies. As evidenced by several researches (Andreu & Brennan, 2012; Archer, 2007) inequality persists in some contexts, for example in regard to what is studied and where. This brings us necessarily to the upstream social and cultural conditions of the higher education system itself, demanding debate on the broader and more substantive meaning of the concept of "opportunity" (Gewirtz 1998; Nussbaum, 2010; Tillman & Scheurich, 2013), and consequently, on the social support that is provided to students in need.

This chapter seeks thus to reflect critically on the indirect effects of Bologna's Process, namely associated with the teleological orientation of what is taught and researched in high education institutions, as well as the impact of these debates in extra European countries like Brazil. Additionally it discusses the presupposition of equality in the access and attendance of high education in the European higher education area and the issues associated with the so-called "social dimension" of the Bologna Process, both in a historical or substantive perspective.

1. The antinomies in the reason of a reform

The Bologna reform was based not only on educational grounds, but also on economic and political motivations. The assertion of a growing European market in the international geopolitical chess, underlined, in the 1990s, the exigency that highly skilled people could be trained and could move freely throughout Europe. To this end, it was crucial to ensure fairly consensual mechanisms for mutual recognition and comparability of diplomas capable of generating confidence in the quality of training offered by the various European higher education institutions. In other words, it was necessary to create a European Area of Higher Education capable of training specialists from different countries and based on unified criteria around certain standards or guiding principles of quality and comparability. Within this scope, higher education institutions began to be also parameterized by reference to their graduates' employability potential in an increasingly wider geographical area.

Thus, demographic issues became particularly acute for some Universities. A 2009 Eurydice study envisaged a reduction of around 15% by 2020 in the European students population, which would necessarily lead to major readjustments in management style and differentiation processes between higher education institutions. In addition, the pronounced aging of the teaching staff across Europe, given the baby boom generation near retirement age, may lead to a sort of "brainwar" (Sursock & Smidt, 2010) for students and academic staff. To this end, higher education institutions are investing in the conquest of the "best", in the search for adequate talents to the achievement of the strategic goal they aim to reach. Clarifying the institution's strengths and potential, and the investment in national and international marketing are, henceforth, the prerogative of universities' action in search for additional financing mechanisms and advantageous ranking positions (in fact, two elements that may feed each other).

1.1. Quality vs utility: Dilemma and strategic choice?

The Report *Trends 2010: A decade of change in European Higher Education* (Sursock & Smidt, 2010) examines the changes that occurred in European higher education institutions in the course of a decade after Bologna's Declaration. As explicitly stated in the document's foreword,

> Europe is perceived around the world as having developed far-reaching policies for education and research. From the point of view of European institutions, however, there is still room for improving the coordination of these two sets of policies. Historically, European universities view themselves as knowledge-based institutions that produce new knowledge and disseminate it through teaching and innovation. The links between research, teaching and innovation is a critical success factor and is all the more important to knowledge-driven societies. Therefore, the condition for successful change in the next decade requires reinforcing the links in the knowledge chain and placing universities, as institutions, at the centre of European and national policies (Sursock & Smidt, 2010, p.4).

On the same Report (Sursock, & Smidt, 2010), it becomes clear those that were, from the respondents point of view (rectors of 20 European universities), the significant changes that have occurred with the Bologna's process implementation: 60% highlighted quality assurance processes; 53% reported increased cooperation between universities; 42% increased cooperation with industry, and 43% acknowledge their autonomy increased. Concerning shifts in university policy, only 28% of respondents claim to have changed their academic policy and 20% their tuition fees. In terms of impacts, 58% of universities' rectors believe that "Bologna's" impacts are very positive, for 3% the impact was null and 38% consider there were gains and losses arising from the process.

A comparison between these results and the assessment obtained in *Trends 2015* (Sursock, 2015), the percentage of respondents who consider the impacts very positive rises to 59%, however the percentage of mixed appraisals decreases (from 38 to 30% of the respondents) and responses of indifferent impact increase, from 3 to 5%. On the *2015 Report*, the context data are particularly emphasized, namely the economic crisis (highly important for 43% of respondents: notably in the Czech Republic, France, Greece, Hungary, Ireland, Italy, Latvia, Lithuania, Portugal, Romania, Slovakia, Spain and Ukraine) and the low demographic growing (highly important to 32% of the responding institutions, particularly in the Czech Republic, Hungary, Latvia, Lithuania, Poland, Portugal, Romania, the Russian Federation, Slovakia and Ukraine).

Although illustrative, these data do not add much to the understanding of what is at stake when identifying the more or less positive impacts of the Bologna process, nor on the meaning attributed to reforms and content of ongoing adaptations. Very little is known, as the reports themselves acknowledge, about what the European higher education area is or should be. The scarcity of debate has even led to some ambiguity between humanistic objectives and technocratic purposes at the heart of the Bologna process. In fact, an ambiguity that has determined in an indelible way, over the last decades, European higher education development.

The attractiveness of the European area in the formation of qualified "human capital" and the competitiveness (especially with Northern American higher education institutions) have become, in reality, key features on the European political and economic agenda, in line with the assumptions of the Lisbon Strategy (2000). In fact, it explicitly inscribes the goal of creating the "most dynamic and competitive economic space in the world", based on knowledge. Europe would, thus, be able to ensure simultaneously sustainable economic growth, job creation and social cohesion. Higher education transmutes into a crucial instrument for this endeavor.

The European Association for Quality Assurance in Higher Education (ENQA), in a Report published in 2006 (p. 9), points out that "higher education, in a context of globalization, has begun to show the characteristics of a market" (cit. in Lima, Azevedo & Catani, 2008, p. 17).

Taking over a competitive edge in the global market is, in effect, explicit in various documents framing the Bologna reform. Higher education institutions hence become, first and foremost, producers of well-trained and flexible professionals to respond to the challenges of the market. It is therefore consistent with the underlying philosophy of the reform that the various choices made are oriented towards guaranteeing employability, measuring and auditing procedures, strategic planning and economic efficiency (within the organizational management of universities itself). Principles derived from the industrial universe, which in their essence do not relate to the founding values and concerns of university education, are henceforth explicitly included in the context of higher education. The credit transfer system, for example, does not only convey a confidence assumption on the quality of skills acquired by the student in a "partner" higher education institution. It also enables saving financial resources since it becomes unnecessary for the same training module to be taught at the student's higher education institution of origin. The same implicit purpose lies in the recognition of professional experience and in the awarding of joint degrees, allowing the assignment of educational costs by various institutions and, as such, reducing the actual cost per student.

Concerns for economic rationalization, standardization and measurement of procedures (paradoxically aggregated under a rhetoric of "quality") are, essentially, transversal to the various axes of the Bologna process and tend to determine choices made regarding, for example, what should be taught and how. This way, appropriate criteria and inherent processes in assessing the quality and consistency of teaching and research (essentially dissociated from external pressures and utility concerns) can be, in some cases, put in a secondary place. This does not mean that economic sustainability of higher education institutions and employability of their graduates should not be considered as important elements of reflection. However such concerns shouldn't be prevalent in substantive options on contents to be taught and on science to be developed. These should stand on its own. As the mathematician Henri Poincaré stated, at the beginning of the twentieth century (1905), science is worth for science, it is not moldable to relativistic perspectives and mere pursuit of solutions. *"On ne peut même pas dire que l'action soit le but de la science; devons-nous condamner les études faites sur l'étoile Sirius, sous prétexte que nous n'exercerons probablement jamais aucune action sur cet astre?"* (Poincaré, 1905, p. 241). The main focus of scientific knowledge is not the solution, but the questioning, is not certainty but the methodical doubt. Applicability is not an end in itself, but only a possible product. In the same way, Michel Messu (2015) points out, in the book *De la Méthode en Sociologie*,

> La science ne se réduit toujours pas à ce qu'elle permet de produire concrètement. Sa fin n'est pas le «produit» lui-même, mais le savoir qui s'y réalise, la théorie qui en rend raison. Partant, sa fin ne connaît pas de marque d'arrêt. Elle s'accomplit quand la science se fait. L'activité

scientifique est en quelque sorte sa propre fin et n'admet aucun terme, aucun point final. Et surement pas celui représenté par le produit qu'elle a contribué à réaliser (p. 77).

However, with the Bologna's process implementation, higher education institutions and the science produced and disseminated by them, are especially linked to the effort of innovation as well as economic and social development. "Higher education institutions are increasingly viewed by policy makers as 'economic engines' and are seen as essential for ensuring knowledge production through research and innovation and the education and continuous up-skilling of the workforce" (Sursock & Smidt, 2010, p. 14). Useful knowledge is thus one that can be applied and produces measurable and adequate results for the fulfillment of the goals of economic growth.

The teleological dimension of higher education emerges at this level as the inescapable debate. Sjur Bergan (2006, *cit*. in Sursock & Smidt, 2010), for example, highlights as aims of higher education, four essential objectives conceived as a whole, reinforcing and complementing each other: "preparation for the labor market, preparation for life as active citizens in democratic societies, personal development and the development and maintenance of a broad, advanced knowledge base" (*cit*. in Sursock & Smidt, 2010, p. 31). From the author's point of view, the purpose of personal development has been neglected and became invisible at the core of the Bologna process while other objectives are only considered in a scarce and incomplete way. A much deeper and multidimensional reflection on the present purposes and challenges of higher education is, therefore necessary.

Within Bologna's framework, the orientation towards the formation of "human capital" adapted to the new demands of the globalized labor market is, as previously mentioned, embraced as paramount. The theory of human capital, developed especially within the scope of the Chicago School in the 1960s (Schultz, 1963), focuses on the assumption that education is a fundamental element in the creation of skills to increase the possibilities of human productivity. In this sense, education would be an investment in individuals and their competencies, aiming for the development of society and economy.

Associated with this perspective there is a strict conception of competences whose origins lie in the traditions of a functionalist and behavioral approach. These traditions emerge in areas such as management, human resources, vocational and career guidance (Mulder, 2007; Sultana, 2009), particularly in the 1960s and 1970s. In this context, "performance culture", established as the nodal element of training and learning strategies, was associated, for that purpose, with processes of measurement and standardization of behavioral indicators to the detriment of more complex and dynamic approaches. Goals were, therefore, focused on the appreciation of what individuals should be able to do (Melton, 1994) in terms of more or less standardized and measurable descriptors. Thereby, obtaining satisfactory performance results (Jessup, 1991) was the crucial factor for weighing the importance, or irrelevance, of educational efforts. However, during the last decade of the last century, the very concept of competence began to be re-equated and, through this, educational guidelines, centered on mere functionalist and static approaches, deeply questioned (Brown *et al.*, 1994). The main criticisms revolved around the impossibility of understanding, through simplistic logics, complex activities and behaviors, or the influence of personal values, professional frameworks, group processes and environmental influence (Barnett, 1994; Hager & Gonczi, 1996). Other criticisms denounced the underlying reductionism of measuring learning objectives by means of results, which are conditioned by predetermined ends, in a kind of "mechanical teaching for testing" (Bates, 1995).

The rhetoric of competences and skills is still pivotal within Bologna process' framework. Based on the same thesis of human capital theory of the 1960s - education as an essential element in the creation of skills to increase the possibilities of human productivity -, the new guidelines underline higher education's relevance for the formation of active and skill full agents able to fit in a global economy and respond adequately and effectively to its challenges. An economy based on knowledge and innovation as advocated by Europe 2020's strategy, following the preceding Lisbon Strategy.

Designing educational programs driven mainly by economic functionality preoccupations is, however, as it was already mentioned, profoundly reductionist. As the American philosopher Martha Nussbaum (2010) points out, that way it is only considered a portion of how citizens develop.

> The ability to think well about a wide range of cultures, groups and nations in the context of an understanding of the world's economy and the history of many national and group interactions is the key to enabling democracies to be able to deal responsibly with problems which we are currently facing as members of an interdependent world (Nussbaum, 2010, p.9).

The antinomies underlying the Bologna process and the consequent paradoxes inherent to its goals and the practices it intends to develop become thus clear: on one hand, the purposes of knowledge and science *per se,* on the other hand, the goals of functionality and employability. On one hand, quality as substance, on the other, quality as a procedure. On one hand, theoretical knowledge, on the other, know-how. Although we can discuss the simplistic dichotomization of these assumptions, it allows to analytically underscore, above all, the current transmutation of higher education's basic principles, in orientations of instrumental, technical and performative focus.

This component associated with the weighting of higher education's goals and the kind of citizens it helps to produce seem to be, in our perspective, one of the essential dimensions in a more complex reflection on the Bologna process and the balance that can already be achieved on it.

2. Bologna's debates in extra European contexts: the case of Brazil

Bologna's process gathered, in the Brazilian context, controversial positions for or against it. This is mainly due to higher education reform initiatives considered more targeted for privatization since the government of Fernando Henrique Cardoso.

In the midst of higher education reform - in fact in parallel with the reform of the State itself continued in the Lula da Silva government (first mandate: 2003-2006) - such initiatives were materialized through PROUNI (University for All Program, 2005), REUNI (New University, later Program for Restructuring and Expansion of Brazilian Federal Universities, 2007), PNAES (National Student Assistance, 2010), and FIES (Student Financing Fund, 2001).

The governmental discourse was that PROUNI, REUNI and PNAES would allow a democratic expansion of access to and permanence in higher education, with a significant increase in the number of students from lower income social classes in public universities. For that, affirmative policies, for example quotas for students of public schools, black, and Indians, were putted in action since then (Brazil, MEC, 2012). Other favorable argument about the Brazilian higher education reform underlined that it would ease student's internal and international mobility. Lima (2003) points out that in 2003 more than one million students studied in private institutions. The number of enrollments in the private network (1,808,219 students) grew thus three times more than in the public one (887,027 students) before the reforms.

Additionally, the argument of the preparation of universities for 21st century societies was presented, overcoming the "Humboldtian paradigm" in the transmission of knowledge linked with research, and the need to change the ways of thinking and preparing the youth for the future.

In the background of this defense of the ongoing reforms is also the assertion of the state's inability to sustain the cost of federal universities. In this sense, between 1995 and 2002, in a compression policy, investments in federal universities were reduced by 30% (Pena-Vega, 2009).

Nevertheless, the reforms triggered a heated debate within teachers and their organizations, and among students, but not within the National Union of Students (UNE). This organization and its leadership, considered to be co-opted by the government (Vieira, 2015), directed its critics, not to the reform ongoing, but to the operationalization instruments of it in the Brazilian higher education system. These were considered instruments of coercion and a synonym of loss of autonomy of public universities, as well as of reduction of financial means or resources. In fact, it was considered that these factors could condition the improvement guarantee in the quality of teaching, research and extension, the quality of the structures of the campuses, the hiring of teachers and the promotion of the existing ones.

The most compelling argument against the reform is however related with its ideological representation. Accordingly to several authors the reform is associated with "a new colonialist movement" and "a new division" in the trade of educational services (Dias, 2009; Santos 2009). However, despite the freedom that each country, ministers and university communities have had in deciding to approve or reject the principles contained in documents without legal force, the reform of higher education in Brazil inspired by the European Bologna Process is now a reality.

The "New University" proposal (materialized by the Decree 6.096, 24th April 2007) aims to "create conditions for the expansion of access and permanence in higher education, at undergraduate level, for the better use of the physical structure and human resources existing in federal universities" (REUNI, 2007, Art. 1º). In the background this reform intends also to stimulate the concurrence between federal Universities, associating the increasing of financial resources to the presentation of reform plans and the definition of measurable goals. In fact, the so called New University reform, pointed out by some authors (Almeida Filho, 2007) as the sheepish miscellaneous between European and Northern American Models, although considered necessary to surpass some of the structural problems of the Brazilian higher education system, must be aware of the risk of "transforming public universities at Liberal Arts Colleges, failing to achieve the standard of first-class USA universities" (Lima, Azevedo, & Catani, 2008, p. 27)

Actually, the balance of results and perspectives after some reforms points to the expansion / internalization of public universities, but also to an exponential growth of private universities[1] and distance education, as well as adaptations and enlargement of physical structures and some public recruitment of new teachers. However, the academic restructuring did not reach yet 50% of institutional projects in terms of innovation: training in cycles, common basic training for all undergraduate courses, basic training in one or more major area courses, interdisciplinary baccalaureate in one or more of the major areas, baccalaureate with two formative itineraries, according to the types of initiatives pointed out by Ramalho Filho (2009). Moreover, the idea contained in the defense of intra, inter and international mobility did not yet, in fact, promote equality, but rather equivalence, a principle that does not materialize the universalization of public higher education. Within this scope, another "social dimension" conception in high education systems cannot be neglected: the one that is associated with what is mentioned in official reform documents as the component of equity and social justice in higher education.

3. Social dimension in the Bologna process: Limitations and paradoxes

During the first years of Bologna's Process implementation, the technical-operative dimension was established as the reform's priority. The design of procedures, guidelines and instruments, whether related to the process of articulation of higher education in the European area (system of accumulation and transfer of credits, transformation of curricula, definition of transversal learning competences for areas of study, etc.), or concerning

---

[1] Data on the number of public and private institutions in the country make clear the direction and intentionality of the higher education reform inspired by the Bologna Process: between 2001 and 2010, Brazil had 67 public higher education institutions and 1,208 private ones, while, in 2010, public institutions reached 99 and private ones reached 2,100, (INEP, adapted by Araújo, 2015).

the functional and organizational model to be adopted by different Higher Education Institutions (in particular the so-called quality assurance system), was, in fact, at the heart of the initial concerns. This process, which is more political than academic, has been largely determined by supranational bodies and heavily governmentalized, without a clear and sufficient public debate. The participation of educational institutions in decision making and in influencing the process was scarce (Lima, Azevedo & Catani, 2008). The technical and methodological dimension of "how to do" overlapped the deontological and hermeneutic dimension of "why to do", with what implications and with what sense. The reform's substantive and social components were thus transferred, at least in the first stage of the Bologna process, to a secondary and grey area of uncertainty.

Although the first reference to the so-called "social dimension" of the Bologna process surfaces on the 19th of May 2001 on the Prague Declaration, it remains overshadowed by the emphasis on evaluation, the definition of comparable academic degrees to enhance student mobility within the European Higher Education Area, the need for students to participate in the process and the attractiveness of students from other regions outside Europe. The Communiqué of the Council of Rectors of Portuguese Universities (CRUP), released on April 17th, 2001, is clear in explaining these priorities as central objectives for the creation of a real European Higher Education Area: student and graduates mobility, employability and greater competitiveness within the European Area and by reference to the other global blocks. Such objectives would be achieved through readability and comparability of academic degrees, by creating a compatible and comparable system of credits (ECTS and Diploma Supplement) and a process of quality assurance of courses and education systems through cooperation in evaluation processes (EPHE, 2006).

In contrast, the social dimension of the Bologna process was emphasized by students on the 25th March, 2001 within the framework of the Student Göteborg Convention. In the Declaration issued by the National Unions of Students in Europe, students advocate the need for a combination of quality, accessibility and diversity in European higher education, a "Europe without boundaries for its citizens". At this level, conditions and social implications underlying the access and attendance of higher education are of particular relevance to the students, who demand the cooperation and responsibility of the States in this domain.

In effect, it were the organizations representative of the students that have most critically positioned themselves regarding Bologna's process technical and mercantile approach as well as the oblivion of the lack of equity at its core. For example, on the Report produced in 2007 - *Bologna with Student Eyes* (ESIB, 2007) - it is precisely underlined the difference between the marketing of the attractiveness of the European Higher Education Area and the real possibilities for mobility and payment of studies by a considerable proportion of students from third countries or from countries with significant economic differentiation within Europe. Mobility grants have, in fact, been decreasing, always demanding a considerable co-payment from families (especially if mobility operates between countries with very different socio-economic levels). Similarly, tuition fees (even in public universities) reach, in some countries (as is the case of Portugal), increasingly high values that try to get close to the "real cost" per student. Students are, in this sense, consumers of educational services. In fact, on the ground of increasing the quality of education and services to students in some European countries there has been an increase in the costs of attending higher education, particularly in the last decade, which can turn into a relevant barrier to equitable access to higher education for all candidates. Nevertheless, the various countries that form the European High Education Area have very distinct realities on this matter at the level of the first cycle of studies. In some cases, free studies, such as in the Scandinavian countries; in other cases mandatory payment of tuition fees, such as in Portugal.

To this end, the paradox between a discourse that proclaims "higher education for all", in conditions of equity and justice, and a practice that tends to favor differentiation and competitiveness has been emphasized for a long time. In fact, although these concerns regarding equity in higher education were highlighted in 2001, it was only in May 2005 (at the Bergen Conference) that social dimension was recognized as an inherent axis of the European High Education Area, being assumed as a necessary strategy to promote its attractiveness and competitiveness:

> The social dimension of the Bologna Process is a constituent part of the EHEA and a necessary condition for the attractiveness and competitiveness of the EHEA. We therefore renew our commitment to making quality higher education equally accessible to all, and stress the need for appropriate conditions for students so that they can complete their studies without obstacles related to their social and economic background. The social dimension includes measures taken by governments to help students, especially from socially disadvantaged groups, in financial and economic aspects and to provide them with guidance and counselling services with a view to widening access (Bergen Communiqué, 2005, p.4).

This orientation was defined even before the Bergen Conference, at the seminar "*The social dimension of the European Higher Education Area and world-wide competition*" (Paris,

January 2005), in which the premises of what is known as the social dimension of the Bologna Process were refined:

> The social dimension includes all provisions needed for having equal access, progress and completion of higher education. Enlarging the existing gap between different parts of Europe should be avoided, and at the national level the gap between those who benefit from higher education and come back later in life and those who never make use of this possibility should be closed. Participants agreed that: • strengthening the social dimension of higher education is one of the conditions for making real a knowledge society, which implies increasing the number of graduates from higher education through lifelong learning; • social and economic background should not be a barrier to access to higher education, successful completion of studies and meaningful employment after graduation; • taking into account the social dimension of the EHEA both at the national level and the European level contributes to the creation of a coherent, balanced and competitive European Higher Education Area (Bologna Seminar, 2005, s.p.).

Taking as a concern the overcoming or minimization of obstacles to a successful learning path, as well as the access to quality higher education for all students, regardless of their socio-economic starting conditions, the definition of actions and measures to meet this target was defined and shaped in national contexts according to their needs and specificities. The definition of such global strategies - for instance, through the collection of comparable data (via Eurostat, Eurydice and Eurostudent) - and national guidelines was explained at the London Communiqué (2007).

This strategy emphasized the importance of collecting comparable and reliable data on students, widening participation, identifying underrepresented groups of students, undertaking peer learning activities between countries of the EHEA, and designing adequate teaching and delivery methods to cater for the needs of all students. (Infosheet, 2014-2016, p. 2).

In this Communiqué (and, in its continuity, in the one of Leuven, in 2009) the aim is to ensure the representation of the diversity of all social groups in the frequency of higher education and define key issues for the achievement of the social dimension in the EHEA. These issues are based on six cornerstones (Eurostat, 2009):

> 1. Equal opportunities for access, participation and completion of higher education (anti-discrimination legislation covering higher education; fair and transparent admission rules);
> 2. Extension of access to and participation in higher education (outreach programs for underrepresented groups, flexible learning pathways, and recognition of prior learning, in particular of a professional nature);
> 3. Improved completion rates and quality of education (provision of academic services: guidance, study resources, teaching and learning methods, retention measures as a flexibility strategy, etc., provision of social services - counseling, targeted support for students with special needs and "non-traditional" students);
> 4. Participation of students in the government of higher education institutions (measures to ensure student participation, for example, in course and program evaluations);

5. Financing to start and complete higher education (adequate and coordinated national financial support systems; targeted support for disadvantaged groups);
6. Monitoring (systematic and periodic collection of student background data, employability graduate tracer studies).

To this end, a set of actions and procedures were established in 2012 (Bucharest) aimed mainly at reducing inequalities through measures and services directed to students, duly adapted to the specificities of national contexts and based on the general *"Strategy for the Development of the Social Dimension and Lifelong Learning in the EHEA to 2020"*[2]: counseling and guidance; flexible and diversified learning strategies (provision of part-time courses, accredited internships, distance learning through the use of ICT, open and creative educational resources); support to teachers' work (pedagogical methodology, continuous scientific deepening, guarantee of academic freedom) for a better monitoring of students' individual development; recognition and accreditation of students' previous experience (namely professional), peer learning (e.g., encouraging entrepreneurship), among others.

All of these measures are, however, designed, according to the spirit of the Bologna process, as strategies of attractiveness and competitiveness of the European Area. According to the underlying rhetoric, concerns about reducing inequalities in access and attendance of higher education increases skills and benefits not only students but society as a whole and its social and economic cohesion. This would generate social justice by guaranteeing equal opportunities for all, not only in access to

---

[2] Strategy for the Development of the Social Dimension and Lifelong Learning in the EHEA to 2020: http://bologna-yerevan2015.ehea.info/files/Widening Participation for Equity and Growth_ A Strategy for the Development of the Social Dimension and Lifelong Learning in the European Higher Education Area to 2020 .pdf

knowledge, but also in the access to employment in societies that require ever more specialized and differentiating levels of qualification.

This formal manifestation, although being an important step in promoting greater equity in terms of access and attendance at higher education, has thus been driven by purposes upstream of social concerns and, as such, has not elicited the debates that would allow appreciate to what extent some of the reforms implemented do not generate or increase (new) inequalities.

An equalization of opportunities is usually associated with measures to compensate for unequal starting conditions, for example through programs of positive discrimination (e.g., specific social support or definition of quotas for certain population groups, as in the Brazilian case). However, these programs and measures do not fail to raise a number of questions that should be considered in a deeper reflection on social justice and policies designed to achieve it. Namely, the perverse negative discrimination effect of positively discriminated groups, or even the absence, or limitation, of real impacts on the transformation of starting conditions, largely marked by supra-individual and / or supra local inequalities. In this perspective, social justice promotion policies can not only focus on higher education, nor have a palliative or merely regulatory focus, but rather embody holistic and complex prerogatives in the basic socio-economic context. Policies that support reconciliation between work and higher education or between family, work and study (for instance, for young parents) are paradigmatic examples.

A study developed in Spain, by Marina Elias Andreu and John Brennan (2012), stresses that the reforms stemming from the Bologna process may actually boost mechanisms of inequality considering the distinct way the entry and attendance of higher education are experienced[3] by students from socioeconomically differentiated environments and, in particular, student-workers.

The economic crisis, accompanied with the exponential increase of tuition fees in some European countries (even in public universities as in Portugal) are, in fact, inevitable elements for a more complex reflection on the real possibilities of access and attendance of higher education. Many students have to work in order to attend higher education, which distances them from university experience and impairs their involvement and the construction of their identity as students (Andreu & Brennan, 2012). Additionally, although there are legal mechanisms in various countries to ensure student-workers' rights to attend classes and assessments, this status is not demanded by many students who fear losing their jobs. Many others cannot even access such status since they do not have a signed work contract. There are, consequently, processes of social and economic structuring, which are previous to the access mechanisms to higher education, and that end up conditioning not only equity in terms of access, but, above all, equity in terms of attendance and conclusion thereof.

Data on the social dimension of access and attendance to higher education in 2009 (Eurostat, 2009), although with significant improvements, also reveal - despite the limitations that statistical studies always present due to their extensive tendency and consequent loss of specificity and relativity in the analyzes - countless structural conditioning factors:

> Increasing participation in higher education is sustained by high percentage of qualifying graduates of secondary schooling. However, in a few countries, entrants in higher education represent less than 60% of qualifying graduates

---

[3] Even the choice of which university to attend is driven by selective premises.

of upper secondary education; when measured directly, the share of students from non-traditional routes entering higher education stood at 15% in England and Wales, but amounted to less than 12% in other countries for which data are available; countries show very marked differences on part-time studying. The share of part time students ranged from less than 10% of the overall student population to slightly more than 50% in Sweden; age is a key determinant when analyzing part-time studying. In fact, at EU-27 level, almost half of students aged 30 and over are part-time students, while this is far less widespread among younger students. The level of education of parents still has an impact on success in higher education; in some countries, less than 10 % of those whose parents have a low educational level graduated from tertiary education; the continuing transmission of disadvantages through family backgrounds tends to affect men and women equally; however, the situation is improving; young people from low educational family backgrounds have better chances of graduating than their elders did in the past (Eurostat, 2009, p.45).

In fact, Andreu and Brennan's study (2012), previously mentioned, and others (ESU, 2015), show that, in the student's opinion, higher education is actually characterized by major elitism. This conception, which seems paradoxical by reference to the assumptions of the Bologna reform, reveals a set of elements that emerge in the hidden side of this process.

Instrumental rhetoric and rapid training, in reality, leave behind a group of students less prepared to respond to such demands. If we add to this aspect some additional factors - the increase of taxes and fees; the association (which occurs in some countries) between social support and merit (linked to school "success"); the most restricted system of prescription of enrollments; the requirement of continuous attendance of classes that hampers the maintenance of employment, among others - the conditions for the accentuation of some iniquities seem to be uplifted, in counterpoint with an official discourse increasingly anchored in the appeal to social justice in higher education (Andreu & Brennan, 2012).

Additionally, processes and mechanisms of social support vary substantially between contexts, presenting students from different countries distinctive challenges and coping possibilities. Social support, in the form of scholarships, exemption or public subsidization of tuition fees (when they exist), or others, which differ from one country to another, tend to focus on criteria that are either compensatory, sometimes universal, or meritocratic, sometimes mixed, as in the Portuguese case that associates the compensatory logic - proof of resources - to the meritocratic logic based on evidences of "school success".

In another dimension, the autonomous student paradigm, core element of Bologna's reforms, raises important issues in terms of equity, especially in a context of mass access to higher education. The so-called "student-centered learning" stems from a set of assumptions that are, in fact, mere rhetorical devices. Firstly, because they disregard the difference of backgrounds, experiences, skills and expectations of the various student profiles; Secondly, because they do not take into account the actual possibilities for teacher monitoring and mentoring of students; Thirdly, because they do not attend the differences regarding quality of previous education and the knowledge then acquired or not; Fourthly, because they place emphasis on what students want and can learn rather than what they should learn. And what they "should learn" is far beyond utilitarian and provisional knowledge.

As already mentioned in the first part of this chapter, higher education should, above all, stimulate curiosity and provide the basis for critical and complex thinking. In this sense, knowledge of historical-philosophical framework, for example, is essential. Thus, student-centered learning cannot be more than a methodological component, adaptable to the goals and contents of what needs to be taught. Moreover, it cannot assume as an *a priori* premise student's full autonomy to learn and set apart what is important or not. In fact, as Leathwood (2001) states, in pedagogical terms, many students, from the United Kingdom, "in the first year felt that they had been expected to be 'independent' too early in their studies and that they had been left to sink or swim" (*cit.* in Andreu & Brennan, 2012, p. 107).

Hence, the application of reforms to different contexts without the necessary adaptation and anticipation of adverse consequences may lead to situations of greater inequity vis-a-vis a system and a European context that applies the same evaluation gauge without considering the starting distinctions.

4. Final remarks

Higher education tends to be directed nowadays - and Bologna, in spite of all the possibilities and advancements it presents, has enhanced such risk - towards the swift development of adaptability skills in different socio-professional frameworks. From a global competitiveness' perspective, promoted in various European and international instances, higher education risks progressively to be reduced to mere logics of learning to produce, learning to undertake, and learning to succeed.

An education that produces more development and, potentially, greater social justice, has to be conceived as an act of liberation, a space of interconnection and cultural learning capable of founding and consolidating a new conception of life and humankind. In this sense, in itself, education (and high education certainly) is both an end and a means. An end, as an essential instance in the acquisition of knowledge; a means of reducing inequalities of origin and building adequate opportunities for access to desired social and economic positions. Inherently, school, and higher education in particular, is an instance of social mobility. In Pourtois's (2006) perspective, this means giving universities an essential purpose: to contribute to the formation of more responsible people, involved in building a more just society, and as such, a vector of social transformation. Underlying these assumptions is the classical question - should higher education prepare for integration into the world as it is, or as it should be? (Pourtois, 2006), or such concerns are and should be oblivious to the basic concerns of higher education?

Educational policies in this regard need to be conceived and evaluated as driving the neutralization of the weight of social disadvantageous circumstances, as well as strategies of empowerment and construction of skills and opportunities, and also of deep and complex formation on the cultural and ethical bases of life in society. In other words, the school and the university cannot be guided by a merely instrumental perspective, which tends to devalue all non-econometric knowledge, for example associated with the humanities and the arts.

In contrast, educational institutions cannot ignore the production of knowledge essential to the demands of today's world, most of which are functional. Even because such a fact would tend to penalize especially the most disadvantaged population, and consequently it would, in another way, replicate basic inequalities (Albuquerque, 2015). Nevertheless, a number of queries emerge, but the answers involve a profound complexity.

The transformation of post-Bologna university training into a rapid and essentially utilitarian preparation for labor market integration does not fail to raise relevant issues, either as regards to the consistency of basic training and the respective depth of knowledge (cultural, philosophical, artistic), or regarding the suspicion of subjecting higher education to market demands and, as such, its transformation into a production institution of technicians and not of professionals and conscious citizens, capable of thinking and acting ethically and globally, in an increasingly complex and plural world.

In our view, as we have tried to advocate, scientific knowledge should not be guided by normative or utilitarian presuppositions or by moral orientations. Its rationale must be the development of scientific curiosity and rigorous data, axes that are not constrained by reference to short-term and instrumental dimensions, but which allow simultaneously to understand and overcome them. In the same way, social conditions and equality in the access and frequency of higher education institutions should be seriously taken in consideration in the European area in the name of a real consistent and cohesive Europe of knowledge and mobility.

References

Albuquerque, C. (2015). Contributos para uma reflexão crítica sobre a igualdade (substantiva) de oportunidades. In R. T. Ens & I. W. Bonnetti (Orgs.), *Educação e Justiça Social* (pp. 73-91). Ijuí. Editora Unijuí.

Almeida Filho, N. (2007). *Universidade nova: nem Harvard, nem Bolonha*. Retrieved from: http://www.twiki.ufba.br/twiki/bin/view/UniversidadeNova/Artigo_n1.

Andreu, M.E. & Brennan, J. (2012). Implications of the Bologna Process for equity in higher education. In A. Curaj, P. Scott, L. Vlasceanu, L. Wilson, L. (eds),

European Higher Education at the crossroads. Between the Bologna Process and national reforms. Part 1 (pp. 101-118). New York, London: Springer.

Araújo, J. O. (2003). O elo assistência e educação: análise assistência/desempenho no programa residência universitária alagoana. Programa de pós-graduação em Serviço Social, Dissertação de Mestrado em Serviço social. Recife: Universidade Federal de Pernambuco.

Archer, M. (2007). *Making Our Way through the World: Human Reflexivity and Social Mobility*. Cambridge: Cambridge University Press.

Barnett, R. (1994). *The limits of competence*. Buckingham: Open University Press.

Barroso, J. (2006). O Estado e a educação. A regulação transnacional, a regulação nacional e a regulação local. In J. Barroso (Org.), *A regulação das políticas públicas de educação* (pp.43-70). Lisboa: Educa.

Bates, I. (1995). The competence movement and the National Vocational Qualifications framework. The widening parameters of research. *British Journal of Education and Work*, 8(2), 5-13.

Bergen Communiqué (2005). *The European Higher Education Area*. Report of the Bologna Follow-up Group to the Conference of European Ministers Responsible for Higher Education. Bergen, 19-20 May. Retrieved from http://www.mctes.pt/docs/ficheiros/Bergen_Comunicado.pdf. 28 jun. 2007.

Berlin Communiqué. *Realising The European Higher Education Area*. Retrieved from: http://www.mctes.pt/docs/ficheiros/Comunicado_de_Berlim.pdf.2003.

Bologna Seminar (2005). *Seminar on the social dimension of the European Higher Education Area and world-wide competition*. Work Programme of the Bologna Follow-up Group 2003-2005. Paris. Retrieved from: https://www.ehea.info/cid102048/social-dimension-paris-2005.html

Brasil, MEC, Ministério da Educação (2012). Lei de Cotas. Lei n. 12.711, de 29 de agosto de 2012.

Brown, L.M. *et al.* (Eds) (1994). *Competence-based training. A collection of readings*. Victoria: Deakin University, 1994.

Crozier, F., Curvale, B., & Hénard, F. (2006). Final Report on The Quality Convergence II Project: promoting epistemological approaches to quality assurance. In F. Crozier, et al., *Terminology of quality assurance: towards shared European values?* (pp. 22-28). Helsínquia: ENQA. Retrieved from http://www.enqa.eu/files/terminology_v01.pdf.

Dias, J.S. (2009). O Processo de Bolonha In E.M.A. Pereira, & M. de L.P. (Orgs.), *Universidade contemporânea: políticas do Processo de Bolonha* (pp. 129-152). Campinas, SP: Mercado das Letras.

ENQA (2006). Quality Assurance of Higher Education in Portugal. Helsínquia: European Association for Quality Assurance in Higher Education. Retrieved from<http://www.enqa.eu/pubs.lasso 2006.

EPHE (2006). Quality Assurance of Higher Education in Portugal. An Assessment of the Existing System and Recommendations for a Future System. European Association for Quality Assurance in Higher Education, Helsinki.

ESIB (2007). Bologna With Student Eyes. London: The National Unions of Students in Europe. Retrieved from http://www.mctes.pt/docs/ficheiros/ ESIB_Bologna_With_Student_Eyes_full.pdfE

ESU, European Student's Union (2015). Bologna with Students Eyes. Time to meet the expectations from 1999. Brussels. Retrieved from: https://media. ehea.info/file/ESU/32/8/Bologna-With-Student-Eyes_2015_565328.pdf.

EUROSTAT (2009). *The Bologna Process in Higher Education in Europe. Key indicators on the social dimension and mobility.* Luxembourg: Office for Official Publications of the European Communities.

EURYDICE (2009). Higher Education in Europe 2009: Developments in the Bologna Process. Brussels: Education, Audiovisual and Culture Executive Agency.

FIES (2001). Student Financing Fund. Lei nº 10.260, de 12 de julho de 2001. Brasil.

Gewirtz, S. (1998). Conceptualizing social justice in education: Mapping the territory. *Journal of Education Policy*, 4(13), 469-484.

Gumport, P.J. (2000). Academic Restructuring: Organizational Change and Institutional imperatives. *Higher Education: The International Journal of Higher Education and Educational Planning*, 39, 67-91.

Hager, P., & Gonczi, A. (1996). Professions and competencies. In R. Edwards, A. Hanson, & P. Raggat (Eds), *Boundaries of adult learning* (pp. 246-260). London: Routledge/ Open University Press.

Infosheet - Social Dimension (2014-2016). *Improving access to and participation in Higher Education: "Supporting the Bologna Process in Malta 2014-2016"*. Erasmus+ Project. Malta: National Commission for Further and Higher Education.

Jessup, G. (1991). *Outcomes. NVQs and the emerging model of education and training*. London: Falmer.

Lima, G.F.C. (2003). O discurso da sustentabilidade e suas implicações para a educação. *Ambiente & Sociedade*, 6 (2), 99-119.

Lima, L. C., Azevedo, M. L. N., & Catani, A. M. (2008). O processo de Bolonha, a avaliação da educação superior e algumas considerações sobre a Universidade Nova. *Avaliação: Revista da Avaliação da Educação Superior*, 13(1), 7-36.

London Communiqué (2007). *Towards The European Higher Education Area: responding to challenges in a globalised world*. Retrieved from http://www.mctes.pt/docs/ficheiros/Londres_Communique_18May07.pdf, 2007.

Melton, R.F. (1994). Competence in perspective. *Educational Research*, 36(3), 285-294.

Meyer, J. W., Ramirez, F. O., Frank, D.J. & Schofer, E. (2007). Higher Education as an Institution. In P. J. Gumport (ed.), *Sociology of Higher Education. Contributions and Their Contexts* (pp. 187-221). Baltimore: The John Hopkins University Press.

Moreau, M.P., & Leathwood, C. (2006). Graduates' employment and the discourse of employability: a critical analysis. *Journal of Education and Work*, 19 (4), 305-324.

Mulder, M. (2007). Competence. The essence and use of the concept in ECVT. *European Journal of Vocational Training*, 40(1), 5-21.

Nussbaum, M. C. (2010). *Not for Profit. Why democracy needs the humanities*. Princeton: Princeton University Press.

Pena-Vega, A. (2009). *O processo de Bolonha no Ensino Superior da América Latina*. Paris: ORUS- Observatório Internacional de Reformas da Universidade. Retrieved from http://www.institut-gouvernance.org/fr/analyse/fiche-analyse-433.html. 02 nov. 2015.

PNAES (2010). Programa Nacional de Assistência Estudantil. Decreto n° 7.234, 19 de julho de 2010. Brasil.

Poincaré, H. (1905). *La valeur de la science*. Paris: Ernest Flammarion Éditeur.

Pourtois, H. (2006). Pertinence et limites du principe d'égalité des chances en matière d'éducation scolaire. *GIRSEF*. Retrieved from https://www.uclouvain.be/cps/ucl/doc/etes/documents/DOCH_159__Pourtois_.pdf.

Praha Communiqué (2001). *Towards The European Higher Education Area*. Retrieved from http://www.mctes.pt/ficheiros/Comunicado_de_Praga.pdf. 28 jun. 2007.

PROUNI (2005). Programa Universidade para Todos. Portaria 2.561, 20 de julho. Brasil.

Ramalho Filho, R.A. (2009). Universidade promove inovações. Retrieved from: http://portal.mec.gov.br/ultimas-noticias/212-educacao-superior--1690610854/11954-sp-1459103587. 9 Mar.2017.

REUNI (2007). New University/ Program for Restructuring and Expansion of Brazilian Federal Universities (Programa de Apoio a Planos de Reestruturação e Expansão das Universidades Federais). Decreto-Lei n.6.096, de 24 de abril de 2007. Brazil.

Santos, B. S. (2009). Para uma pedagogia do conflito. In A.L.S. Freitas & S.C. Moraes (org), *Contra o desperdício da experiência: a pedagogia do conflito revisitada* (pp. 15-40). Porto Alegre: Redes Editora.

Schultz, T.W. (1963). *Economic Value of Education*. s.l.: Hardcover.

Smith, J. P., McKnight, A., & Naylor, R. (2000). Graduate employability: Policy and performance in higher education in the UK. *Economic Journal*, 110 (464), 382-411.

Student Göteborg Convention (2001). *Student Göteborg Declaration*. Göteborg: National Unions of Students in Europe, 25 March 2001. Retrieved from: http://www.yok.gov.tr/en/web/uluslararasi-iliskiler/goteborg-bildirgesi.

Sultana, R.G. (2009). Competence and competence frameworks in career guidance: complex and contested concepts. *International Journal of Education and Vocational Guidance*, 9, 15-30.

Sursock, A. (2015). *Trends 2015: Learning and Teaching in European Universities*. Brussels: EUA Publications.

Sursock, A., & Smidt, H. (2010). *Trends 2010: A decade of change in European Higher Education*. Brussels: EUA Publications.

Tapper, T., & Palfreyman, D. (2000). *Oxford and the Decline of the Collegiate Tradition*. London: Woburn Press.

Tillman, L.C., & Scheurich, J.J. (2013). *Handbook of Research on Educational Leadership for Equity and Diversity*. London: Routledge.

Vieira, J.C.A. (2015). *Avaliação política do modelo de gestão da assistência estudantil na UFRPE: fundamentos gerencialistas e padrões mínimos na provisão de necessidades*. Programa de pós-graduação em Serviço Social, Dissertação de Mestrado em Serviço social. Recife: Universidade Federal de Pernambuco.

DOI | https://doi.org/10.14195/978-989-26-1620-9_8

CHAPTER 8

PROFILES OF MOBILITY STUDENTS

Liliana Moreira

University of Coimbra, Faculty of Sport Sciences and Physical Education.

E-mail: Liliana.moreira0@gmail.com

Rui Gomes

University of Coimbra Centre for Social Studies and Faculty of Sport Sciences and Physical Education

E-mail: ruigomes@ces.uc.pt

In this chapter we present the figure of the international student and how they are perceived by the university institutions and the States. Specifically in the European Union, and based on the division of the European countries in the world-system as semi-peripheral, peripheral and central countries, we analyse the academic mobility data before and after the implementation of the Bologna process. Synchronically, we present the mobility student profiles of a university located at a central country and a semi-peripheral country, respectively the University of Groningen, in the Netherlands, and the University of Coimbra, in Portugal. The methodology used was the questionnaire and a correlational descriptive analysis. The student flows are identified with the colonial past, the neighbouring relations and the demand for central countries.

Introduction

Apart from the traditional roles of teaching and research, universities are currently under pressure to respond to local and transnational problems, in hopes of a prospective answer to still emerging problems. Universities are the product of a geopolitical web of knowledge at a global and local scale (Dale, 1998; Martins, 2005). Turned into companies and managed according to the market, they have a direct responsibility over the country's competitiveness, where innovation is not enough and the scientific outputs must have market value and must be tradable (Oliveira, 2000). In Sousa Santos' vision, "the world-system's central countries moved into a pluriversity knowledge, this being a contextual knowledge in a sense that the organizing principle of its production is its application" (Santos, 2005, p. 29). This means that universities are moving towards being Mode 2 institutions, as defined by Gibbons:

The thrust of the new mode of knowledge production is that research in many important area is cutting loose from the disciplinary structure and generating knowledge which so far at least does not seem to be drawn to institutionalise itself in university departments and faculties in the conventional way. At times, it often seem that research centers, institutes and 'think tanks' are multiplying and the periphery of universities, while faculties and departments are becoming the internal locus of teaching provision. (Gibbons, 1997, p. 7).

The large European universities of the central countries, such as the UK and Germany, try to follow a model that, among other measures, promotes an outreach, universities providing services and responding to the commercial needs. Universities in semi-peripheral countries, although they tend to follow the same paths as those in central countries, are limited exactly due to the characteristics of their countries, because the connection between the market and the universities is fragile, the market is not demanding and thus they remain in the semi-periphery even in Mode 2. For the semi-peripheral institutions, repositioning in the world-system is seen as a solution to authenticate and validate their educational system (Gomes, 2005).

For some authors, like Perry & May, the excellence and relevance of knowledge can be framed, like Weberian ideal types, as analytical resources, in a contextualized or decontextualized manner:

> A decontextualized excellence where the knowledge production processes are separated from the context in which they are produced. The corollary of this perspective is the competitive relevance, where obtaining funding in industry of consultancy activities is seen as being equal to academic funding as an indicator of quality. The contextualized excellence emphasizes the indirect benefits of science and technology for certain spaces and places. Policies are centred around attracting equipment, staff, students or "world class" equipment – through the creation of favourable frameworks – and are based on assumptions over the indirect benefits arising from this. The relevance is contextual. (Perry & May, 2008, p. 112).

The decontextualized excellence is described as a neoliberal globalization of education, equally incorporated in the European political speech that calls on the convergence of a European Area of Higher Education and Research, initiated with the Bologna Process.

Given the educational transnational market, the European Union tried to protect itself, since last century's 80s, by harmonizing the higher education system through a top-down rule of localized globalism which formalized in the Bologna Process, the result of the Bologna Declaration. From its various objectives, we can highlight the competitiveness and the efficiency:

> Specifically, we must bear in mind the objective of increasing the European higher education system's international competitiveness. The vitality and efficiency of any civilization can be measured by how much its culture attracts other countries. We need to ensure that the European higher education system acquires a degree of attraction worldwide that is similar to the one achieved by our extraordinary cultural and scientific traditions. (Bologna Declaration, 19th June 1999).

Considering the European Union as a transnationalization agency, as an entity that can act in the various national arenas, the Bologna Process emerges as an example of educational policy transnationalization (Cortesão & Stoer, 2001), in which a supranational agency overlaps national policies, in a clear model of standardization, interdependence and imposition (Dale, 1999). The original idea of a network of European universities for knowledge sharing is not wrong in itself; what can be criticized is the mercantile vision given to that same knowledge. With the Bologna Process, the pillar of mobility was reinforced with the express pretension of increasing the European higher education system's international competitiveness. Within this framework, the European Union reinforced the mobility programs. The most famous of these programs is Erasmus, which is the result of the first well succeeded mobilities focused on teaching. There was also the need to develop a number of rules shared by the European Union's countries, such as the ECTS (European Credit Transfer System) credits for academic recognition and accumulation of knowledge.

However, "the discrepancy between the values defended and the real practices must be understood as a result of the cultural reception processes which are specific to each country and dependent, among other aspects, on the relative position of a given State in the world as a whole" (Gomes, 2005, p. 66). The impositions arising from the Bologna Process, for example, were considered differently by each adhering country, due to each State's higher education structure and the legislation. As a whole, it reflects the different social production forms of each country, which vary according to the world-system position and the way in which society absorbs change. This way, the Bologna process rules that were meant to be harmonious resulted in different interpretations and led to implementation problems. In a study coordinated by Justyna Pisera (2010) and promoted by the *Erasmus Student Network*, PRIME 2010 (*Problems of Recognition in Making Erasmus*) 8,908 students of 26 countries were questioned and identified a number of issues as the major problems of the system: study program incompatibility, different calculation of credits, recognition of equivalences in classification scales, bureaucratic issues, lecturers' approach and lack information prior to mobility.

Mobility appears as a means and an end in itself of the European educational policies. Seen as a form of obtaining European citizenship, it aims at increasing the competitiveness factor as an attraction for the international student.

In this chapter, and understanding the importance of the international students in the various European Union countries, we propose to register de balance of the academic mobilities within the European Union from 2000 to 2012, the pivotal year being the year of the Bologna Process (2007-2008). We also intend to analyse the flow asymmetry and interpret mobility patterns. In a more synchronic approach, we aim at identifying the profiles of students coming to the University of Coimbra, which is located in a semi-peripheral country, and the University of Groningen, located in a central country of the European Union. These universities were not chosen at random, they are institutions located in two medium cities, with a similar number of inhabitants, whose universities have a similar number of students and faculties. Each one is over four centuries old, Coimbra being the oldest, and both belong to common scientific cooperation networks.

1. The importance of international students

Universities have an important role as institutions in political decisions, because they coexist with other regulating axes from the State and the market. However, they are determinant in promoting the international students, and they can even be seen as catalysts for student mobility. International students are perceived as a reserve and a solution for the ageing population in Europe as well as the sharp decrease in State funding for universities. Much like replacement migration, the notion used by the United Nations in 2000 to characterize labour replacement migration, the international students are comparable to a replacement student, a solution for the decline in the number of national students.

But these are the students who can bring multiculturalism into the institutions, by somehow rejecting the implicit proposals of acculturation in their host countries. It is possible to find a differentiated vision of university, as defended by some authors referring us to a comprehensive internationalization:

Comprehensive internationalization is a commitment, confirmed through action, to infuse international and comparative perspectives throughout the teaching, research, and service missions of higher education. It shapes institutional ethos and values and touches the entire higher education enterprise. It is essential that it be embraced by institutional leadership, governance, faculty, students, and all academic service and support units. It is an institutional imperative, not just a desirable possibility.

Comprehensive internationalization not only impacts all of campus life but the institution's external frames of reference, partnerships, and relations. The global reconfiguration of economies, systems of trade, research, and communication, and the impact of global forces on local life, dramatically expand the need for comprehensive internationalization and the motivations and purposes driving it. (Hudzik, 2011, p. 6).

This vision from Hudzik (2011) rests on the possibility of every student being exposed to internationalization by the comparison of contents as part of their curriculum, the internationalization being seen as skill incorporated in behaviours, offering all students the possibility of experiencing a period of mobility, active incorporation of curricular plans with different perspectives, promoting the integration of foreign students with the national students, all of this in a real commitment with the community. Notwithstanding the general tendency for educational isomorphism, one can see, even in the central countries, some hints of counter-hegemony, namely in those countries where citizenship is lived with awareness and whose curricula incorporate new topics, ethnic studies, less spoken language preservation and indigenous knowledge preservation, among others.

The Higher Education institutions have a larger or smaller degree of internationalization and adopt their political strategies in hopes of attracting international students. However, international students have changed. In general terms, the international students have transnationalized, i.e., over their lives they can combine various learning mobility plans in different moments and in more than one institution or country. Equally, the current form of communication within the IT era, as Castells (2002) would say, also contributes to its global dimension.

The search for education abroad, somehow enhanced by the search for degree legitimation abroad, carries with it part of the social stratification. Only students with a network of economic and social support can study abroad. Within these networks, families are identified as a basic reference, "parental influence is particularly strong among undergraduate students when they are choosing a destination country" (Mazzarol & Soutar, 2001, p. 12). The international students have transnationalized, i.e., they can gather diplomas abroad from more than one institution and this marks a new phase in the identity of these students. It is not rare to find students completing three courses of studies in three different countries. We currently witness the search for a diploma abroad or a period of mobility abroad as a way to enhance the curriculum vitae (Tarrant, 2011). Students are searching transnationally what they cannot find within borders, a new optimistic vision of education that can give them security and social mobility. Barron, Baum and Conway (2007) state that some students consider a diploma obtained abroad as more valuable, "... learning, living and working experience that is a major financial and time investment in the future of both individuals and society at large" (Barron et al, 2007, p. 97).

The new characteristics of the international student are based on the dimensions of the globalized world. The greatest differences are the speed with which they move, the network connection and how they are seen by the type of globalization and by the host institutions. John Urry currently identifies twelve types of mobilities, including student mobility "discovery travel of student, au pair and the other young people on their 'overseas experience' where this can constitute a 'rite of passage' and which typically involves going overseas to civilizational centres" (Urry, 2007, p. 10).

This worldwide movement of students implies rather interesting economic values for various countries, making this phenomenon a segment of the market which is and will be explored by the host central countries and emerging in the semi-peripheral countries. We enter a transnational domain of mercantile university services where consuming education abroad enters the typology of GATS (*General Agreement on Trade and Services*) and consists of the provision of service through the transnational mobility of the consumer. This is currently the big slice of mercantile transnationalization at the universities.

Bhandari & Blumenthal (2011) reveal that the global mobility of students reaches 3.3 million per year, representing a 65% increase since 2000. These numbers reinforce the globalization aspect of this issue, and also the government action to search for this segmented market. In the UK alone, HESA (Higher Education Statistics Agency) reveals that "more recent statistics would suggest this figure has significantly increased and considers the value of educational services to currently stand at £ 10.3 billion" (Barron et al, 2007, p. 88). "An OECD recent study calculated that this business was worth 30 billion dollars in 1999" (Santos, 2005, p. 23). The universities have the following objectives: "not only dominate global university rankings, they produce the most research, control the key journal and other means of knowledge distribution, educate the top Ph.D. holders, employ most postdocs, and are more attractive to the internationally mobile knowledge elites" (Altbach, 2013, p. 103).

The importance of this object of study is its new characteristics, the way in which it is perceived by the Higher Education institutions, how it is seen by the States and the transnational instances.

1.1. The International Students

The definition commonly accepted is linked to the one stated by UNESCO, "students that leave their country or territory of origin and move to another country or territory with the objective of studying" (UNESCO, 2009, p. 36). This definition associating mobility and study goes as far as appearing in the Portuguese legislation, specifically in the legal regime of entering, staying, exiting and moving away for foreigners in national territory, where the long term resident statute defines the higher education student as a national from a third State that has been accepted by a higher education establishment to attend, as their main activity, a full time study program with a view to obtaining an academic degree or a recognized higher education diploma, including preparation courses for those studies or research for obtaining an academic degree (Law no. 23/2007, 4th July).

Evidently, the duration of the stay exceeding one year can result in a criticism to the definition of student and their conceptual framework, pushing the concept to the area of migrations. However, it is expected that no paid activity is implied, which is a characteristic associated to the immigrant. Therefore, as indicated by Glover, "independent of their consecutive length of stay, international students may be classified as temporary residents in their study destination due to their extend stay. This temporary residence may stretch over several years, for example, when students undertake a full degree or enrol in a second degree after finishing their first". (Glover, 2011, p. 181).

Two categories of international student were defined. The first one relates to the student who intends to obtain a diploma by the host university, therefore staying more than one year and defined as regular, often subjected to the same rules of conduct as the national students and to the payment of fees. The other category is related to the international student with a shorter term mobility, without the goal of obtaining a diploma, a student in mobility. Within the European Union, this mobility student is generally identified with the Erasmus program and is the object of its own legislation and the framework of education, training and youth of the European Commission.

1.2. Mobility Patterns Inside the European Union

Internationally, in the perspective of consuming education abroad, international students follow the same migratory flows as the peripheral countries into the central and semi-peripheral countries. McMahon, quoted by Mazzarol (2001),

> found a negative correlation between economic prosperity in sending countries and the volume of international students flows, perhaps because greater educational opportunity counteracts the effect of improved GDP per capita ... a positive correlation was found between the size of host nation and the sending nation's economies. (Mazzarol & Soutar, 2001, p. 4).

The theory of world-systems with regards to student mobility is more centred around the forces acting around education transnationalization, in the sense of capturing students as a result of economic globalization and the dynamics of the educational international markets. The *Observatory on Borderless Higher Education*[1], quoted by Verbik and Lasanowski (2007) identifies the major receptors of international students: United States of America, United Kingdom and Australia. The countries appearing on top are indicated not only due to the English language but also because they easily adjust to the bureaucratic and visa requirements: "various developments have shown that international student and graduate visa schemes are increasingly used as integral parts of recruitment strategies and are receiving more attention in accordance with their perceived importance and strategic value" (Verbik & Lasanowski, 2007, p. 24). The most attractive countries in the world, in terms of international education, alter their policies with regards to scholarships and consular visas.

Within the European Union, the countries were also articulated in the logic of the world-system as central, semi-peripheral and peripheral countries (Wallerstein, 1979). In the study of mobility flows and patterns, we observed the statistical data of mobility students from 2000 to 2012 and from there a descriptive analysis was carried out. In effect, "student and staff mobility is one of the central aims of the Bologna Process and has been promoted by all participants in the Process and enjoys unanimous support" (Harutyunyan & Bonete, 2010, p. 31). Notwithstanding this incidence in mobility, as we can see in Figure 1, 2 and 3, the total number of outgoing mobilities, i.e., the number of students exiting, per country, on a mobility program financed by the European Commission, is not very different pre and post Bologna.

---

[1] The *Observatory of Borderless Higher Education* is a joint initiative of the Commonwealth Universities Association and the Universities of the United Kingdom.

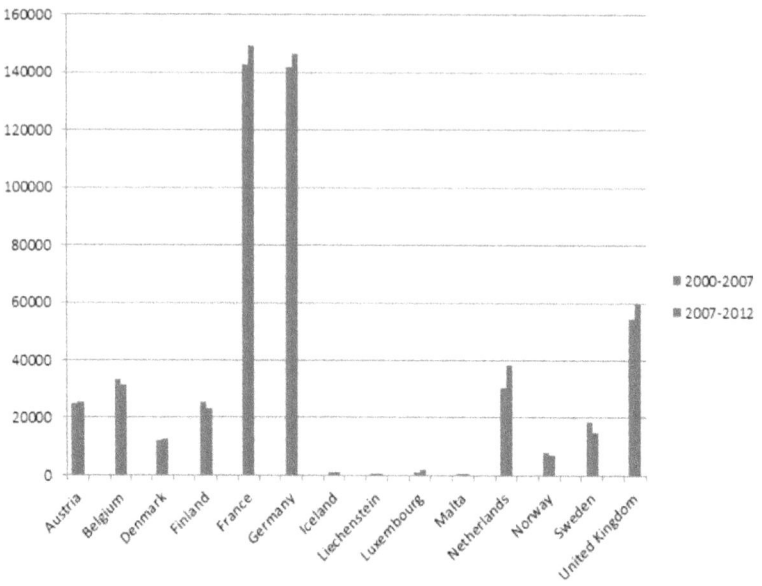

Figure 1. Outgoing flow of students coming from central countries
Source: European Commission, 2014

Within this group of countries, which includes the founding members of the European Union, we do not find significant differences in the outgoing student flow. The numbers are constant and we highlight France and Germany, who also correspond to the countries with a higher demographic density. The mobility in these countries is often reinforced by the use of the English language. These countries recognize the added value of internationalization for its citizens, the enormous advantages of the dialogue between cultures, and therefore they promote practices of mobilities, fomenting cultural participation, as is the case with the Philosophy of DAAD (German Service of Academic Interchange) in Germany.

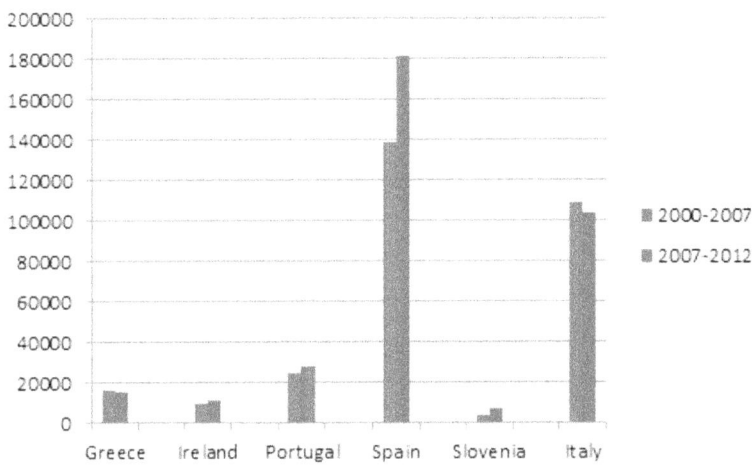

Figure 2. Outgoing flow of students coming from semi-peripheral countries
Source: European Commission, 2014

Spain clearly stands out as the country with the largest demographic density of the group, showing a significant impulse in outgoing mobility after the academic year of 2007-2008. In the remaining countries, with the exception of Italy, there was a slight increase.

These values must be analysed bearing in mind these countries' entry to the European Union, which happened in 2004 for Estonia, Hungary, Poland and Slovakia. Even though these countries only entered the European Union close to the pivotal year in our data collection, some of these countries were already participating in the Erasmus Program, as a condition

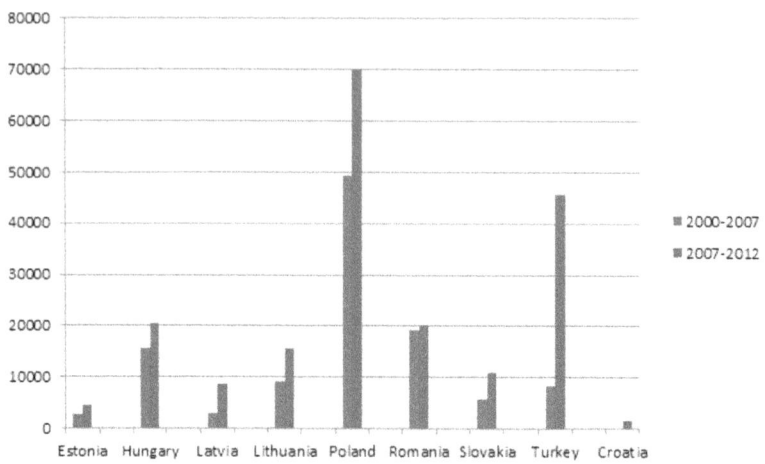

Figure 3. Outgoing flow of students coming from peripheral countries
Source: European Commission, 2014

of adhering country, which explains the maintenance of flows observed for example with Romania, which only entered the European Union in 2007.

If we consider that the student mobility programs, namely Erasmus, date back to 1987, in thirty years we can understand how the reality of mobility was implanted and promoted in the European society from early on, as well as the success of the project. Therefore, the number of students exiting, per country, in a mobility program financed by the European Commission does not differ significantly if we consider the period pre and post Bologna Process in the higher education institutions. In sum, although the global values are, in fact, higher after the

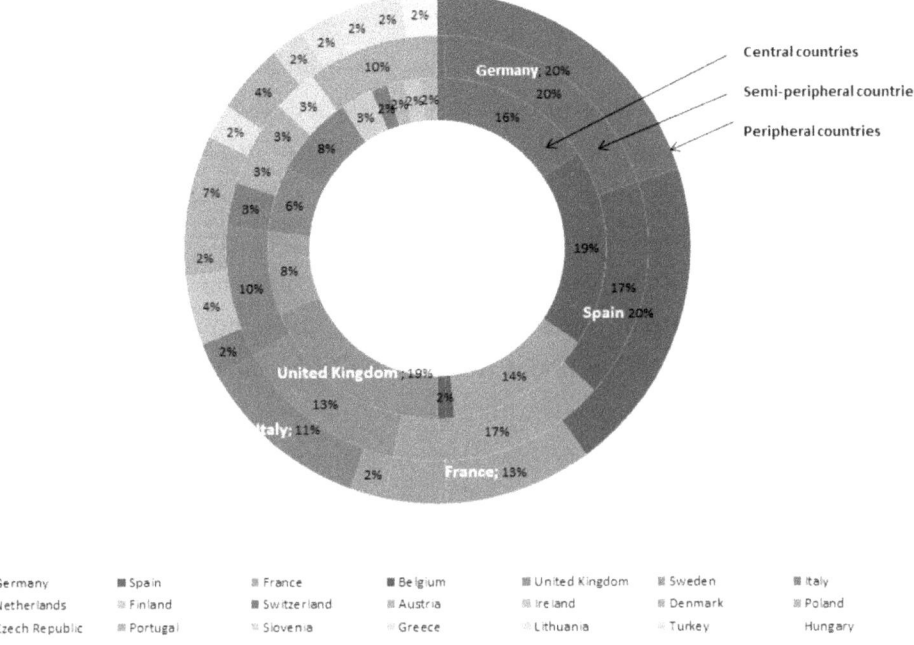

Figure 4. The 5 main host countries for outgoing students in 2011-2012
Source: European Commission, 2014

Bologna Process, 2007-2008, the only significant differences concern Spain and the group of peripheral countries. In the case of the peripheral countries, we can explain the flow increase with the entry to the European Union, and therefore the funding of the Erasmus Program.

Data reveals that the student flows are a well consolidated reality within the European Union, and Figure 4 shows us the mobility patterns.

Figure 4 shows that, within the European Union and in 2011-2012, the following countries stand out as hosts for students: Germany, Spain, France, United Kingdom and Italy. This pattern is maintained independently of the students' country of origin, which shows a group of countries with a profile for hosting students. Academic mobility moves towards central countries with high ranking universities which are more academically productive and with a higher number of post-doctoral positions.

The promotion of student mobility by the European Commission is visible in educational programs promoting this, generally accompanied by funding and organized mainly in Erasmus+. Upon observing the student flows intra EU in 2000 to 2012, it can be noted that the actual number of outgoing mobilities increased, although not significantly. The main difference is in the type of flow, now integrating flows coming from peripheral countries. The Bologna Process did not globally result in a significant flow increase, but rather in an express pretention of harmonizing mobility procedures which resulted in the programs Socrates-Erasmus, followed by Lifelong Learning and the current Erasmus+.

Student profiles

Having identified the mobilities within the European Union, we will now focus more synchronically on the analysis of outgoing student flows into two higher education establishments - the University of Groningen, in the Netherlands, which represents a central country, and the University of Coimbra, in Portugal, a semi-peripheral country. Retrieving the traditional theories of Wallerstein (1979) in political studies, the Netherlands represent centrality and Portugal, by its social and economic indicators, occupies an intermediate, and therefore semi-peripheral, position.

The base-population of the sample will be the group of international students in both universities. We can immediately conclude that the number of international students in the

University of Groningen is higher, specifically the "regular" type. The University of Coimbra, although it has a lower total number of international students compared to the University of Groningen, has a higher number of mobility students. In terms of age groups, the samples are similar: the University of Coimbra has an average student age of 26.1 and the Dutch institution 25,0. We observe a higher percentage of female students in both institutions, which contributes to the higher education feminization rate. As far as the course of studies is concerned, the data from the first course is proportionate in both universities, but in the second and third courses, the University of Coimbra registers a higher number of students in relation to the University of Groningen. The Dutch institution has a higher number of students paying student fees.

With regards to the parents' educational level, we find a significant difference, with the Dutch institution registering a higher family educational capital within its students. The parents of the foreign students enrolled in the Portuguese institution reveal a lower educational level, the highest amount falling on primary education, both for the father and the mother in all courses of study. If we consider that the average age of these students is 26, the parents are probably around 50 to 60 years old, of working age but with an elementary educational level. Inversely, the University of Groningen's students of all courses of study reveal a higher percentage of parents with a higher degree, both father and mother. The family educational capital of Groningen's students is higher. This parent educational level data matches the central countries' indicators showing a higher educational level than the semi-peripheral countries.

The geographical origin of the international students comprising this sample is divided into forty countries for the University of Coimbra and forty seven for the University of Groningen. We note the neighbourhood effect of Spain with regards to Portugal and of Germany with regards to the Netherlands. It is interesting to verify that a large number of students come from countries with a colonial past related to Portugal and to the Netherlands. If we look at some numbers in Coimbra, 47.6% come from Brazil, 44. 5, 4% from Angola, and 4.5% from Cape Verde. In the case of Groningen, 6.6% of the students come from Indonesia and 5.9% from the United States of America.

> The process of economic globalization creates cultural links between core capitalist countries ad their peripheries (...) In many case, the cultural links are longstanding, reflecting a colonial part in which core countries established administrative and educational systems that mirrored their own in order to govern and exploit a peripherical region (...) The diffusion of core country languages and cultural patterns and the spread of modern consumption patterns interact with the emergence of transportation /communication infrastructure to channel international migration to particular core countries. (Massey et al., 1998, p. 40).

This association with the colonial past is also indicated in the literature (Lee & Tan, 1984; and Bhandari & Blumenthal, 2011).

In order to define the student profiles, an online questionnaire was carried out for the students at the University of Coimbra and at the University of Groningen, through a stratified sample proportional to the course of studies. The sample strata were equally divided into regular students, those defined as students that will obtain a diploma by the host university, and mobility students, those who will obtain their diploma with the home university. With the social and demographic data collected from the 507 questionnaires completed, the statistical technician of Multiple Correspondence Analysis carried out the student profiling.

> The description of these groups can contemplate two analytical vectors: 1. Identifying the specificity of the association between the categories of the multiple variables analysed, in order to profile each group. 2. Observing the relative positioning of the various groups. The analysis of the distances between the groups shows the existence of association or opposition relations. (Carvalho, 2004, p.18).

We therefore gathered the following variables: family educational capital (educational level of the parents), home country (recodifying the countries into continents), course of studies, as well as the enrolment status, i.e., regular or mobility.

Given that the profiles can have different results in both universities, we collected the numbers separately and for both we identified two scales, based on the Multiple Correspondence Analysis: education and geographical origin. These scales were recorded as new variables, allowing new possibilities of tests. Two dimensions were identified in the case of UC, with excellent internal reliability indicators $\rho>.90$ following the model *Alpha Cronbach*, with education being 47.2% of the variance and the geographical origin 41.9% of the variance. By analysing the contribution of each variable for each scale, it was possible to identify the profiles of the students at University of Coimbra:

> UC 1: Mobility students coming from Europe, enrolled in the first course of studies, with a low family educational capital.

UC 2: regular students, coming from South America or Asia, enrolled in the third course of studies, with a high family educational capital.

UC 3: regular students, coming from South America, enrolled in the first course of studies, with a low family educational capital.

With the University of Groningen, two scales were determined - education and geographical origin - and they represented very strong indicators of internal consistency $\rho > .90$ verified by the value of *Alpha Cronbach*, the first scale explains 51.5% of the variance and the second 43.9%. We will proceed with identifying the composition of the profiles of the international students in Groningen. Also three were identified:

RUG 1: Mobility students coming from Europe or North America, enrolled in the first course of studies, with a high family educational capital.

RUG 2: regular students, coming from Europe, Asia or South America, enrolled in the second or third course of studies, with a high family educational capital.

RUG 3: regular students, coming from Africa or Asia, enrolled in the third course of studies, with a high family educational capital.

Overall, the University of Groningen hosts more regular fee paying students looking to obtain a degree, especially in the second and third courses of studies. The University of Coimbra hosts more mobility students. In the profile of mobility, which includes the Erasmus students, data confirms the flow patterns amongst central countries, i.e., in the University of Groningen, these students are mainly coming from France, Spain, Germany,

Italy and the UK. With regards to the same profile, the University of Coimbra, and confirming its semi-peripheral status, has mobility students coming from Poland, Spain, Italy, Germany and Turkey.

2. Final comments

The international students might emerge, in a hegemonic plane, as a product of the global educational market, and, in that perspective, the consumption of education abroad carries with it the same social stratification, given that only an elite can access it. Therefore, it appears as an alternative answer to the State decapitalization of higher education, and this answer is clearer within the central countries fully assuming their statute as hosts and having international students as a segment of demand. In the semi-peripheral countries, specifically Portugal, the academic mobility balances between logics of State decapitalization, transnational requirements and private interests, and so the legal advances and setbacks reflect this semi-peripheral situation. Equally, this topic re-centres us in the Portuguese semi-periphery, given that it is a country sending students to central countries and trying to capture students from old colonies. Thus, the search for education abroad by consumer mobility has increased and spread to various countries, and it makes it a very attractive segment of the market. On the other hand, it responds to the problem of ageing population, namely in Europe, reflected in the decrease of national students in the higher education institutions.

However, in this massified demand for international education, something is changing in global terms, such as the increase of new funding initiatives by some countries, different geopolitical motivations, students opting for non-traditional destinations, student retention policies in the traditionally sending countries, thus altering the very object of study as international student flows (Bhandari & Blumenthal, 2011). Additionally, there are new actors in the international arena, such as profit-making and non-for-profit organizations that can work as a booster to this segment of the market.

However, the international students can also be a product of a counter-hegemonic globalization, if we see it in this new perspective of knowledge ecology where students can positively confront their cultures in a selfless search, Hudzik's comprehensive internationalization (2011).

We encounter transnational communities of students, not in the sense of having a hybrid international student with two poles, a home and a host. The hybridism went further and reached the sense of transnationalization. Today it is easy to find examples of students passing through various countries in different courses of studies, which brings us to the similarity of brain circulation "more accurately describe the increasing multidirectional nature of international flow and the growing awareness that such mobility patterns or exchanges are mutually beneficial for sending and receiving countries, albeit in varying ways" (Bhandari & Blumenthal, 2011, p. 16).

Synchronically, we analysed the international students and identified three types of profiles for each institution, where we highlighted the separation between regular and mobility students. We noted that the mobility and regular students differ in terms of country of origin and family education capital. The profiles allow a clearer explanation of the differentiating characteristics of the student population and are important landmarks for new research on academic mobility.

References

Altbach, P. (2013). The world is not flat: the brain drain and higher education in the 21st century. In Anna Glass (Ed.), *The state of higher education 2013*. OECD Higher Education Center, 103-107.

Barron, P., Baum, T. & Conway, F. (2007). Learning, living and working: experiences of international postgraduate students at a Scottish university. *Journal of Hospitality and Tourism Management*, 2, (14), 85-101.

Bhandari, R. & Blumenthal, P. (2011). Global Student Mobility and the Twenty-First Century Silk Road: National Trends and New Directions. In R. Bhandari & P. Blumenthal (Ed.), *International Students and Global Mobility in Higher Education* (1-24) New York: Palgrave Macmillan.

Carvalho, H. (2004). *Análise Multivariada de Dados Qualitativos- Utilização da HOMALS com SPSS*. Lisboa: Edições Silabo.

Castells, M. (2002). *A era da informação: economia, sociedade e cultura*. Lisboa: Fundação Calouste Gulbenkian.

Comissão Europeia (2014) *Erasmus: facts, numbers and trends*. Taken on 20th October, 2015, from http://ec.europa.eu/education/library/statistics/ay-12-13/facts-figures_en.pdf

Cortesão, L., & Stoer, S.R. (2001). Cartografando a transnacionalização do campo educativo: o caso português. In Boaventura de Sousa Santos (Ed.), *Globalização: fatalidade ou utopia?* Porto: Edições Afrontamento, 369-406.

Dale, R. (1998). Globalization: a new world for comparative education. In Jurgen Schriewer (Ed.), *Discourse and comparative education*. Berlim: Peter Lang, 87-109.

Declaração de Bolonha (1999). Declaração conjunta dos ministros europeus da educação acordada em Bolonha [online]. *Web site*. Accessed on 5th October, at http://media.ehea.info/file/Ministerial_conferences/05/3/1999_Bologna_Declaration_Portuguese_553053.pdf.

Gibbons, M. (1997). *What kind of University? Research and teaching in the 21st century*. Beanland lecture – Victoria University Technology, Australia.

Glover, P. (2011). International students: linking education and travel. *Journal of Travel & Tourism Marketing*, 28, 180-195.

Gomes, R.M. (2005). *O governo da educação em Portugal*. Coimbra: Imprensa da Universidade de Coimbra.

Harutyunyan, G.; & Bonete, R. (2010). Enhancing opportunities for students and staff. In European Higher Education Area (Ed.), 1999–2010 *Achievements, Challenges and Perspectives*. Bologna Process

Hudzik, J. (2011). *Comprehensive Internationalization From Concept to Action*. Washington: NAFSA: Association of International Educators.

Lee, K. H., & Tan, J. P. (1984). The international flow of third level lesser developed countries: determinants and implications. *Higher Education*, 13(6), 687-707.

Lei nº 23/2007 de 4 de Julho de 2007. *Diário da República* nº 127- *I Série*. Regime Jurídico de entrada, permanência, saída e afastamento de estrangeiros no território nacional.

Martins, S. (2005). Portugal, um lugar de fronteira na Europa: uma leitura de indicadores socioeducacionais. *Sociologia, Problemas e Práticas*, 49, 141 161.

Massey, D., Arango J., Hugo, G., Kouaouci, A., Pellegrino, A. & Taylor, J. (Eds.) (1998). *Worlds in motion understanding international migration at the end of the millennium*. Oxford: Claredon Press.

Mazzarol, T. & Soutar, G. (2001). "Push-pull" factors influencing international student destination choice. *The International Journal of Educational Management*, 16 (2), 82- 90.

Perry, B. & May, T. (2008). Excelência, relevância e a universidade. *Sociologia, Problemas e Práticas*, 56, 105-128.

Pisera, J.; Dicle, E.; Fellinger, J.; Huang; L; Kalinic, I.Trawinska, J. & Vinca, E. (2010). *PRIME 2010: Problems of recognition in making Erasmus*. Belgium: Erasmus Student Network.

Santos, B. S. (2005). *A universidade do século XXI: para uma reforma democrática e emancipatória da Universidade* (2.ed.). São Paulo: Cortez Editora.

Tarrant, M., Stoner, L. Borrie, W., Kyle, G., Moore, R. & Moore, A. (2011). Educational travel and global citizenship. *Journal of Leisure Research*, 43, (3), 403-426.

UNESCO Institute for Statisti. (2009). *Global Education Digest 2009: Comparing Education Statistics Across the World*. Montreal: UIS.

Urry, J. (2007). *Mobilities*. New York: Polity Press.

Verbik, L. & Lasanowski, V. (2007). *International student mobility: patterns and trends*. United Kingdom: The Observatory on borderless higher education.

Wallerstein, I. (1979). *The capitalist world-economy*. Cambridge: Cambridge University Press.

This paper was supported by the Portuguese Foundation for Science and Technology (FCT) under the strategic project UID/SOC/50012/2013.

DOI | https://doi.org/10.14195/978-989-26-1620-9_9

CHAPTER 9

MAKING BOLOGNA REALLY WORK!

Elmer Sterken

University of Groningen (Netherlands)

E-mail: e.sterken@rug.nl

This chapter contains an optimistic view on the Bologna process. Academic development benefits from cooperation and collaboration. Europe has an ideal history to stimulate international academic cooperation. Universities make progress in internationalization: they move from adjusting the language of instruction to spreading their reputation and to optimizing internationalization at home. In education European universities should work on inclusion – making all students feel welcome in their system – and activation – getting students in an active mode in the educational process. For instance project-based education can both activate students in learning and bring real-life cases into academic training. A strong and collaborative academic Europe benefits all.

Introduction

On June 19th 1999 the Bologna Declaration has been signed. Since 1999 higher education in Europe has developed substantially in terms of quality. Students have become more mobile, universities have opened and standardized their programs and the European Higher Education Area (EHEA) has made serious contributions to welfare. Despite economic and political struggles in the last couple of years the goals of European higher education policy remain the same as in 1999. Cooperation and collaboration continue to be important and welfare-improving objectives for European universities and corresponding nation states.

In this chapter I will strongly support the Bologna process. The main argument is that cooperation and collaboration in higher education bring welfare. I first review the post-Bologna experiences. The main achievements and drawbacks are very well known and can so be dealt with in brief. Next I will sketch the future of internationalization of European higher education. Two current developments affect higher education to a large extent. First, the international labor markets are in a continuous change and show an increasing volatility of jobs and job duration. Secondly, the development of ICT in education changes academic training at a rapid pace. Nowadays, we are able to share information quickly and in an efficient way. Students can get access to knowledge no matter where they live or work. This allows that students can benefit at the maximum of available information and need more training to access information than to remember details. The availability of ICT also allows for better quality of contact hours between lecturers and students. Instead of 'consuming' information alone, students can nowadays interact better with their lecturers. So,

ICT allows for new forms of learning. I see two major lines. First, distance learning opens news ways of learning. Students around the world who do not have access to higher education now can follow basic and even advanced courses offered by top-quality universities. And secondly, ICT also makes campus education more vivid. The main focus of higher education at the institutional campus level should be twofold: (1) inclusion of all students, domestic and foreign, into the local system, and (2) activation of students in the classroom.

How did we get at this previously mentioned high-level stage of educational development in Europe? The signing of the Bologna Declaration in 1999 has increased the speed of internationalization across Europe. Although a simple counterfactual is not an option, we should ask ourselves whether we would have reached the current level of quality of higher education and welfare without the help of the Bologna process. My direct answer would be: without Bologna we would still have a more regional or national approach to education. But before coming to conclusions, let's review how we came to 2016. I start with a view from 1614, the foundation year of the University of Groningen and will illustrate how international education was at that time. Then I shortly discuss the formation of European nation states in different times of war turmoil and finally how we got to the Bologna declaration.

1. The old days

On August 23rd 1614 the local crowd cheered when six professors left the Martini Church in Groningen, a northern city in the Netherlands, at that time at war with Spain. The six professors attented the inaugural session of the university and one of them, Ubbo Emmius, became the first Rector Magnificus. Emmius was a German professor, born in Greetsiel, Ost-Frisia, in Germany, trained in Rostock and had taken experience in travel to universities in European countries, like France, Switzerland and Italy. Emmius was supervised during his studies by the famous Professor David Chytraeus in Rostock, followed his classes in the Michaeliskloster (now the University Library of the University of Rostock) and took over the Humanist ideas as put forward by King Alfonso of Naples in the fifteenth century. Coming to Groningen Ubbo Emmius wrote an 'Eternal Edict' stating the humanist ideas in the University of Groningen setting.

The University of Groningen became a truly international university in the seventeenth century with 40 percent of its students being foreign, although it should be admitted that students coming from today's southern Dutch provinces Brabant and Limburg were considerered to be foreigners. It was popular as a student in those days to travel across Europe to those places and institutions where famous professors were lecturing. All-in-all no wonder that the crowd of Groningen cheered at the inaugural sessions. The city was in an economic upsurge and the Hanze Union and - linkages (for instance with again Rostock) gave welfare to the region. Due to the economic boom increased the need for training of medical doctors, lawyers and referents. New intellectual capital was needed and appreciated.

A few decades before, in 1575, William of Orange founded a university at Leiden. Although this was still at the beginning of the war with Spain, it preluded at the rise of the Netherlands as a powerful state. The Netherlands became a world economic power in the seventeenth century and although European unification was still far out of sight, the general believe was that trade, knowledge and welfare were related. Each of the seven Dutch provinces (in those days called states) was allowed to start a university (five actually did so) and intellectual climate developed quickly. The average income per capita in the Netherlands became the highest of the world in the seventeenth century. Scientic inventions became common and an academic tradition started.

Soon after Leiden, a university started in Franeker, and more would follow after Groningen in Harderwijk, Utrecht and Amsterdam. The lesson to be learned from this seventeenth century experience in the Netherlands had been learned before in many European countries, but most prominently in France, Italy, Portugal, Spain and the United Kingdom. There is a strong correlation between economic and intellectual welfare, between academic development, 'openness' and mobility, between academic autonomy and scientific productivity. Academic success also seems to trigger internationalisation.

The way we look nowadays at collaboration and exchange goes back to the work of the famous economist David Ricardo (1772-1823). Ricardo showed that trade (or exchange of ideas) leads to higher welfare. The main reason is that each individual agent (or researcher or country) has a relative comparative advantage. In a team of researchers or a pool of students collaboration and exchange therefore lead to a higher social welfare. As long as the costs of mobility or collaboration don't exceed these alleged benefits, cooperation and collaboration in higer education pay off. So this holds within the European union: the basis of the Bologna treaty.

The prosperity European countries were able to achieve was decreased during the centuries of political turmoil and wars during the 18th, 19th and first half of the 20th century. In those days more focus was put on the formation of nation states and the protection of national heritage and domestic economic progress. One could argue that may European universities also suffered from religious battles. The result was anyhow that scientific collaboration was at a relatively low intensity, as was the international student mobility. Ending with the Second World War in the 1950s European countries felt again the need to collaborate in the newly-formed European Union. As we know by now, this was good news for academic development. As stated before, in 1999 the Bologna Declaration was signed.

2. 'Bologna' in a nutshell

Before turning to an evaluation of the Bologna-process it is natural to give a quick review of the 'Bologna'-achievements. With the unification of different parts of Europe on the way, it is quite natural to start thinking about creating a European Higher Education Area (EHEA). R&D spillovers are abundant and one wants to avoid that new inventions stop at the border. Intellectual cooperation is therefore seen as a necessity. It was considered to be a public task to bring knowledge to as many European citizens as possible: setting up the European Higher Education Area (EHEA) is still believed to help all Europeans.

Of course it is relevant in this process that mobility of academics increases. An increase of mobility of staff and students can lead and/or help/support to:

> a) getting a uniform credit transfer system (European Credit Transfer and Accumulation System, ECTS),
> b) creating automated transfer of credits between institutions (the *Groningen Declaration*, (2012),
> c) creating of a diploma supplement stating accomplishments,
> d) introducing a uniform quality control process,
> e) adapting uniform learning outcomes,
> f) implementing double- and joint degrees,

g) increasing general cooperation between universities,
h) elaborating the ERASMUS-program,
i) implementing fully the Bachelor-Master-Doctorate-structure (3-cycles).

Besides setting up the EHEA and creating the instruments to speed up mobility of staff and students, additional goals of the Bologna process were formulated after 1999: the pursuit of a "social dimension"; support for lifetime learning; recognition of the global impact of the Bologna process.

Moreover and finally, embracement of important additional stakeholders in Europe was proposed: European University Association; European Students' Union; European Association for Quality Assurance in Higher Education; Business Europe.

The European Higher Education Area has indeed developed successfully. The number of included countries has increased from 29 at the start to 47 members now. Moreover, the eight European Frame Programmes have both stimulated mobility of individual excellence (European Research Council) as well as network formation (via for instance Twinning and Teaming) and there are many more success stories.

As we consider the educational implementation of 'Bologna' there are some serious drawbacks though. First, the completion of national outcomes frameworks is troublesome. The diploma supplement is provided, but acceptance and understanding by employers remains a challenge. Secondly, wide implementation of the three-year bachelor, which requires an efficient curriculum, has made it more challenging for students to consider study abroad. Thirdly, there is a limited convergence of national quality assurance policies: this leads to difficulties in implementing double and joint degrees. Moreover, availability of online descriptions of programmes is still a problem at many institutions.

Next, conversion of results using grading tables and automated transfer is lacking to a large extent. So, there are still many practical issues to be solved.

There are also more serious macro-concerns. Political support for European convergence has decreased in the last years. The economic crisis of 2008 / 2009 has led to a divergence of interests between various European countries and nationalism is a serious threat to internationalization. And finally, the speed of convergence of the accession countries (new-member states) is rather low. These macro-concerns lead to a lower willingness to invest in European harmonization.

Forming the European Higher Education Area needs serious seed money and the economic and financial crisis has made resources scarce. Again, the political will to offset national interests to the favor of international collaboration seems to have lost power. Therefore it remains a big challenge to illustrate the large advantages of international cooperation and collaboration. I will do so hereafter and present some views on modern ways of internationalization of universities.

2.1. Internationalization

Why would a university restrict its recruitment to home country or home region students and staff? Why would talented people only live in the direct vicinity of the institution? Why is it a requirement that both staff an students come from the local culture and speak the native language? Is this fair and does it lead to high local welfare? The way I pose these questions is answering them: it is not.

I am not arguing that universities do not have local responsibilities. Societal impact in the region is a major 'reason to exist', since local tax-payers are most likely to be important fundraisers of the university. But a university can be the 'entrance to the world' for the local community, while research in the region can be considered to be the product of a local living lab. Universities can be considered to be intermediairies for the region to the world.

In this chapter I am not paying too much attention to distance learning and the use of Massive Open Online Courses (MOOCs), but give a stronger emphasis on campus education. Major universities run both operations, distance and campus education, but for sake of simplicity I focus on the campus model.

Internationalisation 3.0

Starting from the observation that talented people can live all around the world, most universities started their internationalization process by adopting the *lingua franca* of science and/or attracting foreign students. In general we call this episode of internationalization phase 1.0. Universities in countries wherein the native language did not have an appeal to incoming students changed their language of instruction to English (like in the case of Dutch universities). Others opened their doors to talented students from abroad. The number of international students increased during phase 1.0: either full degree students or students on an exchange term.

The educational model however did not change too much. Apart from the language of instruction (books, articles, lectures, lecture notes), hardly any attention was given to inter cultural differences and/or backgrounds of students. To some students the cultural shock of studying abroad could be interesting, to others threatening. In class lecturers did not consider the heterogeneous background of students to be an issue.

On the other hand universities understood that apart from inviting foreign students to become their own students, internationalization phase 1.0 did not contribute as such to a better reputation of the institution as such. Each institution strives actively for increasing its academic reputation. Through a better reputation international students will become more eager to come and study. Without a good information market of 'university quality' most universities were/are forced to use the international rankings, such as the Academic Ranking of World Universities (ARWU), the Quacquarelli Symonds World University Rankings (QS) and the Times Higher Education Supplement World University Rankings (THES), to signal quality to outsiders. Partly these rankings are based on surveys that try to measure reputation, but they only can cover partially the full academic standing of participating universities. The concern for increasing international reputation is a characteristic of internationalization phase 2.0.

Spreading the reputation of the institution is getting larger importance in a communication world. It is quite easy for students to access information concerning the quality of a university. The traditional flaw though is that the quality rankings are largely determined by research performance and so much by educational quality. So in many cases the next step of internationalization policy, say phase 3.0, is the adjustment of the educational space at home.

Before describing how the adjustment of the international educational space at home can be done a few words about changes in the environment that have speeded up this process. First, international labor markets have changed and are changing. Today's alumni students need to have more skills and competencies than in the past. They should be able to use their knowledge and level of thinking in a more rapidly changing environment, where job duration has become shorter and shorter. Collaboration and 'project' skills have become more relevant and creativity in the use of academic knowledge has become more prominent than before. The second change is the use of ICT. ICT has speeded up professional life. It has also changed the set of available teaching and learning tools. We can use videos, voting systems, annotation techniques, etc. in education, which has changed or can change the nature of how we teach and/or learn. This phenomenon as such is not new. Like at many other universities lectures used to be very long centuries ago, sometimes up to five hours. And in many universities the introduction of a book instead of using teaching notes has also been under discussion! So, technological progress in education is of all times. But let's turn back to the adjustment of campus education for international students in current days. I am convinced that for a young student the model of moving to a university town, setting up an independent and responsible life as a citizen and becoming an academic is still attractive. This applies to domestic and foreign students.

2.2. Inclusion

For a campus university it is of extreme importance that students feel at home and included in the wide system of the campus. This applies to the domestic students, but even more to the incoming ones. Inclusion applies to both the academic and the non-curricular environment. Language and culture play important roles in this process.

So the first adjustment to the model of a home campus is the creation of the Multilingual and Multicultural Learning Space (MMLS). In a few words this implies that any student, either home-based or foreign, should feel welcome in all the institutions that the university offers. That starts with an introduction of students into the educational model, into the cultural values, into the 'local habits' and so on. It is no big deal that a student needs to pass cultural barriers as long as it is known and explained. It is no big deal that many examples in class are taken from the region as long as it is made clear in advance. It is no serious issue that the local grading system differs, as long as it is made clear to guest students. In general universities need to bring a lot more effort in preparing students before the program starts. The final goal again is that all students feel included and embedded in the local academic scene.

2.3. Activation

The second adjustment is the activation of students. By activation I mean students being active during contact hours with the lecturers. The days that courses were taught by giving large-scale lectures in big auditoria seem to be history. The German poet Wilhelm Busch (1832-1908) once wrote: *'Wenn alle schlafen und einer spricht, diesen zustand nennt mann unterricht"* (When all sleep and one speaks, this situation is considered to be education). And indeed there is ample evidence that many students do not learn during mass lectures.

Another argument to actively engage with students is that the lecturer can benefit from the different, possibly international, diverse backgrounds of students. If students contribute from their perspective or cultural background, discussions/interactions in class become richer. So if in a class on 'corporate governance' students from North America or Asia can tell about their home situations and mingle with Europeans the quality of the course will increase. This is the main argument of the International Classroom: making all students feel included and activate them in class by bringing in their own cases and experiences. In the International Classroom diversity is an asset instead of a liability.

Another argument for 'active learning' is that the student learns more (or at least remembers better the experiences in the course) and it is more fun. Students moreover come to the 'richer' domains of learning, as proposed by Bloom *et al.* (1956). The Bloom Taxonomy of learning domains refers:

1. Remember: recall facts and basic concepts;
2. Understand: Explain ideas or concepts;
3. Apply: use information in new situations;
4. Analyse: Draw connections among ideas;
5. Evaluate: Justify a stand or decision;
6. Create: Produce new or original work.

The hope is that we can push students from the basic phase of remembering to the creative domain as soon as possible. The probability to move up along Bloom's taxonomy is larger if students become more active. It is also likely that students become more entrepreneurial as soon as more activity is required.

The probability that students will become more interested also increases if real-life problems are used in the classroom. In the International Classroom this implies that international real-life cases will trigger more attention than theoretical cases. The main advantage of a real life case is that there is more clarity about the end solution of the issue and the student is forced to think about making assumptions and the choice of the solution methods. In order to complete this argument: in theoretical problems it is precisely the other way round: we know the problem, we know the algorithm to be applied and the outcome in the single unknown issue.

Working with real-life problems and moving up Bloom's taxonomy also contributes to the increasing issue of employability concerns. Students nowadays are more concerned about their future career options than decades ago. Labor market volatility has increase (job duration is shorter) and the probability that an alumnus will serve for the same institution or firm for lifetime is really low. Students like to prepare better for this uncertain future and a very good way to prepare is to gain experience in solving real-life problems.

On the way, we are lucky that ICT has improved. It has improved so much in education that we have ample tools to support active learning. We have many tools that prepare students before class starts: the so-called Flipped Classroom setting. We have better tools that students can use in communication. We have better tools for students to interact (classroom voting). We have better tools to assess the quality of students. We have better tools to give students easy access to all information sources.

2.4. Assessment

One element in this discussion is the attention for assessment of the quality of students. Harvard Professor Eric Mazur calls assessment "the silent killer of education". Students are rational: the study along the prescriptions of assessment. The way assessment is organized is basically the line of learning by students. There are various issues relevant here:

1. Students are rational and apply just-in-time management.
In Kindergarten we start training children to behave

'just-in-time': prepare shortly before the event. This implies if remembering is the largest fraction of required competencies, students will prepare just-in-time even more. There is a lot of evidence that people in the age of about 20-25 can remember quite easily about 80-85% of the material for about 3 days;
2. Most assessment procedures imply an *ex-post* test: there is no feedback of the test on learning;
3. In most cases students are tested in isolation: no connection to the Internet, no textbooks and certainly no contact to fellow students;
4. Most examinations give feedback in one dimension: a single grade;
5. Most assessment forms focus on the 'lower' goals of Bloom's taxonomy.

Linking these observations to the discussion on the adaptation of the International Classroom one can make the observation that classical assessment is not to the benefit of 'inclusion and activation'. From a Flipped Classroom perspective a single assessment ex post is undesired. It is by far better to do a pre-test before class starts: the lecturer than knows where deficiencies possibly are and can cope with it during class. In the Flipped Classroom continuous feedback is a necessity. Feedback could also be given better in line with the pre-set learning outcomes. A student can do great on presenting, but needs some improvement on academic contents or the other way round.

Peer group instruction and assessment also fit better into the International Classroom setting than stand-alone 'isolated' learning and assessment. It is pretty unlikely that an alumnus will have to work in full isolation, without Internet connection, without any form of contact with colleagues. Moreover, for international students it is great to have the interaction with fellow students. Peer group instruction can also use a free and more creative setting: solving real-life problems in a group leads to intensive discussions and interactions, which will be memorized better than simply collecting facts.

Summarizing, phase 3.0 of internationalization will focus on the adjustment of the education at home. Two keywords are relevant: inclusion and activation. Inclusion applies to all students (home-based and international): the university opens its facilities and makes all students feel at home. Next it is activation. More active students learn more and have more fun. Activation of students needs adjustment of the organisation of education: the Flipped Classroom and ICT help. Activation also correlates with a stronger focus on creativity. Finally, the diversity of the student population in class must be considered to be an asset and should be used by the lecturer.

3. Concluding remarks

In this chapter I describe the opportunities for internationalization in Europe. I first gave a short review of the origin and some of the concerns of the Bologna Declaration. Internationalization is nowadays concerned with spreading the reputation of universities and adjusting education to the needs of all, home-based and foreign, students. I described a next step in internationalization of campus universities: the model of inclusion and activation. Inclusion applies to the openness of campus universities to all students in terms of language and culture. Activation implies to the learning and teaching methods applied on campus. The Bologna Declaration has set the scene: now universities should try to improve their campus policies. They should try to open up their institutions a bit better to all international students and they should try to activate students in class, letting them to bring in their own experiences, and use the diversity of the student population in class. Inclusion of all students is instrumental and a necessary step in order to be able to activate them in class. Active forms of learning are known to be successful. Moreover, it is more fun for students.

Changing universities is typically hard. Universities exist for a thousand years in Europe and basically they do the same as centuries ago: combining research and education is a smart way. A radical change is therefore very unlikely. The emeritus professor of the University of Edinburg Geoffrey Boulton (2009, p. 69) has once commented: "Changing a university is like moving a graveyard; you don't get much help from the people inside". In a professional organization administrators can only try to convince staff members to consider a change instead of forcing them into a new educational strategy. Still university managers should do two things. First, talk to their political leaders to strongly support European collaboration. And secondly, they should try to offset all day-to-day disturbances of 'Bologna'- difficulties within their institutions. Next they should work on the 'inclusion and activation'. It is all to the benefit of next generations of academics. We should all focus on: Making Bologna really Work! Maybe in one day the European crowd will cheer again to academic processions, like in 1614 in Groningen.

References

Bloom, B.S., Engelhart, M.D., Furst, E.J., Hill, W.H.; Krathwohl, D.R. (1956). *Taxonomy of educational objectives: The classification of educational goals. Handbook 1. Cognitive domain*. New York: David McKay Company.

Boulton, G. (2009). Global: What are universities for ? *University World News*, 29 March.

www.ingramcontent.com/pod-product-compliance
Lightning Source LLC
Chambersburg PA
CBHW071111160426
43196CB00013B/2534